AZERBAIJAN
MOVING TOWARD MORE DIVERSIFIED, RESILIENT, AND INCLUSIVE DEVELOPMENT

Edited by Aimee Hampel-Milagrosa, Aziz Haydarov,
Kym Anderson, Jasmin Sibal, and Edimon Ginting

AUGUST 2020

ASIAN DEVELOPMENT BANK

ADB

ISBN 978-92-9262-310-4 (print); 978-92-9262-311-1 (electronic); 978-92-9262-312-8 (ebook)
Publication Stock No. SGP200216-2
DOI: http://dx.doi.org/10.22617/SGP200216-2

The views expressed in this publication are those of the authors and do not necessarily reflect the views and policies of the Asian Development Bank (ADB) or its Board of Governors or the governments they represent.

ADB does not guarantee the accuracy of the data included in this publication and accepts no responsibility for any consequence of their use. The mention of specific companies or products of manufacturers does not imply that they are endorsed or recommended by ADB in preference to others of a similar nature that are not mentioned.

By making any designation of or reference to a particular territory or geographic area, or by using the term "country" in this document, ADB does not intend to make any judgments as to the legal or other status of any territory or area.

Please contact pubsmarketing@adb.org if you have questions or comments with respect to content, or if you wish to obtain copyright permission for your intended use that does not fall within these terms, or for permission to use the ADB logo.

Corrigenda to ADB publications may be found at http://www.adb.org/publications/corrigenda.

Notes:
In this publication, "$" refers to United States dollars.

Cover design by Mike Cortes. On the cover: Loans from Access Bank has enabled small businesses a chance to develop and grow. As businesses ramp up operations, job opportunities are offered to women and other members of the community who are socially disadvantaged (photo by Daro Sulakauri); Road Construction in Hajigabul-Kurdamir Region (photo by Daro Sulakauri); ADB supported Power Distribution Enhancement Investment Program with the reconstruction and rehabilitation of the Gakh Substation to improve energy efficiency in power distribution by Azerishiq Open Joint Stock Company(photo by AZRM); Workers fixing a waste-water collection line along Mingachevir road at the North-Western end of the town close to Adgash (photo by AZRM); A loan from Access Bank has enabled Elham Musayev to expand his cabbage-growing venture and employ 40 people for 4 months a year (photo by Daro Sulakauri).

Contents

Tables, Figures, and Boxes

Tables

Figures

Boxes

Foreword

Azerbaijan has set a determined course to diversify the economy's sources of growth to lessen its dependence on oil. The restructuring is being guided by the Strategic Road Maps on the National Economy Perspective and Main Sectors of the Economy. The long-term goal is to have in place by 2025 the policy frameworks and other conditions needed to advance the process of diversification. Beyond 2025, the Strategic Road Maps envision an economy that is more integrated regionally and globally.

It will take time for the transition to get into its stride, but it is important that rapid progress is made. Although a modest recovery is underway after oil prices collapsed in 2014, it would be imprudent for Azerbaijan to rely again on buoyant oil prices to sustain strong growth—as the country did for a decade. Making rapid progress on the reforms already started and undertaking new reforms that can make the economy more resilient to shocks and give the new drivers of growth early impetus will be essential.

Indeed, because oil will remain by far the biggest contributor to Azerbaijan's gross domestic product growth for a long time to come, policy makers should assume—as this Country Diagnostic Study (CDS) advises—that lower oil prices will likely be the norm. That said, it is important to recognize that significant gains have already been made in the transition. These include reforms to strengthen a weak banking and financial regulatory system and improve the quality of vocational education and training, and reforms that limit State Oil Fund of Azerbaijan Republic transfers to the state budget.

This CDS uses growth diagnostics to identify the most binding constraints to growth and the interventions that need prioritizing. The study makes a detailed thematic analysis of three key areas—education, which is failing to match the needs of the job market; infrastructure, where gaps exist that could hamper diversification; and state-owned enterprises, a big sector that has long been a costly drag on the economy.

Diversifying the economy will be essential to secure strong, lasting, and resilient growth, but diversification should not be the be-all and end-all of Azerbaijan's reform agenda. As the transition gets underway, reforms are also needed to mitigate sizable risks to the macroeconomy, including exchange rate instability and the high cost of finance for the private sector. The country must improve its international competitiveness, particularly in agriculture, manufacturing, and tourism post Coronavirus disease (COVID-19). The CDS also underscores the urgency of making progress in increasing the country's human capital, the foundation for building sustained growth.

The CDS was prepared using the One ADB approach. This brings together the Asian Development Bank's expertise and knowledge across the institution—ADB staff members at regional and research departments at headquarters and resident missions, and consultant experts—to effectively implement ADB's new long-term strategy to 2030 for its developing member countries. This approach was effective for managing the knowledge gained from discussions held by parallel research teams, and to build consensus on the CDS's key messages. This study provided valuable inputs to ADB's Azerbaijan country partnership strategy, 2019–2023, which aims to support the acceleration of economic diversification and inclusive growth by strengthening human capital, enhancing infrastructure, boosting private sector development, and raising efficiency in the public sector.

This CDS coincides with the 20th anniversary of the ADB-Azerbaijan partnership which was celebrated in 2019. Our two decades of cooperation spanned an oil boom and a severe slowdown; yet we pushed through with our joint agenda of encouraging new economic opportunities, promoting inclusive growth, and reducing urban–rural inequality. I am confident that our partnership for the next 20 years and beyond will be even more productive.

We are confident that our partnership for the next 20 years and beyond will be even more productive.

Yasuyuki Sawada
Chief Economist and Director General
Economic Research and Regional Cooperation Department
Asian Development Bank

Acknowledgments

In 2017, Azerbaijan's Ministry of Finance and the Asian Development Bank (ADB) agreed on a two-phased Country Diagnostic Study (CDS) to help the government advance its agenda to diversify the economy beyond oil under the Strategic Road Maps on the National Economy Perspective and Main Sectors of the Economy, launched in December 2016. The resulting CDS from ADB uses the One ADB approach. The first phase of the CDS (November 2017–June 2018) was a comprehensive growth diagnostic to identify the binding constraints to economic growth and diversifying the economy. The second phase (July 2018–May 2019) was a detailed analysis of these constraints. The approach to both phases was collaborative and iterative. In November 2019, the CDS was presented and discussed at a high level meeting in Baku between ADB and the Azerbaijan government. This CDS is therefore inclusive in its methodological approach and focused on the sectors that are particularly important for Azerbaijan's efforts to diversify its sources of growth.

Chapter 1, Introduction, was written by Aimee Hampel-Milagrosa with inputs from Amador Foronda, Ruslan Aliyev, and Edimon Ginting.

Chapter 2 on the Growth Diagnostics Framework was written by Aimee Hampel-Milagrosa with inputs from Ruslan Aliyev, Amador Foronda, Kym Anderson, and Edimon Ginting.

Chapter 3 on Strengthening Human Capital was written by Jasmin Sibal and Aimee Hampel-Milagrosa, with inputs from Ilkin Nazarov and support from Aziz Haydarov.

Chapter 4 on Enhancing Infrastructure for Economic Diversification and Competitiveness was written by Neeraj Jain and Aziz Haydarov, with support from Aimee Hampel-Milagrosa.

Chapter 5 on Transforming State-Owned Enterprises into Engines of Growth was written by Michael Schur and Aziz Haydarov, with inputs from Lakshman Ganesharajah and Volha Hrytskevich, with support from Aimee Hampel-Milagrosa. Fakhri Ismayilov and Ahliman Qasimov provided the data used in the chapter.

Chapter 6, Concluding Remarks, was written by Aimee Hampel-Milagrosa.

The background papers, additional data, and the figures and tables were supplied by Amador Foronda (macroeconomy and product space); Daryll Naval, Marie Anne Cagas, and Angelica Maddawin (education); and Reneli Gloria and Denise Encarnacion (infrastructure). Kym Anderson was the economics editor and Alastair McIndoe was the manuscript editor. Kym and Alastair served as proofreaders of the draft chapters. Jasmin Sibal, Amanda Mamon, Roslyn Perez, and Gee Ann Burac were the proofreaders of the final, print-ready, draft. Ricasol Cruz-Calaluan, Amanda Mamon, Yuliya Hagverdiyeva, and Elvin Imanov provided administrative support. Mike Cortes did the layout, cover design, and typesetting.

Three missions were undertaken for the Azerbaijan CDS to present preliminary findings to ministries and government agencies, gather feedback from stakeholders, and exchange information on the implications of the findings of the thematic chapters. The mission team benefited from the participation of Nail Valiyev and Sabina Jafarova of ADB's Azerbaijan Resident Mission. Integral to the CDS was the conduct of the computable general equilibrium modelling training led by Mark Horridge and Gouranga Das, and supported by Rashad Huseynov.

We are grateful to the Government of Azerbaijan, particularly the Ministry of Finance, for its collaboration with the research team and for embracing the One ADB approach. Thanks also go to the following ministries and government agencies, whose engagement was greatly valued: Azerbaijan Chamber of Commerce, Azerbaijan Railways, Azerenerji, Azerishiq, Center for Economic and Social Development, Center for Economic Reforms and Communication, Central Bank of Azerbaijan's Research and Development Center, Financial Market and Supervisory Authority, Institute for Labor and Social Problems, Institute for Scientific Research on Economic Reforms, International Bank of Azerbaijan, Ministry of Economy, Ministry of Education, Ministry of Energy, Ministry of Finance's Department of Budget Policy and Macroeconomic Analyses, Ministry of Labor and Social Protection of the Population, Ministry of Taxes, State Property Committee, and the State Statistical Committee.

Thanks to the European Bank for Reconstruction and Development, International Monetary Fund, Swiss Agency for Development Cooperation, and World Bank for sharing useful insights on Azerbaijan's socioeconomic development, and to ADB colleagues from the Central and West Asia Department and other departments for their feedback on the CDS.

The CDS team is indebted to Emin Huseynov, Azerbaijan's deputy minister of finance (until September 2018); Edimon Ginting, ADB deputy director general of the Economic Research and Regional Cooperation Department; and Nariman Mannapbekov, Azerbaijan Resident Mission country director, for their guidance and advice. During the CDS' final stretch, the study benefited from the advice of Rana Hasan, director, Economic Analysis and Operational Support Division, Economic Research and Regional Cooperation Department.

Author Profiles

Aimee Hampel-Milagrosa is an economist at the Asian Development Bank's (ADB) Economic Analysis and Operational Support Division, a unit of the Economic Research and Regional Cooperation Department. She leads the division's economic analysis of water and urban development projects, and conducts research on enterprise dynamics and urbanization. Before joining ADB in 2017, she was senior researcher at the German Development Institute in Bonn, where she advised the Government of Germany on private sector development and the economic empowerment of women. She has authored over 50 publications, including in peer reviewed journals. Aimee has a PhD in social science (agricultural economics) from Wageningen University, the Netherlands.

Aziz Haydarov is a senior portfolio management specialist at ADB's Azerbaijan Resident Mission. At ADB, he has worked as an economist in the Philippines Country Office; a specialist in public–private partnerships in the Southeast Asia Department's Public Management, Financial Sector, and Trade Division; and an infrastructure economist in the Indonesia Resident Mission. Before joining ADB in 2009, he was the World Bank's country officer for Tajikistan. Aziz has an MS degree in development economics and policy from the University of Manchester, United Kingdom. He did PhD research at the Ruhr University in Bochum, Germany. He is a certified Public-Private Partnership Specialist from the Institute for Public-Private Partnership in Arlington, Virginia.

Kym Anderson is an economics professor at the University of Adelaide and the Australian National University's Crawford School of Public Policy. From 2010 to 2017, he was on the board of trustees of the International Food Policy Research Institute, Washington, DC, and its chair from 2015. He was commissioner of the Australian Centre for International Agricultural Research from 2011 to 2014, and has been the center's president since 2014. He has worked at the World Bank and, in the early 1990s, at GATT's secretariat. He has published some 400 articles and 40 books. Kym is a recipient of an Honorary Doctor of Economics degree from the University of Adelaide and has a Distinguished Alumni Award from the University of New England.

Edimon Ginting is deputy director general of ADB's Economic Research and Regional Cooperation Department and a former director of the department's Economic Analysis and Operational Support Division. At the division, he supervised reviews of the economic viability of ADB projects and led the preparation of country diagnostic studies for ADB's developing member countries. Before joining ADB in 2007, he was an economist at the International Monetary Fund, advisor to the Indonesian Parliament, and research economist at the Productivity Commission, Australia. Edimon is a postdoctoral fellow at Monash University, Australia, and research economist at Gadjah Mada University, Yogyakarta, Indonesia. He has a PhD in economics from Monash University.

Neeraj Jain is an independent international consultant with extensive experience in developing Asia. He is a former ADB economist who has worked in Central and West Asia, East Asia, and Southeast Asia; senior ADB country economist for Kazakhstan, Malaysia, and Philippines; and country director for the Philippines and Tajikistan, where he led ADB teams for policy dialogue with the governments of these countries. Before ADB, he was a lecturer in economics at the University of Delhi prior to joining the Indian Administrative Service. Among others, he served as a development administrator responsible for planning and implementing district development programs and as a senior official at the Department of Economic Affairs in the Ministry of Finance. Neeraj has an MA in economics from the Delhi School of Economics.

Michael Schur has 25 years' experience as a consultant to governments, multilateral agencies, and the private sector on improving the performance and governance of state-owned enterprises, and on delivering infrastructure. He has worked in Central Asia, Europe, Southeast Asia, Africa, Australia, and New Zealand. He is a former treasury secretary and chief economic advisor to the State Government of New South Wales, Australia, on its state-owned enterprises and privatization programs. Michael is managing director of Castalia Strategic Advisor's Sydney office and chair of the Finance and Assurance Committee of the Board of Housing New Zealand Corporation, a government business that provides social housing services to 200,000 New Zealanders.

Ruslan Aliyev is an assistant professor of economics in the School of Business, ADA University in Baku. His areas of specialization are monetary economics, applied econometrics, and economic growth and development. He has a special interest in the effectiveness of government policies in economies that are rich in natural resources. He worked at the Monetary Policy Division of the Central Bank of Azerbaijan from 2004 to 2007. He is a consultant for national and international organizations, including Azerbaijan's Ministry of Economy, Asian Development Bank, Czech National Bank, World Bank, and the United Nations. Ruslan has a PhD from the Center for Economic Research and Graduate Education—Economics Institute, Prague.

Jasmin Sibal is an economics officer at ADB's Economic Analysis and Operational Support Division, where she is involved in operations support for the economic analysis of ADB projects and analytical work for preparing country diagnostic and impact evaluation studies. She is a former consultant at ADB, providing research support for employment diagnostics studies on Cambodia and Fiji, and the *Women in the Workforce* and *Key Indicators for Asia and the Pacific* reports. Before joining ADB, she was a monitoring and evaluation officer for the Philippine Conditional Cash Transfer program at the Department of Social Welfare and Development, and a senior research executive for a market research agency in the Philippines. Jasmin has an MA in Demography from the University of the Philippines.

Abbreviations

BOT	build-operate-transfer
CGE	computable general equilibrium
ECI	Economic Complexity Index
ERA	effective rate of assistance
FDI	foreign direct investment
GDP	gross domestic product
ICT	information and communication technology
IMF	International Monetary Fund
ISP	internet service provider
km	kilometer
Mbps	megabits per second
NPL	nonperforming loan
NRA	nominal rate of assistance
OECD	Organisation for Economic Co-operation and Development
PPP	public–private partnership
RRA	relative rate of assistance
SOCAR	State Oil Company of Azerbaijan Republic
SOE	state-owned enterprise
SOFAZ	State Oil Fund of Azerbaijan Republic
WEF	World Economic Forum

AZERBAIJAN

FAST FACTS

As of 2018 or latest available year

ECONOMY

Value added by sector:
Agriculture: 6.1%
Industry: 53.5%
Services: 40.4%
GDP (current $): 41 billion
Per capita GNI (current $): 4,760 2016
Oil rent as % of GDP: 17.5% 2016

FOREIGN TRADE

Exports: $13.8 billion
Imports: $8.8 billion
Top 3 imports: machinery and
electric appliances, iron/steel
products, and food stuff
Top 3 exports: Petroleum,
natural gas, tomatoes
Top 3 export trading partners:
Italy, Turkey, Israel

SOCIAL INDICATORS

Unemployment: 5.0%
Proportion of population living below
the national poverty line: 5.0% 2015
Gini index: 0.227 2014
Infant mortality rate: 11.1 per 1,000 live births
Access to improved drinking-water sources: 89.2 2015
Human Development Index: High (0.757)

PEOPLE AND RESOURCES

Total population: 10 million
Total fertility rate: 1.9 children per woman
Adult literacy rate: 99.9%
Agricultural area: 4.8 million hectares
(55.5% of Azerbaijan) 2017
Oil production: 286.3 million barrels
Gas production: 19.2 billion m³

This map was produced by the cartography unit of the Asian Development Bank.
The boundaries, colors, denominations, and any other information shown on this
map do not imply, on the part of the Asian Development Bank, any judgment on the
legal status of any territory, or any endorsement or acceptance of such boundaries,
colors, denominations, or information.

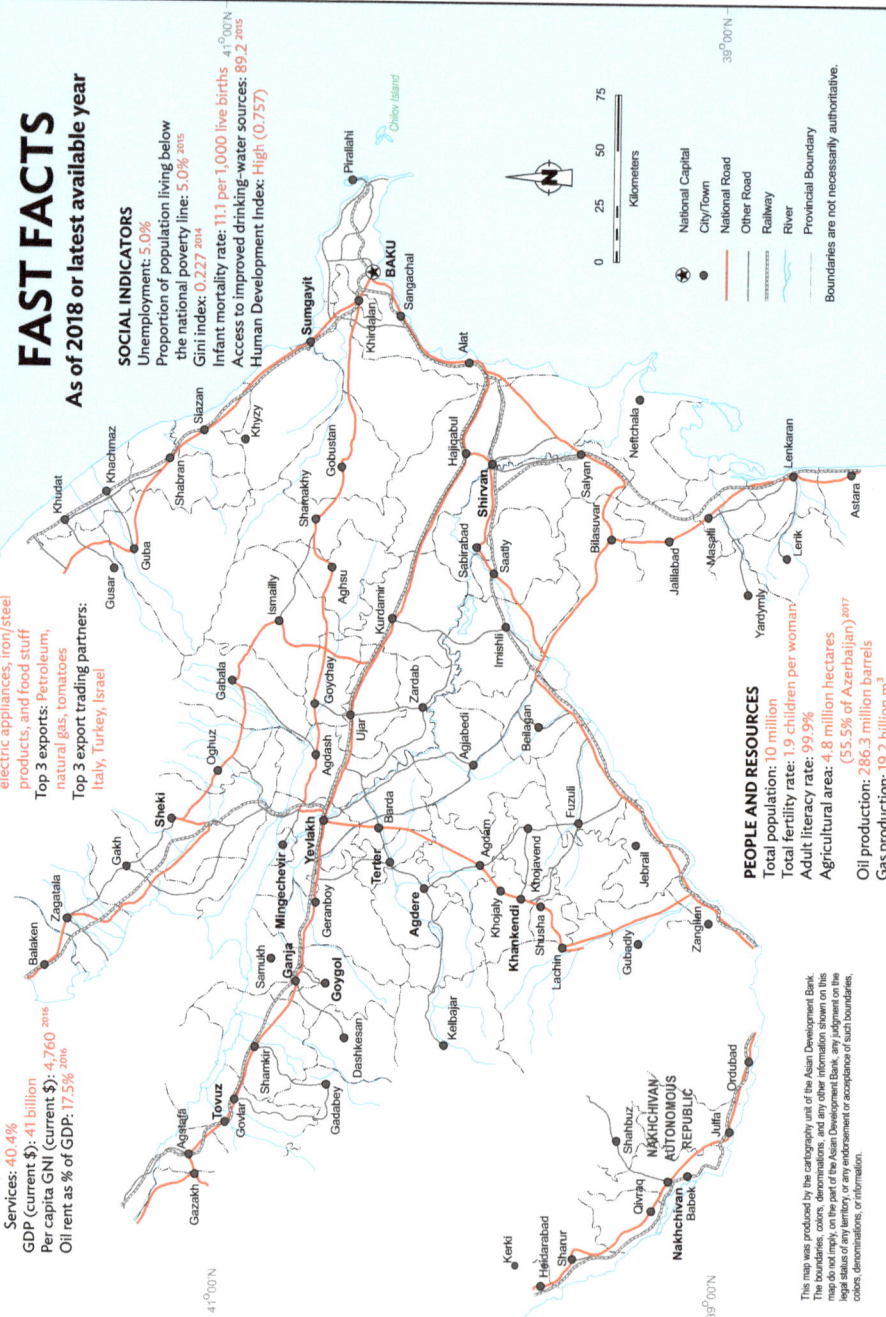

Legend

- ⊛ National Capital
- ● City/Town
- National Road
- Other Road
- Railway
- River
- Provincial Boundary

Boundaries are not necessarily authoritative.

Kilometers
0   25   50   75

50°00'E
46°00'E
41°00'N
39°00'N

BAKU
Sumgayit
Khirdalan
Sangachal
Alat
Neftchala
Lenkaran
Astara
Lerik
Masalli
Jalilabad
Yardymly
Bilasuvar/Salyan
Saatly
Sabirabad
Shirvan
Hajigabul
Gobustan
Shamakhy
Ismailly
Aghsu
Goychay
Kurdamir
Imishli
Bilasan
Beylagan
Aghjabadi
Zardab
Ujar
Agdash
Barda
Fuzuli
Agdam
Khojavend
Jebrail
Zangilan
Lachin
Shusha
Khankendi
Khojaly
Gubadly
Kelbajar
Terter
Agdere
Goranboy
Geranboy
Yevlakh
Mingechevir
Ganja
Goygol
Samukh
Dashkesan
Gadabey
Shamkir
Govlar
Tovuz
Agstafa
Gazakh
Gakh
Zagatala
Balaken
Sheki
Oghuz
Gabala
Khachmaz
Siazan
Shabran
Khyzy
Khudat
Gusar
Guba
Piraliahi
Chilov Island

NAKHCHIVAN AUTONOMOUS REPUBLIC
Nakhchivan
Babek
Qivraq
Shahbuz
Shahbuz
Juffa
Ordubad
Sharur
Heidarabad
Kerki

19-1832 18AZE

CHAPTER 1

Introduction

The remarkably strong growth that Azerbaijan's economy enjoyed since the start of the new millennium came to an abrupt halt when international oil prices plummeted in 2014. Since then, the government has been energetically seeking new sources of growth beyond oil, the economy's mainstay.

Because of the low level of technology used in the oil industry, Azerbaijan's oil reserves were not fully exploited by the former Soviet Union. Since independence in 1991, however, there has been significant oil exploration and development in the Caspian Basin bordered by Azerbaijan. The country also has sizable agriculture land: 57.7% of the total land area and nearly half of this is arable.

Since independence, Azerbaijan's economic development has undergone four distinct stages: regression (1991–1994), reform (1995–2003), oil boom (2004–2014), and slowdown from 2015 (Figure 1.1).[1] It was during the oil boom that the oil and gas sector became the main contributor to the country's strong economic growth up to the collapse in oil prices (Figure 1.2).

---

[1] The country experienced its first oil boom in the late 19th and early 20th centuries. The oil boom of 2004–2014 was in fact a second oil boom.

Figure 1.1: Gross Domestic Product Growth and Gross Oil and Non-Oil Value Added, 1991–2018

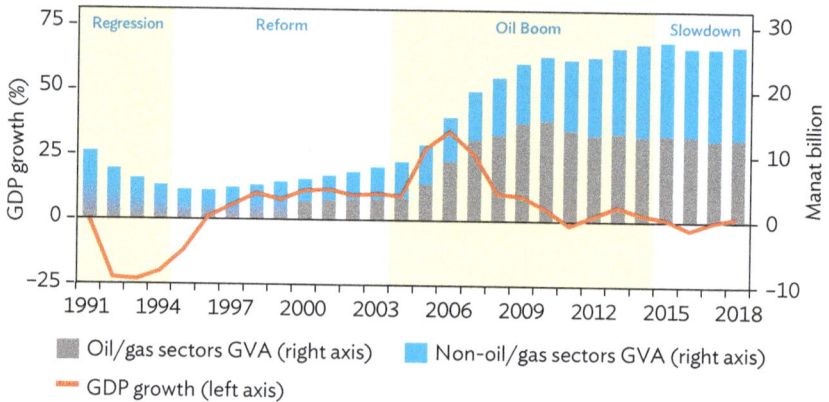

GDP = gross domestic product, GVA = gross value added.
Notes: Data for oil and non-oil sectors available only from 2000. Regression, reform, oil boom, and slowdown are the four stages of Azerbaijan's economic development. Oil and non-oil sector GVA at 2005 constant basic prices. The sum of oil and non-oil sector GVA is equal to GDP at 2005 constant basic prices.
Sources: Estimates based on State Statistical Committee data; and UN Statistics Division database.

Figure 1.2: Growth of Gross Domestic Product of Oil and Non-Oil Sectors, 1991–2018

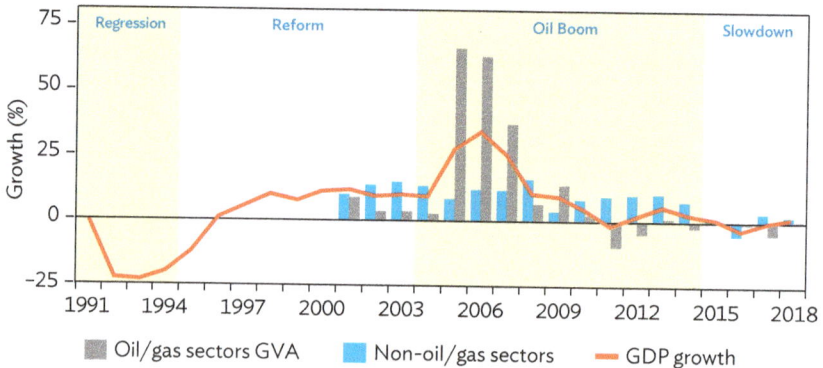

GDP = gross domestic product, , GVA = gross value added.
Notes: Data for oil and non-oil sectors available only from 2000. Regression, reform, oil boom, and slowdown are the four stages of Azerbaijan's economic development. Oil and non-oil sector GVA at 2005 constant basic prices. The sum of oil and non-oil sector GVA is equal to GDP at 2005 constant basic prices.
Sources: Estimates based on State Statistical Committee data; and UN Statistics Division database.

1.1   Rapid Economic Transformation

Azerbaijan has undergone a significant economic transformation since independence. The economy collapsed with the breakup of the former Soviet Union, and by 1995 gross domestic product (GDP) was less than half the 1990 level . But Azerbaijan rose to the challenges it faced, quickly transforming itself into an upper-middle-income country by 2009, when annual average gross national income per capita was $6,093.[2] The poverty rate fell from 60% in 1995 to 13.2% in 2008 and to 4.9% in 2015. Azerbaijan is now classified as a high human development country by the United Nations Human Development Index, with its index in 2017 at 0.757.[3]

Oil remains pivotal to Azerbaijan's economic success. GDP growth started to accelerate from 1995 before plateauing at about 10% in 2000–2004. When oil prices subsequently soared, the oil industry lifted GDP. Oil rents exceeded 15% of GDP during 2004–2014, averaging 28% during the period and peaking at 42% in 2006 (Figure 1.3). Azerbaijan's economy grew fastest during 2005–2010, with annual average GDP growth of 18%. The slump in oil prices since 2014 caused income per capita and the share of oil revenue in the country's GDP to fall.

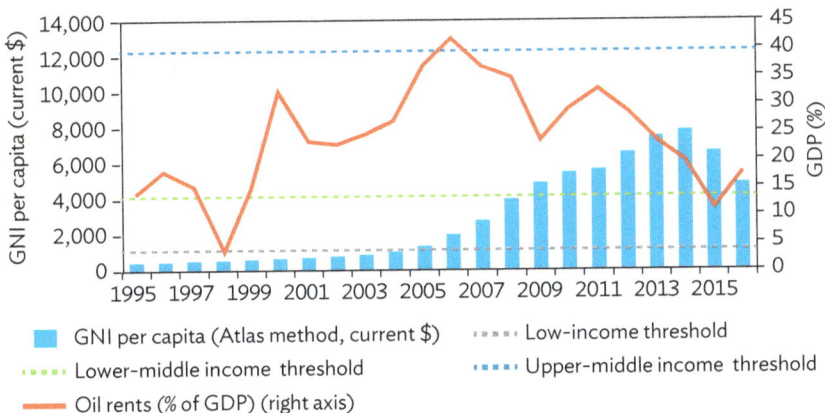

Figure 1.3: Gross National Income per Capita and Oil Rents, 1995–2016

GDP = gross domestic product, GNI = gross national income.
Source: World Bank, World Development Indicators Database.

---

[2]   Under the World Bank's income classification of countries as of July 2018, low income = gross national income per capita of less than $995, lower-middle-income = $996–$3,895, upper-middle-income = $3,896–$12,055, and high income = over $12,055.

[3]   Under the index, low human development = less than 0.550, medium human development = 0.550–0.699, high human development = 0.700–0.799, and very high human development = over 0.800.

During the oil boom years, industry contributed most to GDP growth in both oil and non-oil sectors, averaging 70.9% of total growth over that period (Table 1.1). When oil prices started to fall, GDP growth contracted to –0.8% in 2015, but industry (oil and non-oil) continued to contribute the bulk of GDP, at 248.5%, while the contribution of services and agriculture to GDP growth fell dramatically. Despite adverse economic circumstances, the growth rate of the agriculture sector has, however, slowly picked up, climbing from an annual average of 3.5% during the oil boom to 4.5% during the economic slowdown.

Table 1.1: Major Production Sectors, 1992–2018
(annual average %)

Period	GDP Growth Rate	Agriculture			Industry			Services		
		Growth Rate	Share to GDP	Contribution to GDP Growth	Growth Rate	Share to GDP	Contribution to GDP Growth	Growth Rate	Share to GDP	Contribution to GDP Growth
1992–1994	–21.8	–16.9	32.6	10.4	–24.2	28.8	60.3	–18.2	38.6	29.2
1995–2003	5.9	4.0	18.1	9.0	7.7	44.9	66.8	4.2	37.1	24.3
2004–2014	11.5	3.5	6.2	2.5	13.5	63.7	72.4	9.9	30.1	25.1
2015–2018	–0.1	4.5	6.1	–28.8	–3.0	53.2	212.9	2.7	40.7	–84.1
1992–2018	**3.7**	**1.3**	**6.8**	**3.2**	**4.2**	**66.6**	**54.2**	**3.5**	**34.4**	**30.2**

GDP = gross domestic product.
Note: Financial intermediation services were indirectly measured and included in the services sector.
Sources: Estimates based on State Statistical Committee data; and UN Statistics Division database.

The 2008 global financial crisis had a sharp impact on the economy, with GDP growth decelerating to 0.1% by 2011. Plummeting oil prices, weak regional growth, devaluations in the Azerbaijan manat, and a contraction in oil and gas production quickly reversed some of the gains of the oil boom.

Investment as a share of GDP peaked at 24.1% during the slowdown. But because these investments were mostly in hydrocarbons, the investment growth rate fell sharply, contracting 11.1% during this period because of the oil price shock (Table 1.2). Both investment and savings were quite high before the slowdown, when consumption buffered the economy. In late 2016, global oil prices started to pick up and Azerbaijan's oil exports began to rebound in 2017.

Table 1.2: Expenditure Components, 1991–2017
(annual average %)

Period	Consumption			Government			Investment			Net Exports			
	Growth Rate	Share to GDP	Contribution to GDP Growth Rate	Growth Rate	Share to GDP	Contribution to GDP Growth Rate	Growth Rate	Share to GDP	Contribution to GDP Growth Rate	Exports Growth Rate	Imports Growth Rate	Share to GDP	Contribution to GDP Growth Rate
1991–1994	-23.4	75.4	-7.6	-12.0	23.9	-12.3	-44.6	15.6	213.3	-19.3	-38.1	-14.9	-93.4
1994–2003	3.8	68.5	32.9	-0.5	13.4	-1.5	22.0	32.2	93.3	11.7	18.4	-14.2	-24.7
2003–2014	10.1	39.4	38.7	2.7	10.1	2.0	6.7	23.5	20.8	15.6	9.1	26.9	38.5
2014–2017	4.3	56.3	-237.0	2.1	11.5	-15.4	-11.1	24.1	360.5	-1.8	-3.3	8.0	-8.1
1991–2017	**2.8**	**47.2**	**64.2**	**-0.3**	**10.8**	**6.9**	**1.5**	**24.2**	**-43.4**	**7.6**	**3.7**	**17.7**	**72.3**

GDP = gross domestic product.
Note: Share to GDP and Contribution to GDP Growth Rate do not sum to 100% because of rounding.
Sources: Estimates based on State Statistical Committee data; and Asian Development Bank. 2010 and 2017. *Key Indicators for Asia and the Pacific*. Manila.

In addition to the economic challenges that Azerbaijan has faced since independence, it has had to deal with a war with the separatist region of Nagorno-Karabakh that broke out in the late 1980s and ended in 1994. The effects of this undermined the country's early postindependence economic progress. After the war, Azerbaijan still faced major social concerns. The incidence of poverty in the mid-1990s was high, with more than 60% of the population considered poor. In 1995, real per capita GDP was just 39% of its 1990 level. It was at this low point that Azerbaijan embarked on a strategy to rehabilitate oil production through an ambitious investment plan.

1.2   Oil Boom 2004–2014

The first wave of foreign investments in oil and gas exploration in the Caspian Sea in the mid-1990s transformed Azerbaijan into an exporter of fossil fuels, setting off the next stage of the country's economic development. By 1994, 10% of total exports came from oil; by 2017, the share was 76%, (gas exports in that year accounted for 11% of total exports) (Figure 1.4).

Figure 1.4: Exports by Sector, 1992–2017

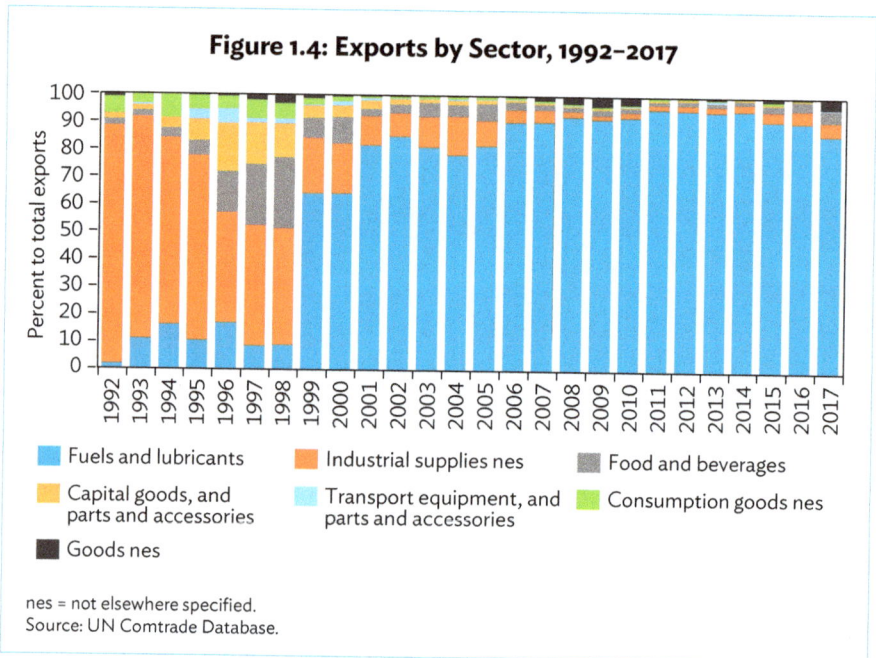

Legend:
- Fuels and lubricants
- Industrial supplies nes
- Food and beverages
- Capital goods, and parts and accessories
- Transport equipment, and parts and accessories
- Consumption goods nes
- Goods nes

nes = not elsewhere specified.
Source: UN Comtrade Database.

Azerbaijan's first major oil contracts for exploration and production with international firms were signed in 1994; these were production sharing agreements between the State Oil Company of Azerbaijan Republic (SOCAR) and international oil companies. In the following year, the country's stabilization and structural reform program got underway to help secure macroeconomic and financial stability, gain better control of inflation, and reduce the fiscal deficit. By the early 2000s, chronically high inflation had been brought under control. The completion of the Baku–Tbilisi–Ceyhan oil pipeline in 2005 marked the country's transition to being a significant oil-based economy, as it was in the early 20th century.

Boosted by huge oil revenue, the economy enjoyed robust growth rates; large foreign reserves, which peaked at $15.8 billion in 2014; more revenue for social protection; and lower foreign debt. Continued inflows of foreign direct investment into the oil industry were largely behind Azerbaijan reaching upper-middle-income status by 2009.

In 2006, economic growth accelerated to 34.5% on the back of a 63.2% rate of growth in the oil and gas sector—this was the highest rate of GDP growth of any country worldwide in that year, according to the World Bank's World Development Indicators. But there was clearly no prospect of sustaining that level of growth after the global financial crisis triggered a global economic slowdown. And by 2011, growth in Azerbaijan had withered to 0.1%, with the oil and gas sector contracting 9.2%.

The new Azerbaijan manat was issued on 1 January 2006 to strengthen reforms and to put the economy on a more stable footing. The new currency appreciated until it was hit by falling oil prices, losing 56% against the dollar by 2016. Since then, the exchange rate has stabilized on the Central Bank of Azerbaijan tightening policy, increasing oil revenue, and low imports (Figure 1.5).

Azerbaijan started to show signs of Dutch disease since the new currency was introduced.[4] High oil prices from the country's fast-growing oil and gas industry resulted in a strong exchange rate against the dollar. After the new currency was issued, inflation rose to 16.7% in 2007 and 20.8% in 2008, and average monthly nominal wages rose by 21% in 2006 and 45% in 2007. Inflation,

---

4   Dutch disease happens when an increase in economic development in one sector (for example, natural resources) results in a decline in other sectors (for example, manufacturing and agriculture). This can be detected by looking at the movement of exchange rates, wages, and imports and exports. Appendix 1 has a more detailed discussion on the economics of Dutch disease.

Figure 1.5: Nominal and Effective Manat Exchange Rate versus the Dollar, 2000–2018

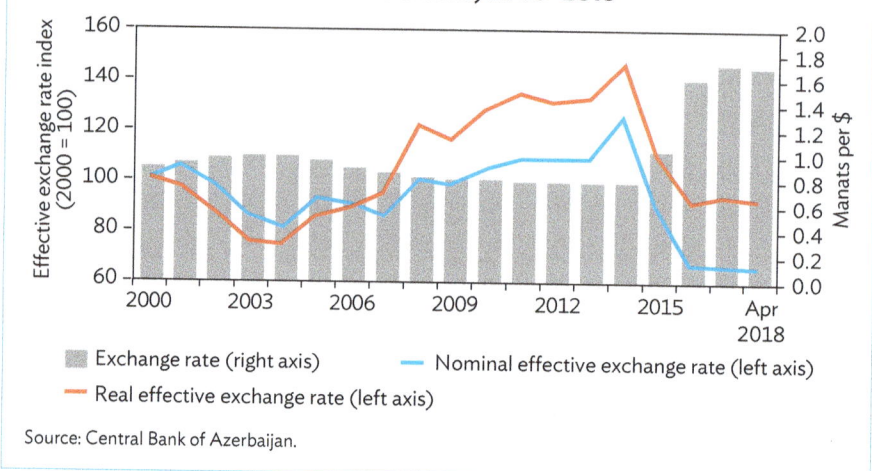

Exchange rate (right axis)   Nominal effective exchange rate (left axis)
Real effective exchange rate (left axis)

Source: Central Bank of Azerbaijan.

higher wages, and the sharp inflow of foreign currency into Azerbaijan, including foreign direct investment, triggered a rise in imported goods and the consumption of nontradable goods and services. This resulted in a decline in the competitiveness of the country's manufacturing and agriculture exports, and a continuing expansion in oil and gas exports.

1.3   Slowdown from 2015 to 2017

It is important to assess the effects of a sharp decline of global market prices of oil on the macro economy. This section presents how Azerbaijan responded to the shock and began its journey toward diversification. From 2015 to 2017, the government swiftly responded to the fall in oil prices by reducing production.[5] Because of worsening bank balance sheets and increasing dollarization, the central bank closed troubled banks; restructured state-run International Bank of Azerbaijan, which was in financial difficulties;[6] and lowered limits on dollar lending. The measures triggered aftershocks in the form of rising inflation, a big drop in the current account surplus, a fiscal deficit, and concerns among

---

[5]   The period 2015-2017 was labeled as "Slowdown", to differentiate it from the previous rapid growth period labeled "Oil Boom". This does not imply that growth has been continuously decelerating since then; on the contrary, in 2018 growth accelerated from a negligible 0.1% in 2017 to 1.4% on gains of 0.6% in the dominant petroleum sector, but with stronger gains (1.8%) in the rest of the economy. Growth is expected to strengthen further in 2019 and 2020.

[6]   International Bank of Azerbaijan, an open joint stock company, is the country's largest bank.

the public over the reliability of the financial sector. The 2016 budget, which increased capital and current spending, resulted in higher public sector wages, pensions, and social protection spending. To help reduce the pressure on inflation, monetary policy was tightened in 2016 and the refinancing rate raised by 1,200 basis points to 15%, which helped to prop up the manat. In accordance with the Decree #760 of the President of the Azerbaijan Republic, dated 3 February 2016, Financial Market Supervisory Authority (FMSA) was established as the public legal entity. In May, 2016, FMSA adopted principles of responsible borrowing and sound lending, and defined limits for credits in foreign currency based on these principles.

During the oil boom, job creation lagged far behind the country's economic transformation. Despite substantial economic development, about one-third of the labor force still works in agriculture, while oil—the most productive sector—employs only 1% (Table 1.3).

Table 1.3: Employment Shares and Productivity by Sector, 2000–2016

Sector	Employment Share (%)				Productivity (current LCU/worker)			
	2000–2005	2005–2010	2010–2016	2000–2016	2000–2005	2005–2010	2010–2016	2000–2016
Agriculture	38.9	38.4	37.2	36.0	580	1,154	1,765	1,232
Mining and quarrying	1.0	1.0	0.9	0.9	58,470	330,639	503,905	510,198
Manufacturing	4.9	4.9	4.9	5.0	2,739	7,305	11,153	11,460
Electricity, gas, and water	1.3	1.4	1.2	1.2	1,952	6,621	17,506	18,246
Construction	5.1	5.5	7.1	7.3	3,452	9,464	17,799	18,650
Trade	15.8	15.6	14.7	14.9	805	2,674	6,454	6,782
Hotels and restaurants	0.6	0.7	1.2	1.2	1,652	8,106	18,972	20,319
Transportation, storage, and communication	5.1	5.2	5.4	5.5	3,450	10,149	15,754	16,118
Financial services	0.4	0.5	0.6	0.7	5,455	21,992	40,303	43,080
Other services	27.1	26.8	26.8	27.2	894	2,688	6,220	6,516
Total	**100.0**	**100.0**	**100.0**	**100.0**	**1,739**	**6,653**	**11,172**	**11,440**

LCU = local currency unit.
Source: Estimates based on Asian Development Bank. 2017. *Key Indicators for Asia and the Pacific 2017*. Manila.

The employment share of other low-productivity sectors, such as trade, were also stagnant over 1991–2017. With about three-quarters of workers in non-oil sectors, labor productivity has made a minimal contribution to economic growth (Figure 1.6).

Figure 1.6: Labor Productivity Contribution to Growth, 2000–2016

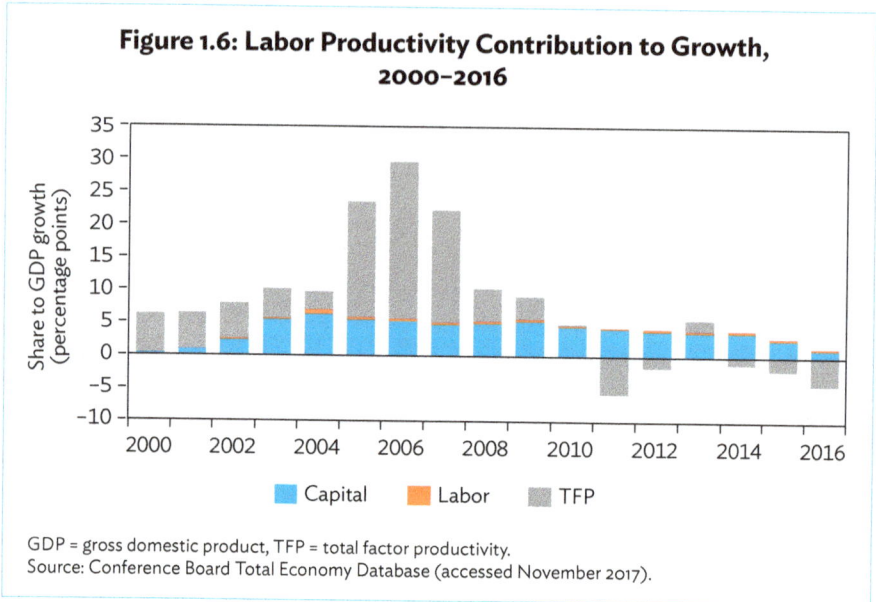

GDP = gross domestic product, TFP = total factor productivity.
Source: Conference Board Total Economy Database (accessed November 2017).

ADB, the IMF, and the World Bank project growth and no contractions for Azerbaijan during 2019 and 2020, with the economy mainly driven by fiscal expansion supported by higher oil prices and natural gas production. Making progress on diversifying the economy over this period will make it easier for the country to adjust to future fluctuations in its terms of trade. There is an urgency to make progress on this because oil prices, although higher, are expected to remain subdued, and the recovery of Azerbaijan's main trading partners is expected to be slow. Aggressive economic policy reforms are therefore still needed to increase the country's resilience to external shocks.

The steep fall in oil prices that started in 2014 and lasted until 2017 exposed Azerbaijan's overreliance on oil and gas, and the economy's lack of diversification (Figure 1.7). The abrupt rebound in oil prices in 2011–2012 was the biggest spike in oil prices on record. Because of this, Azerbaijan should plan its economy on the assumption that lower oil prices—rather than the higher prices from 2004 to 2013—will tend to be the norm (Figure 1.8).

Figure 1.7: Average World Oil Price and Azerbaijan's Crude Oil Production, 1995–2017

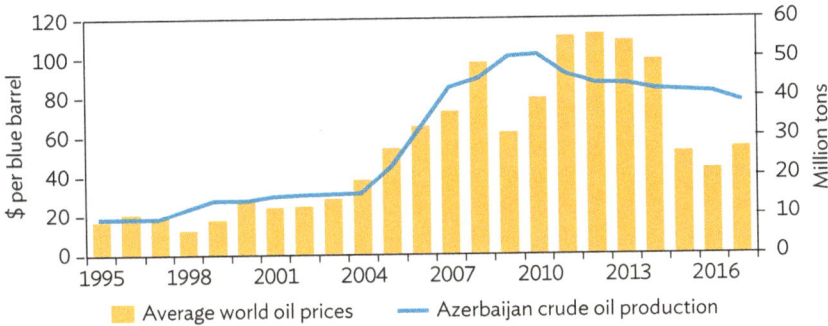

Notes: 1 blue barrel = 42 gallons. World prices are based on Brent prices. Azerbaijan's crude oil production includes gas condensate.
Sources: World Bank, Commodities Price Data; and State Statistical Committee.

Figure 1.8: Real International Crude Oil Price (January 2019 $), 1968–2018

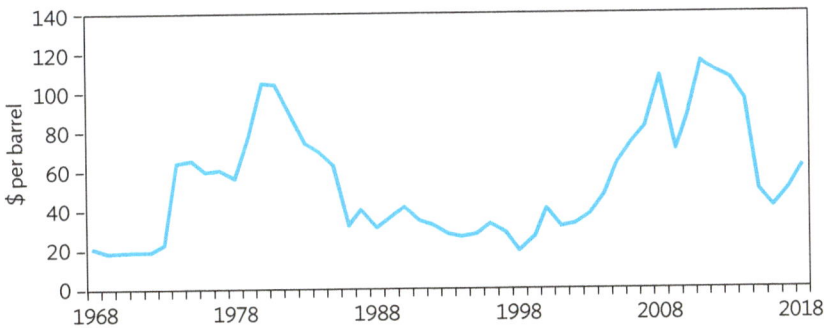

Source: US Energy Information Association, Short-Term Energy Outlook, January 2019.

1.4 Government Reform Initiatives

To tackle the economic slowdown, the government implemented major reforms to tighten fiscal, monetary, and exchange rate policy; improve the management of the State Oil Fund of Azerbaijan Republic (SOFAZ); and undertake financial market reforms. The reforms that were carried out in the country were mainly aimed at retaining the main social-economic results of the rapid economic growth and ensuring medium-term and long-term strategic sustainability of economic development.

From the outset of the oil price shock, the government tried to reduce the economy's dependence on oil revenue by cutting spending financed by this. The percentage of SOFAZ's revenue that goes to the state budget has fallen continuously since 2013 (Chapter 2 discusses this in detail).[7] Another important action taken by the government to reduce this dependency was the 2018 amendment to the Budget System Law to more tightly control the non-oil fiscal deficit and to limit oil-related revenue to a certain margin.[8] By taking these actions, the government wants to isolate the main source of vulnerability—reliance on oil—from the rest of the economy. The next stage will be overseeing the implementation of the new rules on fiscal expenditure and revenue.

To complement these actions, SOFAZ's operations are being improved. To comply with the "Golden Rule" in the Strategic Road Maps on the National Economy Perspective and Main Sectors of the Economy, transfers from SOFAZ to the state budget are to be kept at a sustainable level to protect against oil price fluctuations, and to enable SOFAZ to accumulate reserves and support low levels of public debt.[9] The actual level of transfers from SOFAZ had, at the time of writing, not yet been set. Even though oil prices have risen slightly since 2016, the government is pursuing a conservative spending strategy on oil revenue. In 2018, for example, SOFAZ transfers to the state budget represented 45% of total state budget, a relatively low level compared with years when oil prices were at similar levels. SOFAZ is also improving the effectiveness of its asset management strategy and increasing transparency in its operations. A 2018 survey by the Sovereign Wealth Fund Institute, which analyzes public asset owners, including sovereign wealth funds, ranked SOFAZ's chief executive 10th out of the 100 most impactful public investors.[10] And SOFAZ, alongside sovereign wealth funds in Australia, Canada, Norway, Singapore, and the United States, received the highest score of 10 in the 2018 Linaburg-Maduell Transparency Index, an international rating method on the public transparency of sovereign wealth funds.

---

[7]   Set up in 1999, SOFAZ is mandated to manage sovereign revenue accrued from the country's oil exports. Its primary tasks are to preserve macroeconomic stability through fiscal transfers and to generate wealth for future generations through investments. SOFAZ is overseen by a supervisory board led by the prime minister and it reports to the president.

[8]   The upper bound for next-year fiscal expenditure is set at 103% of current year fiscal expenditure. The next-year ratio of the non-oil fiscal deficit to non-oil GDP in the next year is targeted to be lower than the current year.

[9]   The stricter transfer mechanism between SOFAZ and the Ministry of Finance, called the Golden Rule, may offer better protection of public expenditure—and thus GDP growth—from oil price fluctuations. By stabilizing the amounts transferred to state funds, the Golden Rule allows for the available funds for the state and exchange rates to be forecast, which in turn increases macroeconomic stability and trust in the manat.

[10] For the rankings, see https://www.swfinstitute.org/public-investor-100-2018/ (accessed 10 November 2018).

The Central Bank of Azerbaijan faced considerable policy challenges arising from macroeconomic conditions during the oil price shock that included severe downward pressure on the manat. To tackle this, the central bank switched to a managed floating exchange rate regime, aggressively devalued the manat twice (by 25% in February 2015 and 32% in December), and allowed the currency to depreciate further after these devaluations. As a result of these measures, the oil revenue-backed consumption of imported products fell sharply and the short-term competitiveness of domestic production increased, which together contributed to a healthier trade balance.

The central bank's credibility fell after the economy was hit by surging inflation caused by falling oil revenue and troubled banks coming to light. The central bank responded by tightening monetary policy and strengthening the financial system through reforms. It reduced money supply, with the M2 measure falling from AZN203.0 billion ($193.2 million) in 2015 to AZN89.4 billion ($52.1 million) in 2017, and raised lending interest rates from 3.5% in 2014 to 10.0% in 2018.

Among the most significant financial reforms was the government setting up the Financial Market Supervisory Authority in 2016 to regulate and supervise securities markets, investment funds, insurance companies, bank and nonbank credit organizations, and payments systems operations. Numerous amendments were made to the Law on Banks of 2004, passed after the oil price shock, to improve administration and efficiency in the banking system, and to create an accountable and transparent financial regulatory system. As a result of these measures, the licenses of a significant number of troubled banks and nonbank credit organizations were revoked. The latest amendment to the banking law, in April 2017, determined the personal responsibility of bank administrators in bank operations, and set a legislative framework for agriculture insurance, mutual funds, and microinsurance instruments.

Under the reforms, several specialized financial institutions were established, including the Azerbaijan Credit Bureau, the Azerbaijan Mortgage and Credit Guarantee Fund, and the State Registry for Encumbrance of Movable Property.[11] These institutions have wide mandates that include increasing the transparency of financial institutions and setting up databases on financial obligations. They provide state credit guarantees and are mandated to increase the range of collateral and to encourage the mobilization of movable assets.

---

[11] As of 30 September 2019, the State Registry for Encumbrance of Movable Property has entered 39,281 encumbrance notifications. Through guarantees from Azerbaijan Mortgage and Credit Guarantee Fund, authorized banks provided loans to entrepreneurs in amount of AZN41 million (guarantee scope constituted AVN22 million). Average term of credits was 28 months, average interest rate 16.3%. Azerbaijan Credit Bureau receiving a total of 3.9 million requests and 2.1 million scoring requests.

The Azerbaijan Credit Bureau, as of April 2018, was exchanging information with the central bank and 117 organizations, including all 30 operating banks, 14 liquidated banks, 47 nonbank credit organizations, 22 insurance companies, and three public utilities.

1.5   The Strategic Road Maps on the National Economy Perspective and Main Sectors of the Economy

Reducing the economy's dependence on oil to achieve a more sustainable pattern of economic growth will require attracting significant levels of foreign direct investment and domestic private investment in non-oil sectors. The government's national plan to 2025 was formulated to help achieve this objective and to sustain economic growth after the country's oil reserves will have been largely depleted in about the span of a generation.

On 6 December 2016, President Ilham Aliyev signed a decree launching the Strategic Road Maps on the National Economy Perspective and Main Sectors of the Economy (Strategic Road Maps).[12]

The national plan comprises 12 road maps: the Strategic Road Map on the National Economy Perspective and 11 sector road maps. The Strategic Road Maps outline the government's strategy for inclusive economic development for 2016–2020 (short term) and proposed targets until 2025 (long term) and beyond 2025. The main objective for 2020 is to achieve widespread macroeconomic stabilization and to make the economy more resilient to future oil price shocks. The long-term objective is to ensure the economy is more diversified and to advance economic development through new drivers of non-oil growth. The long-term strategy aims to further increase the country's competitiveness. Deepening Azerbaijan's integration into the regional and global economy is among the objectives beyond 2025. For the government, the Strategic Road Maps are a way to cement a path for strong, sustained, and shock-resilient growth.

The Strategic Road Maps have four core targets: (i) to strengthen fiscal sustainability and adopt a sustainable monetary policy, (ii) to facilitate privatization and reforms for state-owned enterprises, (iii) to develop human capital, and (iv) to develop a favorable climate for business.

---

[12]   Presidential Decree No. 1138.

The Strategic Road Maps underscore the government's commitment to economic diversification, and they acknowledge that a substantial effort will be needed to achieve this. The 11 sectors identified as sources of economic development are:

- Strategic Road Map on the Oil and Gas Industry, including Chemical Products
- Strategic Road Map on the Production and Processing of Agricultural Products
- Strategic Road Map on the Production of Consumer Goods in Small and Medium Enterprises
- Strategic Road Map on the Development of Heavy Industry and Machine-Building
- Strategic Road Map on the Development of a Specialized Tourism Industry
- Strategic Road Map on the Development of Logistics and Trade
- Strategic Road Map on the Development of Affordable Housing
- Strategic Road Map on Vocational Education and Training
- Strategic Road Map on the Development of Financial Services
- Strategic Road Map on the Development of Telecommunication and Information Technologies
- Strategic Road Map on the Development of Communal Services (Electricity and Heat Energy, Water and Gas).

The Strategic Road Maps estimate that AZN5 billion ($2.9 billion) will be needed to achieve their objectives. They emphasize that the private sector will be the main engine of economic development and that public investments will only be used to mobilize private entrepreneurship. The new strategic development period requires restoring a high, sustainable, inclusive economic growth rate. The main direction here is more about the growth having quality and being diversified, rather than the growth rate itself.

1.6 Initial Results of Diversifying into Agriculture and Tourism

Agriculture and food processing

Primary and processed agriculture products in the 1990s accounted for 15% of Azerbaijan's total exports, with cotton making up more than a third of this.

Since 2009, these products accounted for about 3.6% of total exports. Food and other agriculture imports are rising. They accounted, on an average, for 15% of all goods imports since 2000, rising from 14.8% in 2012 to nearly 18.5% in 2016. The dollar value of Azerbaijan's farm exports remained fairly constant in the first decade of moving to a market economy from 1992, and these exports have generally grown steadily.

Figure 1.9 shows that imports of agriculture and processed farm products have grown faster than exports since 1992.

Figure 1.9: Exports and Imports of Agriculture and Food Products, 1992–2016

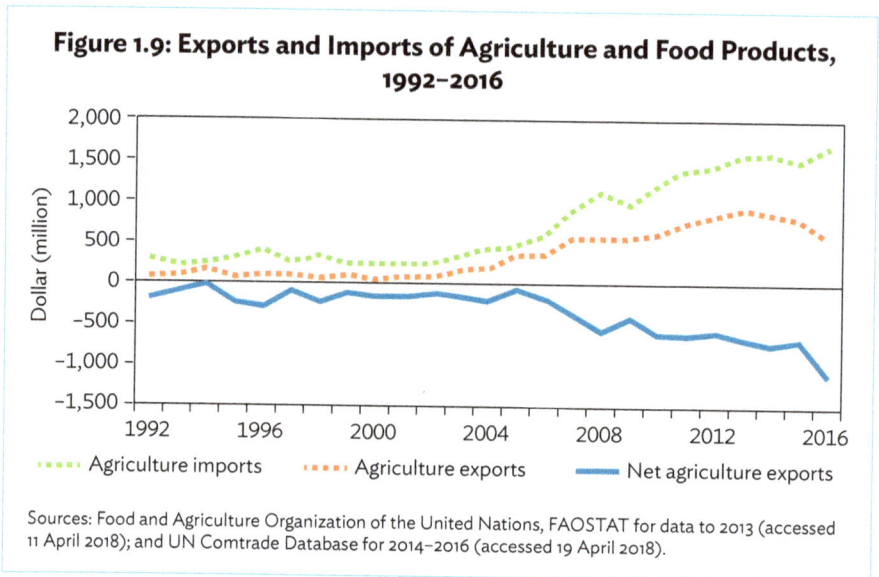

Sources: Food and Agriculture Organization of the United Nations, FAOSTAT for data to 2013 (accessed 11 April 2018); and UN Comtrade Database for 2014–2016 (accessed 19 April 2018).

It is not surprising that the international competitiveness of Azerbaijan's agriculture and food processing exports came under pressure during the oil boom. But it is surprising this continued after the collapse in oil prices in 2014. Agriculture's share of GDP rose little in the period before and after the oil shock, accounting for 5.4% in 2011–2012 and 6.4% in 2015–2016. This pattern is consistent with the signs of Dutch disease. Food processing was also little changed over these periods, accounting for about a quarter of manufacturing GDP.

The level of government spending on agriculture in Azerbaijan is not much different than in neighboring countries. Agriculture output would obviously expand if the government subsidized producer prices, but this would be welfare-reducing for the economy. Protecting farmers and food processors from import competition would encourage more domestic production, but this would be even more wasteful than producer-price subsidies because it would raise domestic food prices. A far better use of public spending to support agriculture would be to invest more in research and development, rural infrastructure, basic education, and technical and vocational education and training.[13] Critical for the transformation of the agriculture sector will be ensuring effective implementation of the government-supported agriculture insurance scheme (to unlock flow of credit to farmers) and facilitation of the agriculture processing industry.

Tourism

Tourism revenue accounted for little more than 1% of all goods and services in 2006, while spending by foreign tourists accounted for just 2.5% of import revenue. Since 2008, however, tourist arrivals have taken off, as Figure 1.10 shows, in part because of the government's efforts to host international events to help promote the country as a tourism destination. Tourism growth has been affected by swings in the manat. Tourism revenue in 2016 was $884 million.

Figure 1.10: Shares of Tourism and Travel Services in Total Exports of Goods and Services, 2000–2016

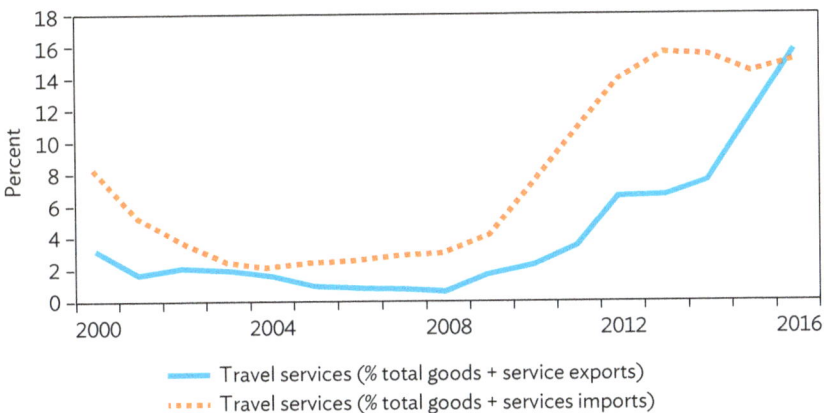

Travel services (% total goods + service exports)
Travel services (% total goods + services imports)

Source: World Bank, World Development Indicators Database.

---

[13]   The number of higher education institution student admissions in the agrarian fields financed through the state budget has increased by almost 3.4 times in the last 5 years.

Despite the encouraging take off in tourism since 2008, the sector needs to be properly developed to attract tourists in sufficient numbers to make a meaningful contribution to economic growth. The COVID-19 pandemic has dealt a serious blow to the country's tourism industry and therefore reforms and investments benefiting this sector have an underlying significance. To this end, the government should provide affordable financing to develop the industry, particularly for upgrading and expanding tourism infrastructure.[14] If the financing constraint can be eased, it will go a long way toward advancing the industry's expansion.

To attract tourists from abroad to Azerbaijan's remoter destinations, such as its ski resorts, the quality of rural roads, and telecommunications and internet connectivity, must be upgraded. Many tourism services are labor intensive, but this is also an industry in which higher levels of skills are needed, particularly in the culinary arts and fluency in foreign languages. Here, further improving the quality of basic education, and vocational education and training, is needed to expand the stock of these skills.[15]

This Country Diagnostic Study aims to contribute to achieving the objectives of the Strategic Road Maps by examining the most binding constraints to achieving sustained and diversified economic growth, and the areas that should be prioritized to advance the government's reform efforts. To do this, the growth diagnostics framework formulated by Hausmann, Rodrik, and Velasco (2005) was applied to Azerbaijan. Chapter 2 explains the framework's methodology and results, and the reform implications of the results for Azerbaijan's economy.

References

Asian Development Bank. 2017. *Key Indicators for Asia and the Pacific 2017.* Manila.

_____. 2010. *Key Indicators for Asia and the Pacific 2010.* Manila.

Hausmann, R., D. Rodrik, and A. Velasco. 2005. Growth Diagnostics. *Faculty Working Paper.* Cambridge, MA: John F. Kennedy School of Government, Harvard University.

---

[14] According to the 2020 Doing Business, Azerbaijan ranked 1st based on the indicator of receiving loans. The main reasons for such an improvement are launch of the credit bureau and set-up of the registry for encumbrance of movable property.

[15] During 2016–2019, the number of qualifications taught in English increased from 39 to 69, and the number of admission places for English-taught programs rose by almost 161%.

CHAPTER 2

The Growth Diagnostics Framework

This chapter draws on the growth diagnostics framework of Hausmann, Rodrik, and Velasco (2005) to offer guidance on how to navigate the reforms that will be needed to achieve Azerbaijan's short-, medium-, and long-term economic targets. The growth diagnostics framework can be used to provide answers to two key questions on Azerbaijan: What are the most binding constraints to sustainable and diversified economic growth? And which areas should be prioritized to advance the country's reform efforts? By focusing on a few areas that represent the biggest hurdles to growth, Azerbaijan—and, indeed, other countries using the growth diagnostics framework—will be more likely to achieve success from their policy and institutional reform efforts.

Building on this theme, Hausmann, Rodrik, and Velasco (2006) introduced the decision tree to summarize these constraints to growth (Figure 2.1). To start the tree, the diagnosis asks questions on the constraints. Take, for example, the question, What is keeping the level of private investment and entrepreneurship low? Is the answer low returns to economic activity or the high cost of finance? If it is the cost of finance, is it high because of limited international finance or an underdeveloped local finance market? If it is underdeveloped local finance, is this because of low domestic savings or poor intermediation between banks, savers, and investors, or government?

Figure 2.1: Growth Diagnostics Decision Tree

Low levels of private investment and entrepreneurship

Low return to economic activity

High cost of finance

Low social returns

Low appropriability

Bad international finance

Bad local finance

Poor geography

Bad infrastructure

Low domestic savings

Poor intermediation

Low human capital

Government failures

Market failures

Micro risks: property rights, corruption, taxes

Macro risks: financial, monetary, fiscal instability

Coordination externalities

Information externalities: "self-discovery"

Source: R. Hausmann, D. Rodrik, and A. Velasco. 2005. *Growth Diagnostics.* Cambridge, MA: John F. Kennedy School of Government, Harvard University.

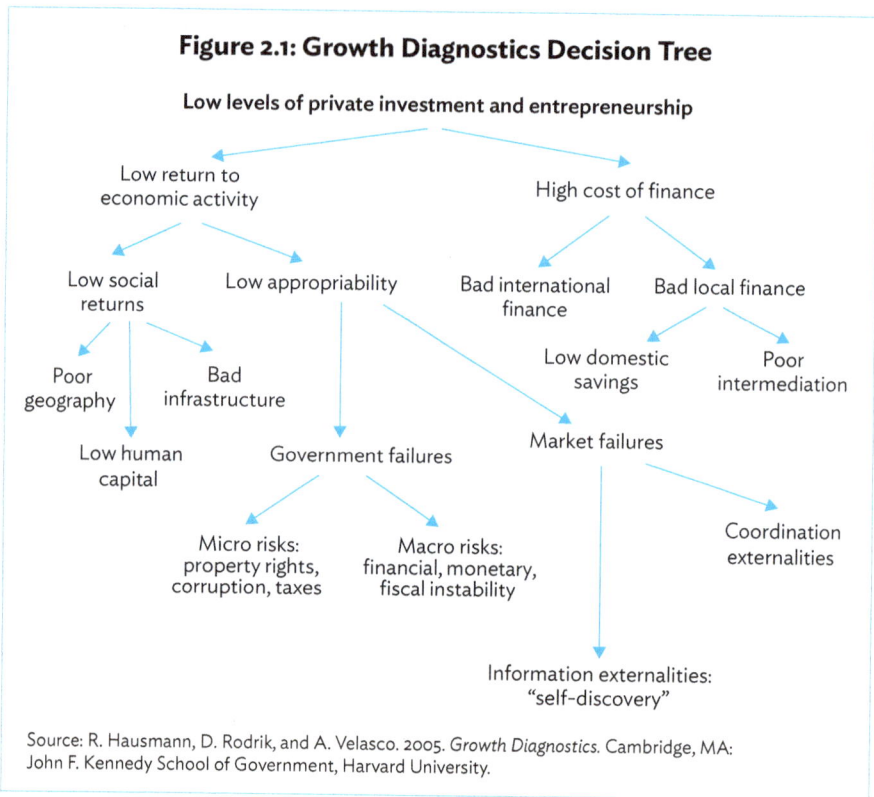

In a theoretical accompaniment to the growth diagnostics approach, Hausmann, Klinger, and Wagner (2008) offer a structured list of tests to help validate findings using the decision tree and eliminate alternative explanations. This "matrix of tests" is not meant to be exhaustive, but it is a useful starting point for matching economic symptoms to the severity of a constraint. The data permitting, the diagnostics draw on the matrix of tests to confirm or reject a hypothesis. To complete the diagnostics after conducting the matrix of tests, this chapter validates the results against the World Economic Forum's (WEF) *Global Competitiveness Report 2018*. Here, Azerbaijan ranks 69th out of 140 countries for overall competitiveness.[1] The following four sections of this chapter correspond to each major branch of the growth diagnostics decision tree: (i) high cost of finance, (ii) low social returns to investment, (iii) government failures, and (iv) market failures.

---

[1]   In 2019, Azerbaijan further moved 11 spots compared to the previous year and ranked 58th among 141 participating states in the *Global Competitiveness Report 2019*. Georgia ranks 74th on that list. It is worth mentioning that, there is an increasing trend of loan portfolio in past 2 years. Also, thanks to reforms carried out in financial sector, the trend of de-dollarization is also observed in loan portfolio (as of 30 September 2019, this indicator is 34.8%).

2.1   High Cost of Finance

Poor access to finance before and after the oil price shock

Various sources point to access to affordable finance as a significant constraint to economic growth in Azerbaijan. According to the World Economic Forum's Executive Opinion Survey, access to finance is the biggest hurdle for doing business in Azerbaijan. World Bank (2018) shows that Azerbaijan substantially lags behind other upper-middle-income countries for getting credit. In an International Monetary Fund (IMF) report on Azerbaijan's finance sector, 30% of firms polled in a survey cited poor access to finance as the biggest obstacle to their businesses (Naceur and Quillin 2014). Firms in Azerbaijan also excessively rely on internal funds for their financing needs, because access to affordable finance is difficult (World Bank 2018).

The banking system's tight credit policies in part reflect the severe stress the sector came under after the economic downturn, when 11 banks lost their licenses in 2016. Another result of the downturn was a fall in the share of local currency deposits in total bank deposits, from 50.1% in 2014 to 24.7% in 2016. Because of uncertainties in the economy affecting the repayment capacity of borrowers, banks further tightened already conservative lending policies, resulting in higher liquidity but low profitability. The high dollarization in the banking system, which accounts for 75% of its deposit base, is also restricting lending and impeding economic growth.

Azerbaijan's underdeveloped nonbank financial institutions and weak governance in the banking sector are the main causes for the lack of access to and the high cost of finance. Microfinance accounts for only about 3% of the overall banking portfolio and contributed to just 5% of gross domestic product (GDP) in 2015. Many recommendations in the 2015 Financial Sector Assessment Program have yet to be implemented. Furthermore, the growth of nonbank credit institutions and credit unions remains slow. Central Bank of Azerbaijan data show the credit portfolio of nonbank institutions totaled AZN454 million ($256.3 million) in January–February 2017, 23.7% less than in the same period of 2016. Weak governance in the banking sector is manifested by a lack of independent members on the supervisory boards of banks. And there is no proper guidance for banking industry regulators to evaluate the processes used by banks to select board members and senior management. Azerbaijan's banks also fail to comply with timely reporting requirements, which undermines transparency.

To evaluate the role of the financial system in the country's economic growth it is useful to look at the sector structure of credit to the real sector. Panel a in Figure 2.2 shows how credit volumes in different sectors have changed since 2000, with the total volume rising until 2015 and then falling sharply on the sudden economic downturn—a pattern that vividly illustrates the country's high dependence on oil revenue. Most credit belongs to households, and here mortgage credit continually rose even after the sharp manat devaluations of 2015 and fall in oil revenue. This was another sign of banks switching to the safer option of savings (Figure 2.2, panel b). The share of credit to households is greater than the share of credit to manufacturing, agriculture, trade, and services—the sectors driving growth—combined. Credit trends have largely been influenced by oil revenue. Before and after the oil boom, nonperforming loans (NPLs) had a higher share in total credit (Figure 2.2, panel c). The share of NPLs remains significant. Slow progress was made in resolving these loans in 2016 and 2017—and there is a risk that the level of NPLs could be drag on economic growth. Unresolved NPLs hold back the economic activity of overextended borrowers, who focus on deleveraging, with these loans trapping resources in unproductive uses.

In terms of the structure of loans by credit institutions, the total volume of loans by all types of credit institutions declined in 2016 and 2017, while the loan share of private banks soared. The number of nonbank credit institutions—47 as of June 2018—and the size of their credit portfolios have risen since 2016. Some banks obtained the licenses of nonbank credit institutions after losing their licenses because of stricter rules on credit. The role of nonbank credit institutions in financing is still trivial and needs to be strengthened.

High interest rates

Azerbaijan's high interest rates suggest that, historically, the cost of finance remains a pressing economic issue. Since 2004, the correlation between the growth rate of real non-oil GDP and the average interest rates on loans has been strong. Indeed, this relationship shows a solid association between the cost of finance and economic growth in Azerbaijan.[2] Figure 2.3 shows average lending rates in Azerbaijan compared with three other countries that were chosen to assess Azerbaijan's relative position.[3]

---

[2] Presently, thanks to the decreased discount interest rates by CBAR and reforms implemented in this sector, we observe a declining trend in interest rates. Hence, as of 30 September 2019, local banks offer consumption credits on average by 23% per year, and business loans by 8% per year.

[3] Georgia is a neighboring country with a very similar past and has embraced bold reforms. The Czech Republic and the Republic of Korea are model developed countries that have experienced exceptional economic growth rates in recent decades.

Figure 2.2: Sector Breakdown of Loans

a. Credit to the Economy by Sector, 2000–2017

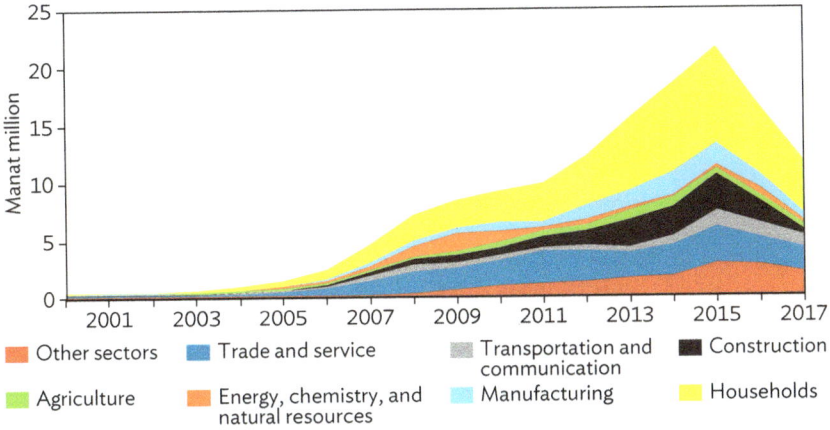

Other sectors | Trade and service | Transportation and communication | Construction
Agriculture | Energy, chemistry, and natural resources | Manufacturing | Households

b. Structure of Credit to Households, 2006–2017

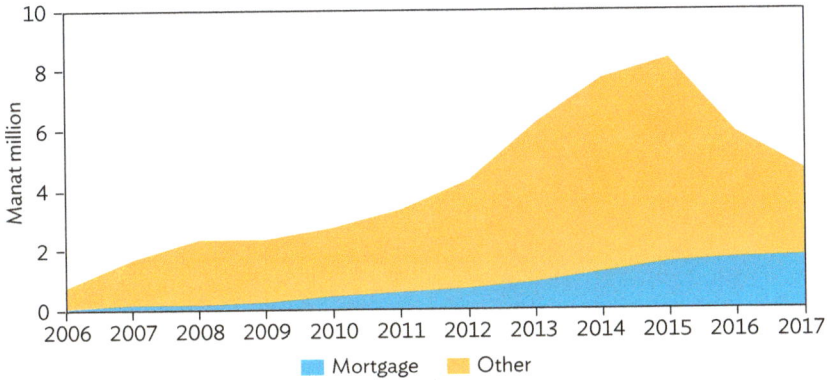

Mortgage | Other

c. Nonperforming Loans, , 2008–2017

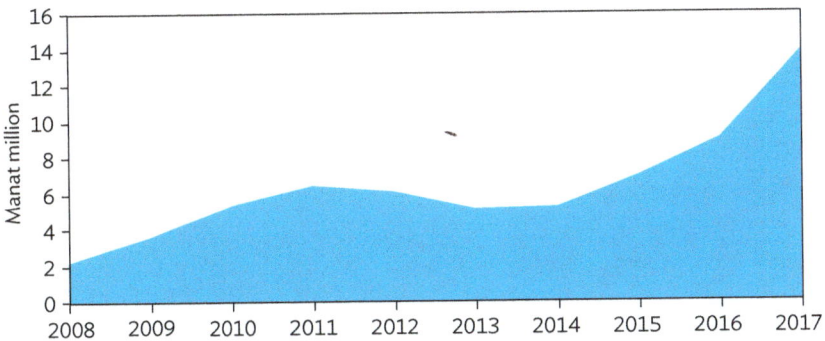

Source: Central Bank of Azerbaijan.

Figure 2.3: Average Lending Interest Rates in Azerbaijan and Selected Countries, 2003–2017

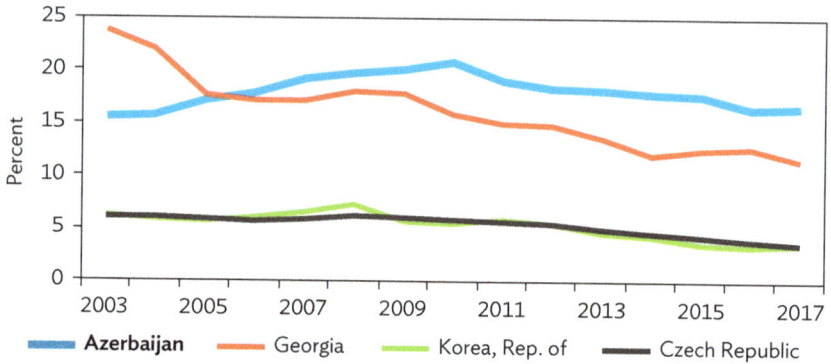

Note: The lending rates in Georgia, despite being previously higher than Azerbaijan's, have begun to taper off, as was the general trend in the region. Lower rates could be partly explained by a more competitive banking sector and a vibrant banking and NBFI in Georgia.
Source: World Bank, World Development Indicators Database.

While historical lending interest rates reflect the high cost of domestic and external finance in Azerbaijan, it is not possible to know whether the problem is rooted in savings, investments, or financial intermediation. To evaluate the supply side of loanable funds—the most evident and direct indicator—deposit interest rates are analyzed. Figure 2.4 plots the historical average of these rates in Azerbaijan with the same countries in Figure 2.3. Despite a declining trend since about 2009, average rates have been high in Azerbaijan, indicating that the government and banks may have restricted access to domestic and foreign savings.[4] A high tax burden can also reduce savings by affecting household incomes. Under amendments to the tax code, households do not pay taxes on interest income for 7 years, starting from 2016, which shows that high taxes on savings cannot be a constraint to growth in Azerbaijan.[5]

A symptom that hints at low foreign borrowing is a negative relationship between economic growth and the current account. The link is straightforward: improvements in the current account signal declining country risk, leading to lower lending interest rates and, ultimately, higher economic growth.

---

[4]   Currently there is a decreasing trend in interest rates of the credits. We would like to note that, (as of 1 October 2019 the average interest rate of retailing loans was over 22 %) consumption credits decreased from 22.6% to 22.3%, and business credits from 9.8% to 8.6% during the last quarter. This trend is expected to continue amid declining discount rates of CBAR.

[5]   Amendments No. 454-VQD and No. 102-VQD.

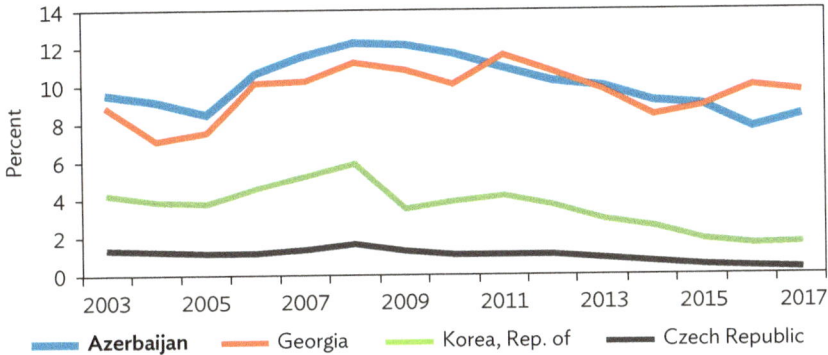

Figure 2.4: Average Deposit Interest Rates in Azerbaijan and Selected Countries, 2003–2017

Source: World Bank, World Development Indicators Database.

Azerbaijan's current account balance and the growth rate of real non-oil GDP move together, implying a strong positive correlation between these variables. Unfortunately, Azerbaijan's current account balance is dominated by oil exports, which have strong direct and indirect positive effects on domestic non-oil production.

Ease of access to foreign finance can be gauged by the sovereign risk and credit ratings of international credit rating agencies. The "oil factor" has a significant influence on these ratings. When oil revenue was high in Azerbaijan, the country's credit ratings were lower-medium grade (BBB–). When oil revenue fell after 2014, the rating agencies lowered their ratings to non-investment grade (BB+) and speculative grade (BB). A consequence of these downgrades has been to restrict access to international finance. Uncertainty over the direction of exchange rates can restrict access to foreign savings. The sharp manat devaluations of February and December 2015, and the currency's further depreciation since then, show how dependent the currency is on the price of oil. The reforms implemented in the country's banking sector, continued dynamic development in national economy, as well as the state support to this sector were among the key aspects that spurred Moody's rating agency to revise the banking system forecasting in Azerbaijan from stable to positive in 2019.

High cost of financial intermediation

The diagnosis of the high cost of finance also looks into problems of financial intermediation.[6] The difference between the average lending rate and deposit rate—the spread—is a direct indicator of risk and inefficiency in the finance sector. As Figure 2.5 shows, the spread has always been historically high in Azerbaijan. It is important to note this is not because of high inflation or uncertainty over exchange rates—the spread has remained high regardless of the level of both. The reason is the considerable risk, cost, and taxation of financial intermediation in Azerbaijan.[7] High operating costs, low consolidation, and inflation are important drivers of Azerbaijan's interest rate spread.[8]

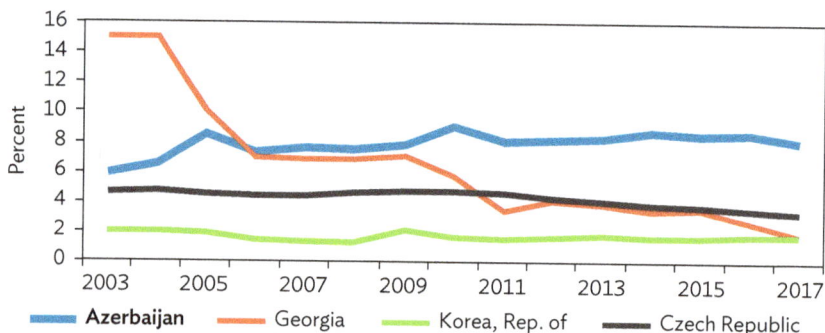

Figure 2.5: Average Interest Rate Spreads in Azerbaijan and Selected Countries, 2003–2017

Source: World Bank, World Development Indicators Database.

The interest rate spreads shown in Figure 2.5 are based on averages and hide useful information. Breaking down the spreads into their components shows how fluctuations in global oil prices and, hence, oil revenue have shaped interest rates in Azerbaijan. This exercise also shows the spread is higher, especially since 2017, for individuals holding foreign currency.[9] The spread for individuals holding manats and legal entities holding both is relatively low and has fallen further since 2015.

---

[6] Currently we observe a decline in costs of financing by the banks. Thus, compared to 2017, a decrease in the interest rate ceiling assigned by the Deposit Insurance Fund allowed the banks to decrease their interest rate costs. Currently the Fund defined the ceiling for annual interest rates for protected deposited in national currency as 10%, and deposits in foreign currencies as 2.5%.

[7] These determinants are extensively studied in Naceur and Quillin (2014).

[8] Inflation has affected the spread of banks. There is a decrease in the operational costs of banks in recent years, which indicate optimization of costs related to digitalization efforts.

[9] The principles adopted by FMSA in May 2016 defined limits for loans issued in foreign currency. Thus, individuals who do not generate income in foreign currency were restricted to receive a loan in foreign currency. The interest rate for deposits in foreign currency is 2.5%.

The observed patterns in different interest rates reveal important information on the structure of savings. The devaluations in the manat obviously affected the structure of savings, with economic agents, especially households, switching from manat to foreign currency or to real estate and other reliable assets. After the devaluations, the weight of total manat deposits dipped in favor of foreign currency deposits. These movements indicate that the devaluations led to dollarization. Following double devaluations, the tendency of dollarization observed in deposits has declined. Thus, while the percentage of deposits in foreign currency constituted 79.7% in 2016, this indicator made up 56.2% as of 30 September 2019.

Oil revenue is an important but indirect determinant of interest rates in Azerbaijan. Interest rates and the average interest rate spread decline when oil revenue falls, and both stabilize when oil revenue rises. When financial resources are scarce, banks are under pressure to carry out reforms and become more efficient.[10] Furthermore, interest rates in Azerbaijan are not completely indicative of the cost of and access to finance. A deeper analysis of how constraints to finance can impede economic growth in Azerbaijan goes beyond the standard symptoms suggested in Hausmann, Klinger, and Wagner (2008). Figure 2.6 shows that in Azerbaijan declining interest rates result in a significant reduction in credit to the economy, which is counterintuitive to the approach in Hausmann, Rodrik, and Velasco (2005). Here, the especially sharp decline in long-term credit to the economy is alarming, because loans directed to long-term investments induce growth.

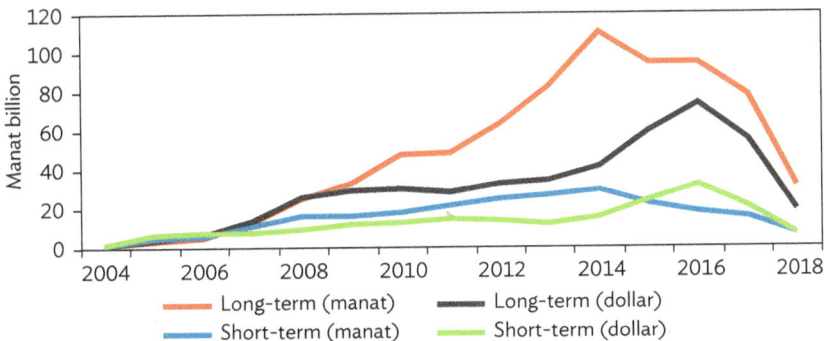

Figure 2.6: Credit to the Economy by Maturity and Currency, 2004–2018

Source: Central Bank of Azerbaijan.

---

[10] The decrease observed in credit portfolio mainly had to do with the transfer of distressed assets to "Agrarkredit" CJSC defined by the International Bank of Azerbaijan within framework of activities that focused on improving the performance of the bank and the closure of several banks.

Other reasons obstruct firms in Azerbaijan from using financial resources to meet their investment needs. Because of this, firms have preferred to use internal rather external sources of financing for their investment needs. According to the State Statistical Committee, only 14% of investment is financed through banks, with 53% coming from firms' internal sources. It should also be noted that the share of government resources rose substantially when oil revenue was high before dropping in 2014 on the falling oil price—a pattern that shows the unquestionable influence of oil revenue on investments to fixed capital.

Azerbaijan's financial institutions do not enjoy a high level of public trust. In most Commonwealth of Independent States countries, formal savings are low compared with other countries in Central and West Asia, but only 15% of adults in Azerbaijan have a bank account, according to the World Bank's Global Financial Development Database. This is a sign of the low level of trust in the country's financial institutions and financial system. Another factor supporting this view is that 46% of banked Azerbaijanis hold savings in cash (World Bank 2016). There is little expectation among financial services users of institutional or government protection. Formal complaints against financial services' providers are rarely made when disputes arise; this is because of a widespread perception that the country's financial institutions are too powerful to take on and that government procedures do not work.

The diversification of banking sector profits is low. According to Azerbaijan's Financial Market Supervisory Authority, the aggregate operating profit of banks is mainly generated by interest income on loans, estimated at 72% of total interest income. A sign of the sector's high level of operating inefficiency is that non-interest expenditure is unusually high and almost equal to interest expenditure.

The fault lines in Azerbaijan's financial system were long hidden by the country's high oil revenue. During the oil boom, the finance sector was buoyed by growing credit and high profits. But falling oil prices and the consequent reduction of oil revenue revealed problems in the sector that pose serious constraints to economic growth. The authors would like to note that, in post-devaluation period, credit activity was slowly restored. Thus, while lending in bank sector was AZN5 billion in 2017, it rose to AZN7.6 billion in 2018. In general, 57% of the loans issued in 2018 were allocated to real economy.

The oil factor also had implications on the validity of the growth diagnostic test results. Initial results show that the growth diagnostics methodology is not ideal for economies whose fiscal health is strongly influenced by their hydrocarbons sector. The analysis for Azerbaijan, wherever possible, uses the oil factor in the tests recommended by Hausmann, Klinger, and Wagner (2008). As a result, some findings were counterintuitive. For instance, decreasing interest rates and spreads were accompanied by declining credit to the Azerbaijan economy. So for the finance branch of the decision tree, other economic symptoms, in line with the argument put forward by Hausmann, Rodrik, and Velasco (2005), had to be examined.

From the growth diagnostics results, it is possible to show that the main reasons behind the high cost of finance can be classified under two general groups: high risk in the real sector and high inefficiency in the finance sector. In the real sector, doing business is perceived to be risky in Azerbaijan.[11] Investors tend to seek short-term, high-return, and high-risk projects, undermining the actual production of goods and services in the economy. Banks, in turn, react to high-risk projects by reducing access to credit. Azerbaijan's mostly inefficient banks, which operate in the country's rather special financial environment, have limited capacity to accurately assess the riskiness of proposed business ventures. Because of this, they artificially raise interest rates or simply turn down loan applications. As noted earlier, banks generate more profit by setting high interest rates spreads. And the lack of public trust in the financial system means that savings are not entrusted to banks, which pushes deposit rates up.

The WEF's 2017 financial market development competitiveness indicators ranked Azerbaijan 79th out of 137 countries, behind Georgia, which placed 63rd. Azerbaijan's rankings were particularly low for the soundness of banks (85th) but better than Kazakhstan (114th) and the Kyrgyz Republic (107th). Ease of access to loans (57th) and the availability of financial services (44th) were also cited as issues hampering competitiveness. In 2019, Azerbaijan improved and ranked 58th among 141 participating states in the 2019 Global Competitiveness Report. Azerbaijan ranks 77th (in 2018 the rank was 92nd) according to the "Soundness of banks" indicator, which was used in developing the overall index. The value of collateral for a loan is very high compared with Europe and Central Asia or lower-middle-income countries (World Bank 2013).

---

[11] This statement may contradict with the results of the World Bank's Doing Business project. As Hausmann, Rodrik, and Velasco (2005) found, focusing on thriving firms in an economy might not be correct. They argue that the focus should instead be on the problems of struggling firms. The issue with the Doing Business project is that it is based on surveys of already established firms, while struggling firms are ignored.

2.2 Insufficient Investments in Human Capital and Infrastructure

Low gross enrollment ratios and student outcomes

Azerbaijan's gross enrollment ratios in preprimary and tertiary education have long been considerably lower than the average for Europe and Central Asia. In 2017, the preprimary ratio was 36%, compared with an average of 74.8 % in Europe and Central Asia, and 27.1% for the tertiary level, compared with 66.6% (Figure 2.7). The gross enrollment rate in tertiary education in Azerbaijan is lower than other countries in the region, including Kazakhstan (49.6%) and Kyrgyz Republic (43.7%). To be able to tackle low enrollment in higher education, the government needs to find ways of further increasing school admission rates.[12]

Figure 2.7: Gross Enrollment Ratios, 1991–2017

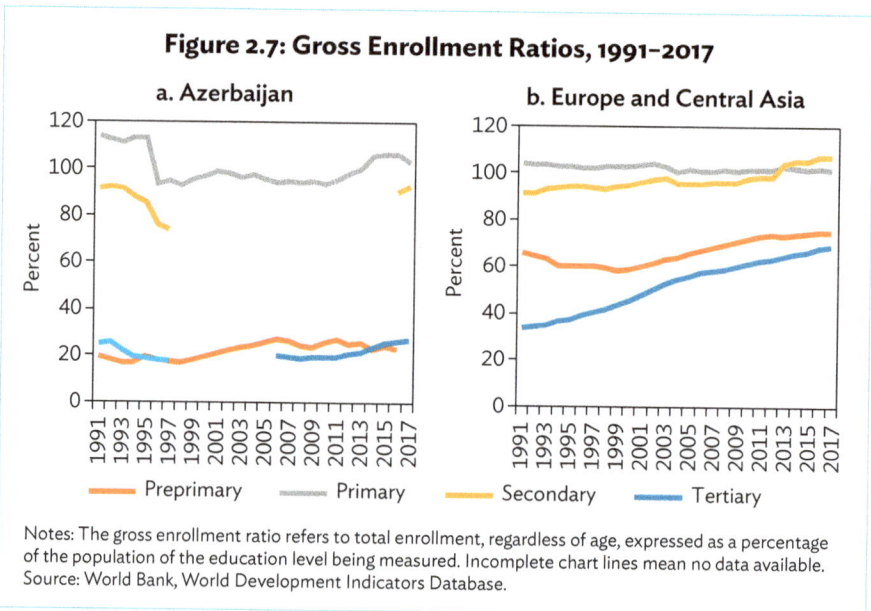

Notes: The gross enrollment ratio refers to total enrollment, regardless of age, expressed as a percentage of the population of the education level being measured. Incomplete chart lines mean no data available. Source: World Bank, World Development Indicators Database.

Azerbaijan's student outcomes compared with those in Europe and Central Asia also reflect the poor quality of the country's education. In the 2009 Programme for International Student Assessmenttest for 15-year-olds held

---

[12] To increase admission rates in tertiary education, in 2019–2020 academic year the government raised number of budget funded places in undergraduate programs of higher educational institutions from 12,300 to 20,500 (42% of all admissions). Also, the Law on Education has been amended to enable college graduates to receive higher education: in 2019, for the first time, 4,774 sub-bachelors were admitted to higher educational institutions without competition.

in 65 countries, Azerbaijan ranked 63rd in science and 64th in reading. It did better in math, placing 45th. Compared with other Central Asian countries, government spending in Azerbaijan on education has been historically low and is generally declining. Education spending as a percentage of GDP has been below 5% since 1998, with the share of education in total government spending falling from 18.8% in 1998 to 8.6% in 2018. For higher education, spending declined from AZN150 million ($190 million) in 2011 to AZN109 million ($138.8 million) in 2014 to AZN160 million ($92 million) in 2017 while the number of students rose from 120,000 to 153,000 in the same time period. This represents a drop in government spending per student, suggesting the need to increase government spending on higher education.[13]

Azerbaijan has the second lowest pupil–teacher ratio at the primary level (14:1) and 4th lowest at the tertiary level (10:1) in Central Asia. A low pupil–teacher ratio typically means that teachers have more time to attend to the individual needs of students. But the low ratio in Azerbaijan, as noted in World Bank (2015), is because of a decline in the number of students. This has been attributed to concerns over the quality of teaching, itself a result of low standards for hiring teachers. Low salaries at all levels of education discourage the qualified and competent from becoming teachers.[14] In 2015, only 52% of total spending on public education institutions went to teacher salaries. The comparable figure in Europe and Central Asia was 69%. In 2019, more than 83% of the funds allocated to public education institutions at all levels of education were allocated for teacher salaries. In general education, the number was 96.8%. In 2020, it is expected to be 84.6% and 97%, respectively. Azerbaijan's centralized education system limits the capacity for more autonomous decisions on curricula, education practices, and budget planning and implementation to be made at the local level, to better fit the needs on the ground.

A World Bank commissioned study for Azerbaijan points to gaps in the quality of Azerbaijan's postsecondary education (Onder 2013). Results from this

---

[13] While the number of students that studied in higher educational institutions In 2018-2019, there were 176,700 students in higher education institutions, including 99,900 self-paid students. In the 2019-2020 academic years, this number is 181,100, including 93,200 of self-paid students. The total higher education student expenditures (own spending and state budget) was AZN400 in 2018 and AZN474.3 million in 2019. This translates to total per student expenditure of about average AZN2,200 in 2018 and AZN2,600 in 2019.

[14] Since 2010, the government has incentivized young teachers (below 35 years old) to work in general education institutions in the rural areas (Decision ff the Cabinet of Ministers No. 67 dated 14 April 2010). The incentives include housing rent and utilities compensation of AZN60, if young teachers stay at rural schools for 3 years; allocation of permanent land plots for settlement; AZN100 top-up to the monthly salary for 3 years, if the general education facility is located more than 20 km away from the regional center. Based on the Ministry of Education's knowledge and skills assessment of the general educational teachers in 2014-2018, the weekly teaching load of more than 150,000 teacher increased by 1.5 times and their salaried doubled.

study also suggest inequalities in higher education attainment between urban and rural regions, and across income groups. The Strategic Road Maps on the National Economy Perspective and Main Sectors of the Economy (Strategic Road Maps) acknowledges that the country has a skills gap.[15] The results of the World Bank's 2013 STEP Skills Measurement Program for Azerbaijan show this shortage is most pronounced for highly skilled workers, such as machine operators, professionals, technicians, and managers.[16] The survey also shows the skills most often lacking are job-specific technical skills, problem-solving skills, and soft skills, such as leadership, teamwork, and openness to experience. The WEF's *Global Competitiveness Report 2018* says Azerbaijan's inadequately skilled workforce is one of the major factors hindering business, along with weak governance, poor access to finance, foreign currency regulations, and inflation.

Data from the 2018 European Union Business Climate Survey shows that employers are concerned about the shortage of skilled labor in Azerbaijan. The survey found that only 31% of businesses were satisfied with the availability of skilled workers. Forty-seven percent were satisfied with the qualifications of their employees and 44% with their productivity. Forty-one percent of employers were dissatisfied with the education their employees had received; 41% were dissatisfied with the technical and vocational education and training system. The skills shortage suggests the education system is not responding to the demands of employers. The mismatch reflects weak cooperation between national and public bodies, and between industry and learning institutions, and is aggravated by a lack of adequate labor market information (ETF 2015).

Impact on health care from oil revenue

Health is integral to human capital development. The increase in oil revenues during the oil boom enabled the government to sharply increase public spending on health, most of which went to free medicine and medical supplies, and upgrading health care infrastructure (Bonilla-Chacin, Afandiyeva, and Suaya 2018). In 2015, about 23% of Azerbaijan households incurred catastrophic health expenditures, allocating more than 20% of their total consumption to health, according to World Health Organization estimates.[17]

---

[15] The Strategic Road Maps say: "The lowest quality human capital indicator in education and employment among various age groups in Azerbaijan relates to the 15–24 age group and the highest indicator relates to 55–64 age group. This means that the best human resource potential in Azerbaijan is accommodated by the old-age generation, while the weakest human resources are among young people."

[16] The World Bank STEP Skills Measurement Program measures skills in low- and middle-income countries, and includes household and employer surveys.

[17] World Health Organization, Global Health Expenditure Database.

Out of pocket payments for health has been historically high in Azerbaijan; in 2016, 79% of health spending in Azerbaijan was from patients' own payments, the highest rate for this in the region. Note that although per government health expenditure decreased in absolute dollar terms from 2014 to 2016, it has increased in purchasing power parity. Poor health outcomes in the population could impede economic diversification, because it results in low workforce productivity. To this end, despite undergoing GDP slowdown, the government initiated compulsory health insurance with pilots ongoing in three districts in 2019. Hausmann et al (2008) identified education and not health as the critical element in the "matrix of tests" needed for an exhaustive diagnostics. Health is briefly mentioned here to acquire a holistic view of Azerbaijan's human capital stock.

Self-generation and income inequality

The skills shortage should push Azerbaijan's private sector to develop strategies to overcome the lack of qualified workers. Hausmann, Rodrik, and Velasco (2006) argue that this is the private sector's response to bypass constraints to growth. To apply this to Azerbaijan: if the country's human capital constraint is binding, the "self-generation" of a highly educated and skilled workforce by large firms to ensure a continuous flow of quality employees should be observed. Figure 2.8 shows that during 2009–2013, the share of workers in Azerbaijan with intermediate education fell and the proportion of workers with advanced education rose. But in the same period, the share of workers with only basic education also increased.

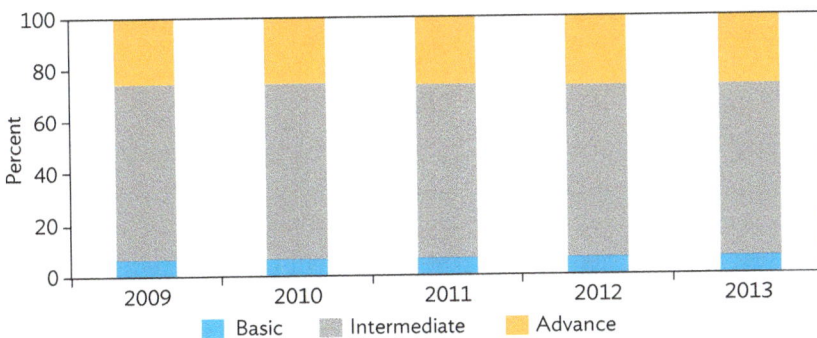

Figure 2.8: Education Attainment of the Employed, 2009–2013

Source: International Labour Organization, ILOSTAT Database.

World Bank (2015) notes that tertiary school graduates tend to specialize in education, health, and oil-related manufacturing, but fewer graduates are produced in services, agriculture, and non-oil-related manufacturing. In Azerbaijan's oil and gas industry, the demand for human capital is so great that several foreign firms have set up university courses and learning centers to educate prospective employees. For example, BP PLC, a major investor in the country's oil and gas industry, partnered with Qafqaz University to set up a large training center to expand the curriculum to cover undergraduate education in chemical engineering, mechanical engineering, petroleum engineering, and other engineering disciplines (World Bank 2015). Educating prospective employees in this way will enable private firms to develop and sustain their own pool of locally hired oil and gas industry workers. In the non-oil sector, a growing number of government agencies, including the Ministries of Tourism, Border Services, National Security, Customs, and Emergency Situations, have opened their own training and learning centers to train future officials on ministry-specific skills.

The adult literacy rate is positively correlated with real gross national income per capita. The World Bank's World Development Indicators show that Azerbaijan workers earn slightly more than their equally educated counterparts in Uzbekistan, but less than counterparts in Kazakhstan and the Russian Federation. Across sectors, however, higher wages have been paid in the hydrocarbon sector since 2010 than in other sectors (Figure 2.9). If this wage gap persists, it could impede economic diversification because of the difficulties in recruiting highly skilled workers for lower-paid jobs. The disparity in wages between the oil and non-oil sectors also distorts the labor market, and is a disincentive for sector mobility and productivity.

Azerbaijan has one of the lowest gross tertiary education enrollment ratios in Central and West Asia. The ratio, at 27.1% in 2017 and 41% in 2019, lower than in Kazakhstan (53.2% in 2018) and the Kyrgyz Republic (43.6% in 2017). In 2017, the average net enrollment ratio for middle-income countries was 35.58% and 52.1% for upper-middle-income ones.[18]

The WEF's 2016–2017 competitiveness indicators for higher education and training show the overall quality of Azerbaijan's education system is moderately good, with the country placing 78th out of 138 countries. But it ranked only 94th for the gross tertiary education enrollment rate and 89th for quality of management schools. The WEF's 2018-2019 competitiveness indicators rank Azerbaijan 54th in overall skills (15th in digital skills and 32nd in graduates' knowledge and skills) and 49th in the quality of vocational education.

---

[18] Source: World Bank, World Development Indicators Database.

Figure 2.9: Average Monthly Nominal Wages and Salaries by Sector, 2007–2016

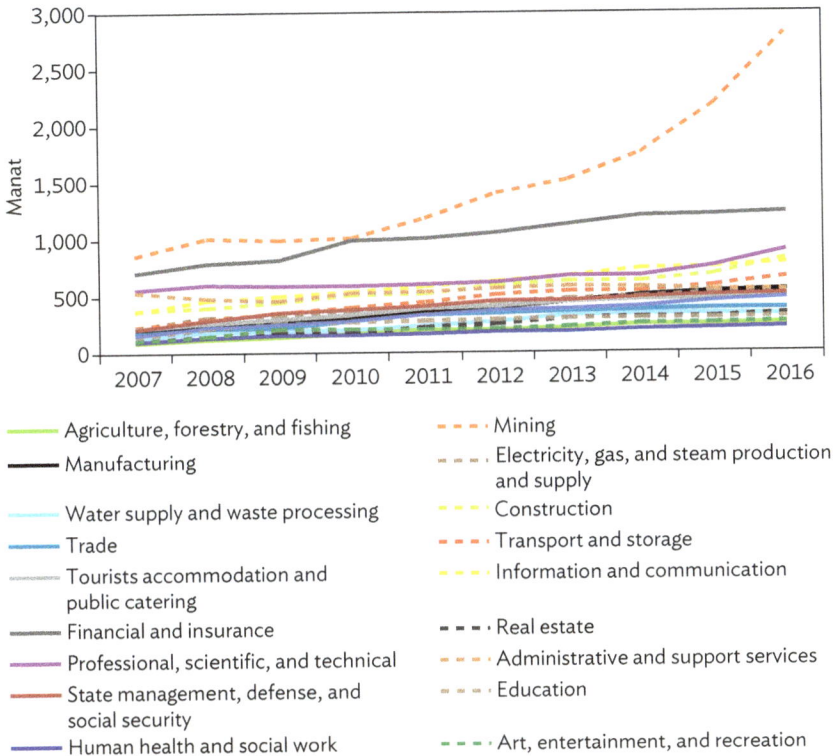

Source: State Statistical Committee.

Infrastructure Quality Varies Across Types

The bulk of Azerbaijan's infrastructure was inherited from the former Soviet Union. Compared to other Central and West Asian countries, the overall quality of the country's infrastructure is good, despite some negative survey findings. Differences in quality can, however, be seen across types of infrastructure (Table 2.1). Heavy investment in upgrading infrastructure since independence has greatly improved electricity supply. But water supply and the rail infrastructure is in generally poor condition. Transport infrastructure has been historically important to Azerbaijan because of its oil and gas industry. An extensive network of pipelines enables the country to reach world markets for its oil and gas exports (Ibrahimov 2016).

Table 2.1: World Economic Forum Infrastructure Indicators: Azerbaijan and Comparator Countries, 2017

Country	Overall Score and Rank	Overall Infrastructure	Roads	Rail	Ports	Airports
Russian Federation	4.9 (35)	4.0	2.9	4.5	4.2	4.6
Azerbaijan	**4.5 (51)**	**5.0**	**4.8**	**4.7**	**4.7**	**5.6**
Kazakhstan	4.2 (68)	3.9	2.9	4.1	3.2	4.0
Georgia	4.2 (69)	3.9	3.8	3.8	4.1	4.3
Tajikistan	3.3 (99)	4.2	4.1	3.7	2.0	4.3
Kyrgyz Republic	3.0 (109)	3.0	2.7	2.4	1.4	3.1

Note: Score: 1 = lowest, 7 = highest, rank out of 137 economies.
Source: World Economic Forum. 2017. *Global Competitiveness Report 2017–2018*. Geneva.

Poor condition of roads, sharply rising vehicle ownership

Roads service over 80% of Azerbaijan's total passenger movements when measured in passenger kilometers (km), and more than 60% of goods, when measured in tons per kilometer. Although most freight is still carried by rail, road freight turnover increased from 7.5 billion ton-kilometers in 2005 to 16.8 billion ton-kilometers in 2016. The contribution of roads in the overall transport sector is expected to substantially increase in the coming years (ADB 2019).

The nonurban road network comprises 25,000 km of roads, including 4,498 km in the Nagorno-Karabakh secessionist region and 2,078 km in the Nakhchivan Autonomous Republic.[19] The network consists of 7,016 km of state roads and 17,997 km of municipal roads. Fifty-one percent of roads are sealed; 60% of the road network is in poor condition. The rate of motorization per 1,000 population is growing rapidly. There were 1.30 million vehicles in 2016, compared to 983,000 vehicles in 2010, and only 612,000 in 2005. And in Baku, vehicles have six times since the early 1990s; there are now 200 per 1,000 inhabitants (ADB 2019).

Azerbaijan's transport network cannot meet the needs of its expanding and diversifying economy. The country has, for example, just 285 km of four-lane highways. Despite the budget for road maintenance increasing from AZN3.3 million ($5.7 million) in 2001 to AZN42.2 million ($72.0 million) in 2011, the level is still insufficient—and because of this a large part of the road network is rapidly deteriorating. Vehicle overloading is contributing to the

---

[19]   The Nakhchivan Autonomous Republic is an enclave of the Republic of Azerbaijan and is connected by air transport from Baku and by road from Iran.

rapid deterioration of the country's pavements. The poor condition of roads results in high transport costs, delayed delivery times, and many accidents. Poor connectivity outside Baku and in rural areas is a problem, with 80% of local rural roads in a dismal condition (World Bank 2015).

The private sector plays a vital role in providing road transport services, accounting for more than 95% of freight and passenger traffic. Most state-owned operators that once dominated the transport market are now mostly in private hands. The road freight market was opened to foreign operators in the early 2000s.

Rapidly deteriorating rail system

Azerbaijan has 2,133 km of rail track: 1,169 km of electrified track and 803 km of double-track. State-owned Azerbaijan Railways, a closed joint stock company, transports an average of 22.3 million tons of freight and 4.8 million passengers annually. In 2018, Azerbaijan Railway transported 13.9 million tons of freight and 2.8 million passengers, making the railway a vital mode of transport. Azerbaijan Railways has failed to adequately reinvest earnings in infrastructure and rolling stock. This has resulted in a rapid deterioration of rail assets and a chronic decline in the serviceability of its locomotive and wagon fleet, which desperately needs upgrading. Tracks are in poor condition, causing speed restrictions on 183 km of the 502 km east–west line and 126 km of the 211 km north–south line that reduce the efficiency of the rail network. With no track rehabilitation program, railway maintenance costs are expected to rise by 20% a year and average train speeds decline to 15 km per hour every year. The electric power system and substations are in poor condition, especially along the east–west line. The 27 substations need to be completely refurbished in the coming years. The rail network's overhead catenaries are close to failing (ADB 2014a, ADB 2019).

Civil aviation expanding

Air transport in Azerbaijan has vastly improved since independence. Government spending on civil aviation, totaling $200 million since then, has gone into buying modern aircraft, upgrading flight management systems, training, and building, in 1999, a new international airport in Baku. Heydar Aliyev International Airport is used by some 60 airlines and is the busiest airport in the Caucasus. Azerbaijan has five other international airports, and 11 regions in the country are connected with Baku by air. In 2018, 4.43 million domestic and international aircraft passengers used Heydar Aliyev International Airport, far more than the number of passengers using other international airports in

Central and West Asia. Georgia's Tbilisi International Airport had 3.8 million domestic and international passengers in 2018, while Tashkent International Airport domestic and international passengers were estimated at 3 million in 2017 (European AIS Database). By 2020, 7 million passengers are forecast to use Heydar Aliyev International Airport (Azernews 2018). Azerbaijan vastly expanded its air cargo operations with the opening of Baku Cargo Terminal in 2005. This is one of the biggest and most technically advanced cargo terminals in the region, and has helped turn Baku into an important cargo transfer point. In 2017, the volume of Azerbaijan's air transport freight was 737 million tons/km. Baku Cargo Terminal serves as a secondary hub for Cargolux, the eighth largest cargo airline.

Logistics underperforming

The World Bank's 2016 Logistics Performance Index ranks Azerbaijan below Georgia, Kazakhstan, and the Russian Federation in the logistics performance of roads, rail, and port infrastructure. Azerbaijan placed 118th out of 160 countries on the index, a lower score than in 2012. Its highest score was for the quality of trade and transport infrastructure (2.71 out of out of a possible top score of 5); its lowest score was for tracking consignments and on-time delivery (2.14) (Figure 2.10).

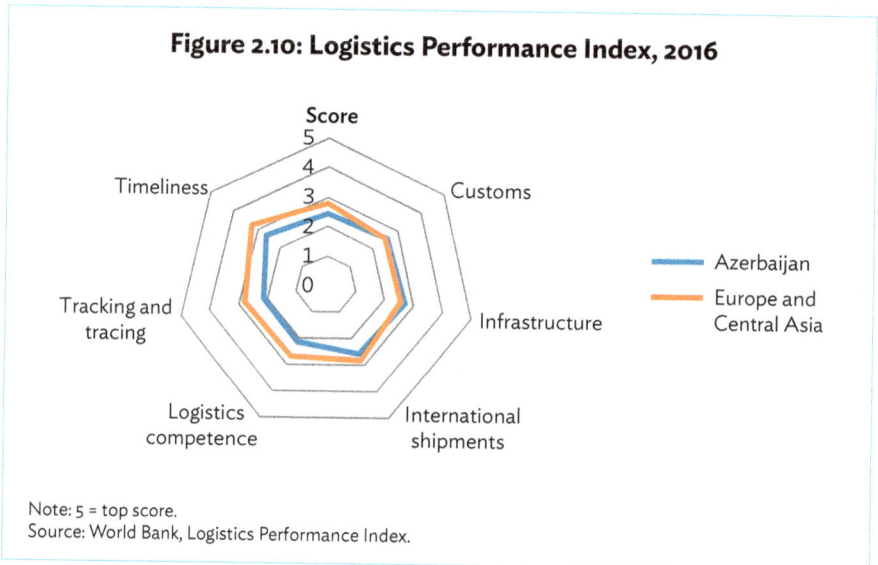

Figure 2.10: Logistics Performance Index, 2016

Note: 5 = top score.
Source: World Bank, Logistics Performance Index.

Baku's traffic congestion

Azerbaijan has the highest population density in the region and traffic congestion is a potential constraint to growth. The main urban traffic congestion problems are in Baku. Economic growth and new urban development, coupled with booming vehicle ownership, are overstretching Baku's transport system. A lack of parking in the city center has resulted in unregulated street parking, which severely impedes the flow of traffic (ADB 2014). All major roads in the capital are congested and therefore a health concern. And because the road network was poorly built and is poorly maintained, accidents have increased over the years.

The government recognizes the need to modernize and expand Baku's bus network. This has about 220 routes, but bus lanes are needed on them. Baku's bus networks are not integrated, underscoring the need for a transport authority for the capital. Public transport fares are too low for operators to cover a significant part of their operating costs and to replace assets (ADB 2014).

In 2010, the World Bank identified urban transport priorities for Baku, which included

- improving the transport industry's coordination of planning, budgeting, and management;
- a road maintenance policy to reduce the environmental impacts of traffic and the socioeconomic costs caused by traffic accidents;
- modernizing public transport to make it faster and safer;
- a parking strategy with cost-effective solutions involving the private sector; and
- implementing a traffic management and information strategy.

Some of these priorities have been implemented, as have other urban transport reforms. But Baku still does not have a master plan for a comprehensive and sustainable strategy for transport, which is organizationally fragmented. Indeed, there is no urban transport strategy for the country as a whole.

2.3 Government Failures

Improvements in regulatory quality

Hausmann, Klinger, and Wagner (2008) state that distortions in regulatory quality, such as the poor protection of property rights and weak governance, tend to discourage private investment. In the Heritage Foundation's 2018 Index of Economic Freedom, Azerbaijan scored 53.6 out of 100 on property rights—lower than the Kyrgyz Republic, the Russian Federation, Tajikistan, and Uzbekistan, but higher than Georgia and Kazakhstan.[20] In the World Bank's Worldwide Governance Indicators, Azerbaijan's regulatory quality is at about the same level as neighboring countries, and has slightly improved since 1996, when the indicators were started.

Hausmann, Klinger, and Wagner (2008) find that high taxes are indicators of micro risks stemming from government failure and can pose binding constraints to economic growth. Figure 2.11 shows Azerbaijan's performance against comparator countries in Central and West Asia and other countries in terms of tax rates. In this group, Azerbaijan is among the countries that have a high marginal tax rate for individuals, but its marginal corporate tax rates are comparable with these countries. Azerbaijan also has the lowest total tax burden as a percentage of GDP in this group.[21] And it is at about at the same level as these countries on performance measures for property rights and governance.

Figure 2.11: Income and Corporate Tax Rates in Azerbaijan and Selected Countries, 2018

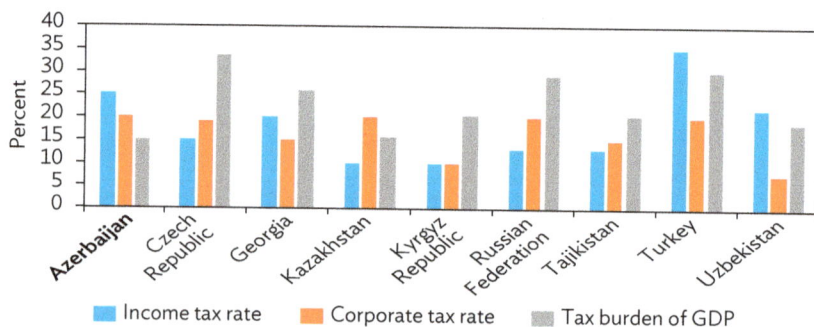

Note: GDP = gross domestic product.
Source: Heritage Foundation, 2018 Index of Economic Freedom (accessed 1 March 2018).

---

[20] Heritage Foundation, 2018 Index of Economic Freedom. https://www.heritage.org/index/.

[21] Azerbaijan's tax burden was not reported as a strong obstacle to doing business, according to World Bank (2013).

Doing business in Azerbaijan

The World Bank's Doing Business project provides information on the business climate and regulatory quality in countries around the world. The project measures the time, cost, and number of procedures to get specific transactions in a business completed. Azerbaijan's ranked 57th out of 190 countries in 2018, a slight improvement from 61st in 2017 (World Bank 2018).[22] The country was commended by the Doing Business project for reforms to make it easier to get credit, protect minority investors, and strengthen contract enforcement to make it easier to resolve insolvencies.

In the Doing Business project Azerbaijan ranked poorly on getting credit (122nd), dealing with construction permits (161st), getting electricity (102nd). The World Bank's 2013 Enterprise Survey for Azerbaijan shows that access to finance is biggest obstacle to doing business (Table 2.2).

Table 2.2: Survey Results of Top Business Environment Obstacles for Firms, 2013

Indicator	Percentage of Surveyed Firms
Access to finance as the biggest obstacle	31.3
Informal sector as the biggest obstacle	29.7
Tax rate as the biggest obstacle	11.9
Tax administration as the biggest obstacle	5.9
Business licensing as the biggest obstacle	5.3
Trade regulations as the biggest obstacle	4.5
Transport as the biggest obstacle	4.3
Corruption as the biggest obstacle	3.5
Access to land as the biggest obstacle	1.4
Courts as the biggest obstacle	1.5

Notes: The survey covers 390 firms operating in Azerbaijan and 15 business environment obstacles. Owners and managers were asked to choose the biggest obstacle to their business.
Source: World Bank. 2013. Enterprise Survey: Azerbaijan Country Profile. Washington, DC.

In 2015, the World Bank launched its distance-to-frontier indicator as a new measure of quality in the Doing Business project. This measures the distance of an economy to the best performance observed on each of the indicators in the Doing Business project since 2005. An economy's distance to frontier is measured on a scale from 0 to 100, where 0 is the lowest-performance frontier and 100 the highest. Azerbaijan's distance-to-frontier score is 70.2, close to the Russian Federation's 75.5, which had a higher overall ranking of 35th compared with Azerbaijan's 57th.

---

[22] Doing Business project rankings range from 1 to 190, with 1 being the easiest country in which to do business.

Ease of trading across borders is important for the efficient exchange of goods and services with neighboring countries, and particularly if a country is diversifying its economy toward agriculture and tourism—as Azerbaijan is trying to do. Azerbaijan ranked 83rd out of 190 countries in 2018 in the Doing Business indicator of trading across borders (Table 2.3). Data on the time and cost it takes to comply with border and documentary requirements for exporting and importing suggest this is more expensive in Azerbaijan compared with Europe and Central Asia. It also takes longer in Azerbaijan to export from and import to other countries compared with these regions. The WEF's Enabling Trade Index also highlights the challenge Azerbaijan faces in improving how it trades across borders. The country's 2016 index score for foreign market access was 2.85 out of a possible 7 points, lower than its 3.90 score in 2014.

Table 2.3: Trading Across Borders Indicators for Azerbaijan and Comparator Countries, 2017

Country (rank out of 190 countries)	Time to Export: Border Compliance (hours)	Cost to Export: Border Compliance ($)	Time to Export: Documentary Compliance (hours)	Cost to Export: Documentary Compliance ($)	Time to Import: Border Compliance (hours)	Cost to Import: Border Compliance ($)	Time to Import: Documentary Compliance (hours)	Cost to Import: Documentary Compliance ($)
Georgia (54)	14	383	2	35	15	396	2	189
Kyrgyz Republic (79)	20	445	21	145	37	512	36	200
Azerbaijan (83)	**29**	**214**	**33**	**300**	**30**	**423**	**38**	**200**
Ukraine (115)	26	75	96	292	72	100	168	212
Kazakhstan (119)	133	574	128	320	2	0	6	0
Russian Federation (140)	96	765	26	80	96	1,125	43	160
Tajikistan (144)	75	313	66	330	108	223	126	260
Europe and Central Asia	28	195	27	111	26	202	26	191

Source: World Bank. 2018. *Doing Business 2018: Reforming to Create Jobs.* Washington, DC.

The WEF's Global Competitiveness Report 2018 ranked Azerbaijan 40th out of 140 countries for the efficiency of its labor market. This growth diagnostic finding is in line with Azerbaijan's ranking in the WEF's indicator for the efficiency of product markets, placing 37th out of 140 countries. The country also ranked high in terms of the time it takes to start a business (17th) and the effect of taxation and subsidies on competition (20th).

Fiscal dependence on oil revenue

The dominant share of oil in exports and government revenue make Azerbaijan highly vulnerable to international oil price shocks and shocks in oil extraction. The country's dependence on oil is its biggest macroeconomic risk, with oil shocks transmitted into the economy mainly through the fiscal channel. The government tried to lessen the impact of an external shock from this source by setting up the State Oil Fund of Azerbaijan Republic (SOFAZ) in 1999, and since then SOFAZ transfers have accounted for a significant portion of the annual state budget. The fund has helped the economy overcome several external shocks. After the global financial crisis, for example, its contribution to the state budget increased from 9.7% in 2008 to 58% in 2013. SOFAZ's budget transfers have declined since then, in part due to lower oil prices (Figure 2.12).

Figure 2.12: State Oil Fund Transfers to the State Budget, 2003–2017

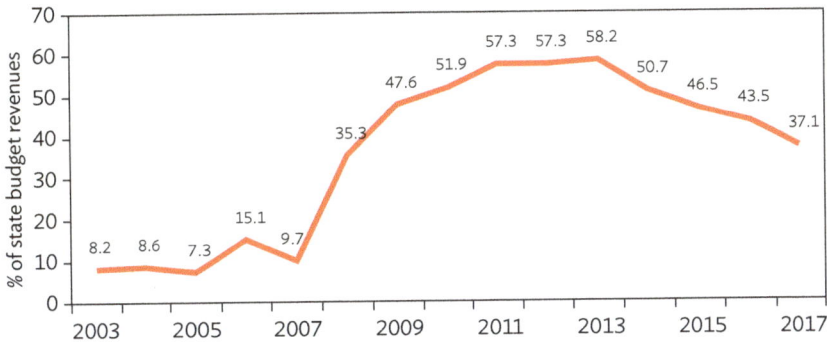

Source: State Oil Fund of Azerbaijan Republic. 2016. Annual Report. Baku; and Ministry of Finance.

Azerbaijan's dependence on oil for fiscal revenue is risky. Figure 2.13 shows what the fiscal deficit would look like with and without SOFAZ transfers. With SOFAZ transfers, the fiscal balance remained stable from 2001–2017. Without SOFAZ transfers, the balance started to turn into deficit in 2002, with the deficit rising until 2013, just before the oil price crash. SOFAZ transfers to state revenue and, consequently, the non-oil fiscal deficit started to decline when oil revenue fell and the government tightened fiscal policy. Subtracting SOFAZ transfers from total revenue does not yield a purely non-oil fiscal balance, since other revenue items—directly or indirectly—depend on oil revenue (for example, tax revenue contains revenue financed through oil). Even so, this approach illustrates the main effect of oil revenue on the fiscal balance, and is a simple illustration of fiscal expansion motivated by windfall revenue from high oil prices in the short-term.

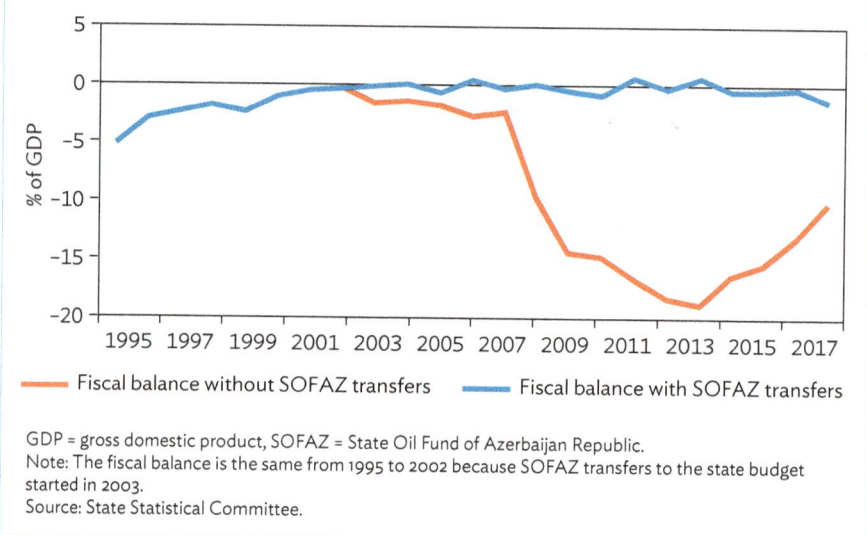

Figure 2.13: Fiscal Balance with and without State Oil Fund Transfers, 1995–2017

GDP = gross domestic product, SOFAZ = State Oil Fund of Azerbaijan Republic.
Note: The fiscal balance is the same from 1995 to 2002 because SOFAZ transfers to the state budget started in 2003.
Source: State Statistical Committee.

The government has had some success in maintaining macroeconomic stability by using SOFAZ as a buffer against external shocks. But SOFAZ has yet to produce sustained results in advancing economic diversification. And despite its attempts to sterilize a large part of the country's oil revenue, the economy is showing signs of Dutch disease.[23]

Dutch disease and falling foreign direct investment in hydrocarbons

Two distinct signs of Dutch disease in Azerbaijan are the increasing real exchange rate and high inflation stemming from rising revenue from oil exports. During some boom periods, the government's large public investment program and fiscal support to the economy have been accompanied by higher inflation and a further appreciation in the real effective exchange rate (Figure 2.14).

---

[23] Appendix 1 discusses the economics of Dutch disease.

Figure 2.14: Annual Average Inflation, 1996–2017

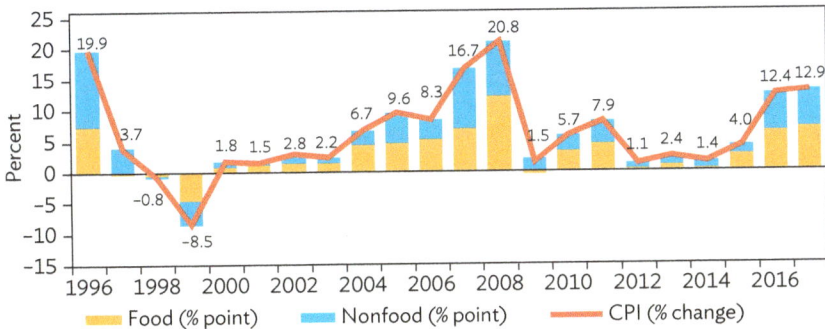

CPI = consumer price index.
Source: Estimates based on State Statistical Committee data.

As experienced in many countries, a fixed exchange rate regime, which prevailed in Azerbaijan for many years, results in increased exposure to foreign currency financing, and a vulnerable currency position for the government and businesses. The policy shift to a managed exchange rate by the Central Bank of Azerbaijan in 2015, and the subsequent depreciations of the manat in February and December of that year, put additional pressure on the balance sheets of private firms, banks, and the government.

FDI has provided significant support for economic growth, though its contribution declined after the global financial crisis. Because large amounts of FDI have gone into the oil sector, the fall in oil prices from 2014 and the consequent slowdown in growth led to a big drop in FDI (Figure 2.15). Lower oil revenue also reduced the country's gross international reserves and increased the government's external debt, from 16% of GDP in 2014 to 25% in 2015 and 37% in 2016.[24]

A series of policy responses to the oil price shock by the government and central bank produced early positive results. Economic growth became positive again in 2017, supported in part by a stronger global economy and a moderate increase in oil prices. The current account also returned to surplus in 2017 because of a sharp drop in imports (Table 2.4). Goods exports, however, have continued to decline, their value in 2017 being less than one-third of that in 2011's.

[24] Government of Azerbaijan, Ministry of Finance. 2018. Medium and Long-Term Debt Management Strategy for Debt Management of the Republic of Azerbaijan. Baku. Adopted through Presidential Decree # 424 dated 24 August 2018. Note that the 2019 value is 17% according to MOF. The government's public debt management strategy adopted in August 2018 envisages the government external debt to GDP ratio to decrease to 20% by the end of 2025. Government defines its external debt as the sum of outstanding sovereign debt and the annual expected fiscal exposure under the outstanding sovereign-guaranteed debt.

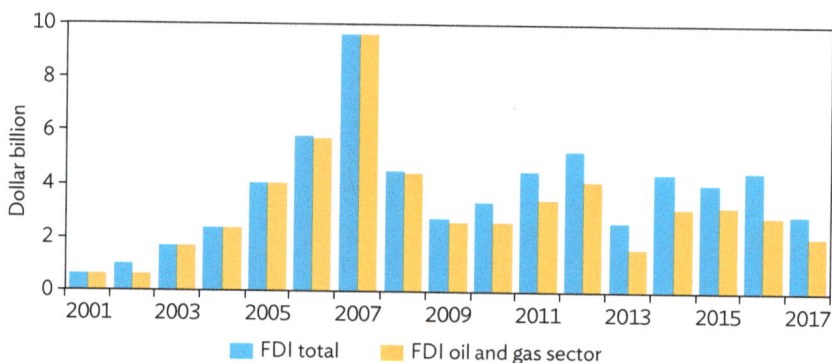

Figure 2.15: Foreign Direct Investment, 2001–2017

FDI = foreign direct investment.
Source: Central Bank of Azerbaijan.

Table 2.4: External Indicators 2005–2017

Item	2005	2010	2011	2012	2013	2014	2015	2016	2017
Current account balance ($ million)	167	15,021	17,155	14,881	13,079	10,431	(222)	(1,363)	1,685
as % of GDP	1	28	26	21	18	14	(0)	(4)	4
Balance on trade in goods	3,299	19,712	24,337	22,182	21,382	18,928	5,812	4,206	6,115
Exports of goods	7,649	26,374	34,393	32,374	31,703	28,260	15,586	13,211	15,152
Imports of goods	4,350	6,662	10,056	10,192	10,321	9,332	9,774	9,004	9,037
Balance on trade in services	(1,970)	(1,733)	(2,996)	(2,924)	(4,189)	(6,090)	(4,229)	(3,155)	(3,379)
Balance on primary income	(1,646)	(3,467)	(4,860)	(4,327)	(4,121)	(2,582)	(2,028)	(2,472)	(1,760)
Secondary income credit	484	509	673	(50)	7	174	222	57	709
International reserves ($ million)	1,178	6,409	10,274	11,277	15,014	15,549	7,910	7,142	6,681
Months of imports	2	5	5	5	7	7	4	4	4
Exchange rate (Manat/$)	0.945	0.803	0.790	0.786	0.785	0.784	1.025	1.596	1.721

( ) = negative, GDP = gross domestic product.
Sources: Asian Development Bank, Central Bank of Azerbaijan, and International Monetary Fund.

Revenue from oil and gas exports has served Azerbaijan well. It contributed to high economic growth, enabled large foreign exchange reserves to be accumulated, reduced debt, and attracted substantial FDI into the oil and gas sector. This revenue has helped to significantly reduce poverty and increase household consumption. But the monetary and exchange rate policies that were effective in stabilizing the macroeconomy from the negative impact of plummeting oil prices did not influence the growth of exports from non-oil sectors. Although SOFAZ has tried to sterilize part of the country's oil revenue, the manat still appreciated significantly during the oil boom, making it difficult for non-oil exports to expand. Lack of export diversification has made Azerbaijan vulnerable to external shocks, and this is expected to continue for some time because oil and gas will remain an important driver of the economy. A more stable exchange rate has been achieved since 2015 because of the central bank's strict monetary policy and by rising oil revenue. This policy stance will help the country cope with similar external shocks in the future. It will, however, have short-term adjustment costs because of increased liabilities in some sectors. And this might affect the capacity of banks, the private sector, and government to support non-oil growth in the short term, because the new currency regime will heighten perceived currency risks until the market adjusts to the new policy setting.

From 2015 to 2017, Azerbaijan's foreign debt averaged 34% of GDP, far higher than the average of 13% during 2005–2014.[25] The external public debt consists of the direct obligations of the state, contingent liabilities from sovereign guarantees, loans from international financial institutions to finance infrastructure projects, and government bonds issued in international financial markets. Fiscal sustainability is not expected to be a risk in the long term because of the country's expected economic recovery. But declining oil and non-oil revenue are reducing the government's ability to support growth in the short term. The overall macroeconomic risks are also partly reflected in the country's sovereign ratings.

The growth diagnostic results for macroeconomic risks are reflected in Azerbaijan's ranking on the WEF's competitiveness indicator for macroeconomic environment. In the *Global Competitiveness Report 2018*, Azerbaijan placed 126th out of 140 countries for this indicator, significantly weaker than the country's overall competitiveness ranking of 69th.

---

[25] Debt values were sourced from International Debt Statistics while GDP values were sourced from World Development Indicators. Azerbaijan MOF estimates the same parameter averaged 21% of GDP from the same time period (Government of Azerbaijan, Ministry of Finance 2018. Medium and Long-Term Debt Management Strategy for Debt Management of the Republic of Azerbaijan. Baku).

2.4 Market Failures

Missing market links

Market failures can greatly dampen economic growth. Production is a complex process, but markets keep this process running and any market malfunctioning may adversely affect productivity. For industries that depend on each other, missing clusters of production create a chicken-and-egg problem. Here, the government's role in identifying the missing link and fixing the problem is essential. Hausmann, Klinger, and Wagner (2008) suggest that the market for tradable inputs should be less complicated for this because these inputs can be imported. Yet in Azerbaijan, high transport costs and exchange rate depreciation make the lack of tradable inputs a binding constraint on growth. In this situation, complex production processes that depend on these inputs will not develop properly or simply will not exist, thereby reducing the number of products in which a country has a comparative advantage. Because of Azerbaijan's special situation in this regard, the analysis of market failures does not distinguish between tradable and nontradable inputs.

Low levels of export sophistication in non-oil sectors

The diagnosis for market failure uses tests that evaluate productivity and innovation across sectors. Increasing productivity and innovation require markets that allow for the flexible mobility of labor, create business-friendly regulatory environments, and support competitive financial systems (Calvo 2006). Market malfunctions caused by coordination failures and information externalities can prevent profitable projects getting off the ground.

This section looks at five measures of economic and export sophistication, beginning with the PRODY value and EXPY index, as proposed by Hausmann, Hwang, and Rodrik (2007). This seminal paper argues that "some traded goods are associated with higher productivity levels than others and that countries that latch on to higher productivity goods ... will perform better." The PRODY value uses the weighted average of the GDP per capita of all countries exporting a certain good, and thus suggests a notional level of income associated with that good. Its authors also show that richer countries export more technologically sophisticated goods, and that countries producing goods that richer countries export tend to grow more rapidly. As a rule of thumb, products with a PRODY value of less than $10,000 are considered to be low-income goods, those between $10,000 and $20,000 are mid-income goods, and those above $20,000 are high-income goods (Aslanli et al. 2013). Figure 2.16 shows examples of Azerbaijan's main non-oil exports in 2011 that have PRODY values exceeding $20,000; these include metal pipelines, ethylene polymer, medicines, oil resin, and acyclic carbohydrates. The country's other main non-oil export products, including tea, vegetable oil, sugar, and raw materials for making margarine, have low PRODY values (below $10,000). According to the Central Bank of Azerbaijan, 61% of Azerbaijan exports have PRODY values of less than $15,000, far below the global average.

Figure 2.16: PRODY Index for Major Export Products, 2011

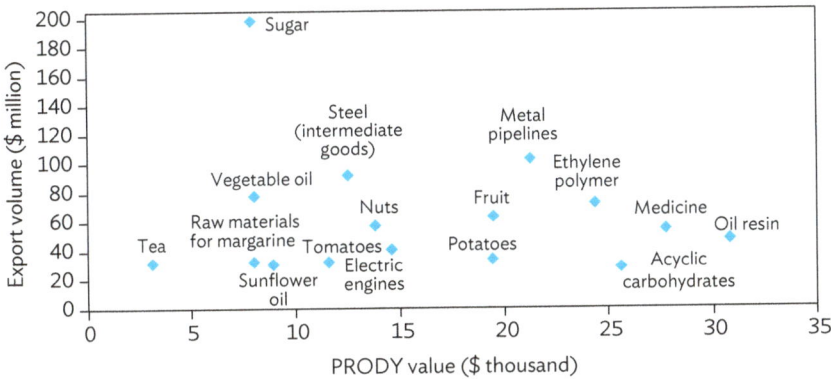

Source: Central Bank of Azerbaijan.

EXPY is a summation of the PRODY weights by the value share of the products in a country's total export basket. Hausmann, Hwang, and Rodrik (2007) show that a country's GDP per capita converges toward its EXPY, meaning that countries with low EXPY for their level of income experience some form of market failure. Figure 2.17 is a scatter plot that shows country rankings on the EXPY index and their exports per capita (both in logs). There is a high positive correlation between these variables ($R^2 = 0.78$), but Azerbaijan's exports per capita are low compared to countries with almost similar levels of export sophistication. Interdependent industries are needed to manufacture sophisticated products that can compete in world markets. The low levels of export sophistication in Azerbaijan indicates there are missing industries or missing links between industries.

Figure 2.17: EXPY Index and Export Performance in Azerbaijan and Selected Countries, 2011

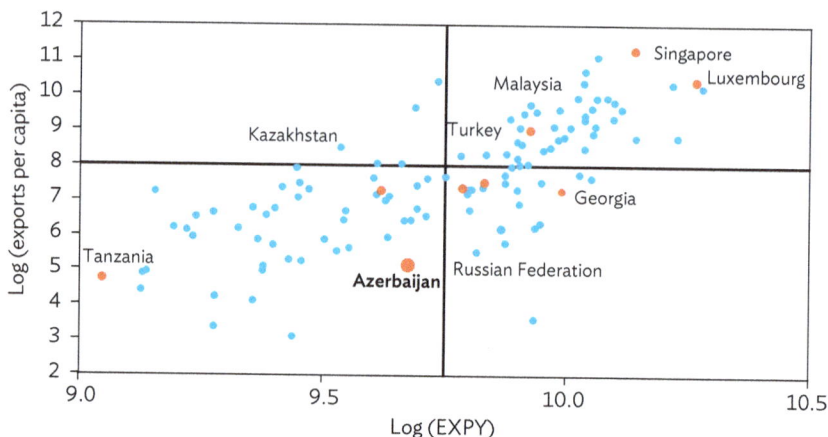

Source: Central Bank of Azerbaijan.

The Economic Complexity Index (ECI) is another informative measure of economic sophistication. It calculates the knowledge intensity of the products that a country exports. The ECI+ Index measures the total exports of an economy corrected by how difficult it is to export each product. Figure 2.18 shows the ECI and ECI+ Indexes for Azerbaijan and five other countries from 2011 to 2015. Azerbaijan's ECI lags far behind comparator countries and ranks close to oil-exporting Nigeria, a country famous for its inefficient management of natural resources. Azerbaijan's ECI+ rankings are better than its ECI rankings, but they are still far behind the other countries. Note, too, that Azerbaijan's ECI has not risen over time, indicating that diversity of production did not improve during 2011–2015. In 2015, Azerbaijan's ECI was –1.64, placing it 104th among the 124 countries in this index.

Product space is another measure of export sophistication. This is a network that connects products that are likely to be co-exported, and can be used to predict the evolution of a country's export structure. Figure 2.19 shows Azerbaijan's product space compared with two other oil-exporting countries, Indonesia and Norway. As the figure clearly shows, only a few sectors—mainly agriculture and petroleum—are located nearby Azerbaijan's production structure, and that important links are missing.

To measure the position of a country in the product space, Hausmann and Klinger (2006) propose another indicator—the Open Forest Index, which

Figure 2.18: Economic Complexity Index and Economic Complexity Index+ of Azerbaijan and Selected Countries, 2011–2015

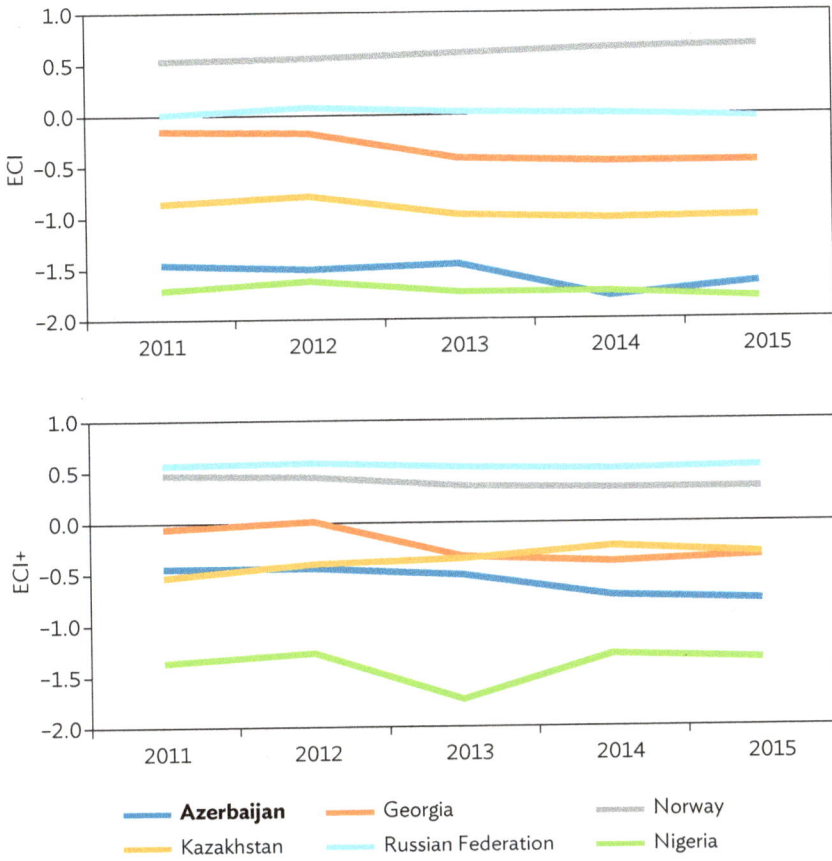

ECI = Economic Complexity Index.
Source: Observatory of Economic Complexity.

measures the presence of "nearby" goods. These authors, as well as Hidalgo et al. (2007), argue that the presence of nearby goods is important because they determine a country's comparative advantage. In the Open Forest Index, Azerbaijan is located well below the densest country clusters, which can be another sign of market failure, according to Hausmann, Klinger, and Wagner (2008). Comparing growth diagnostic results with the WEF's global competitiveness indicators in terms of market size, Azerbaijan ranks 63rd out of 137 countries, weaker than its overall ranking on the index of 35th.

Figure 2.19: Product Space Map for Azerbaijan, Norway, and Indonesia, 1995 and 2016

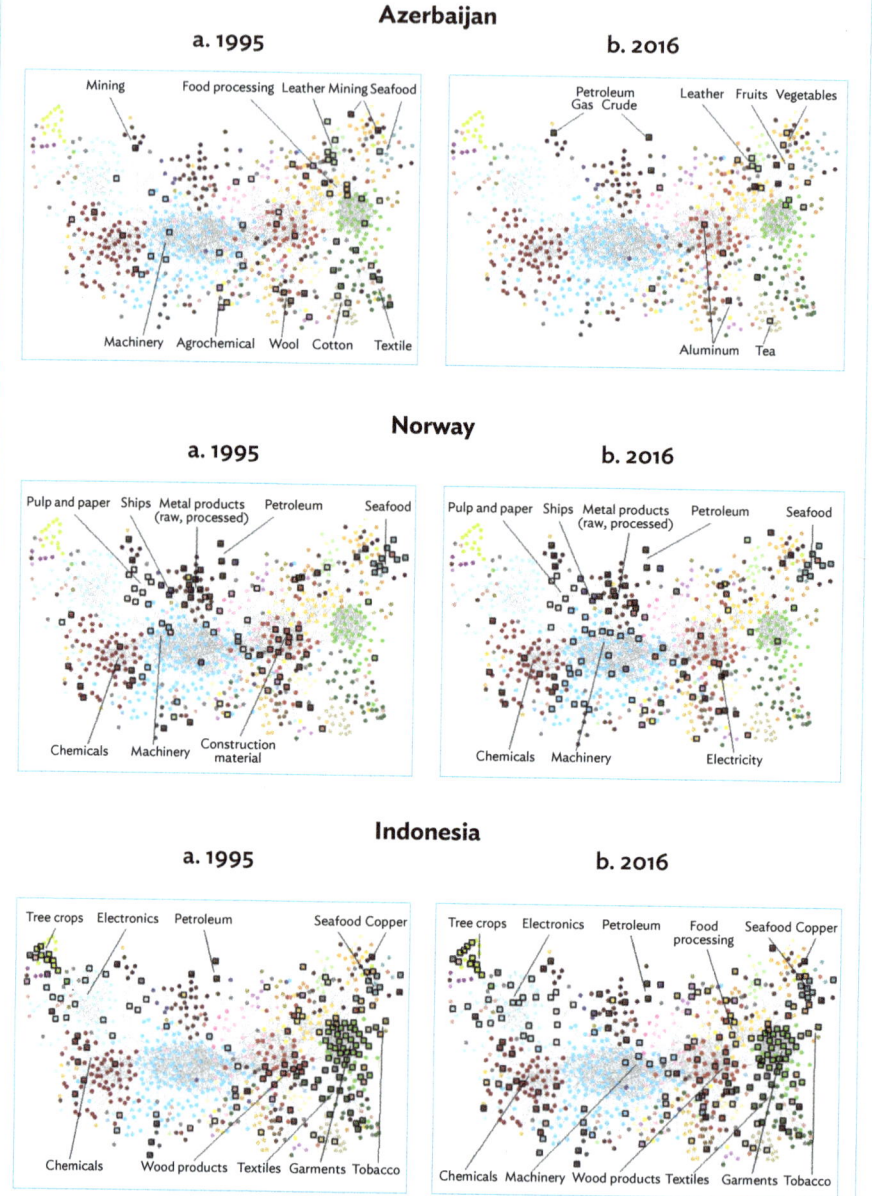

Azerbaijan

a. 1995

b. 2016

Norway

a. 1995

b. 2016

Indonesia

a. 1995

b. 2016

Note: Each square is an export product, with a Revealed Comparative Advantage Index greater than 1; that is, when a product's share of a country's export basket is greater than its share of world exports.
Source: Asian Development Bank estimates based on UN Comtrade data.

Box 2.1 Bangladesh: Consolidating Export-led Growth

In 2015, ADB published the Bangladesh Country Diagnostic Study. The CDS explained how the country transformed its economy over the last two decades while maintaining an average annual growth of 5%–6%. It also outlined a reform pathway that the economy will need to "switch gears" to consolidate the growth momentum over the medium term. This Box presents an excerpt of the findings which may be useful for drawing possible parallels with Azerbaijan.

"Underlying Bangladesh's success has been the reduction in the population growth rate and the dependency ratio and a decline in the volatility of output. The movement of surplus labor from the primary sector into more productive manufacturing activities characterized the structural transformation of the economy. External inflows have soared, spurred by exports of garments and remittance inflows. Much of the successful outcomes were the result of a deliberate strategy by successive governments to promote industry in the context of the government's ambitious 5-year plans. Improved fiscal and external macroeconomic stability have also helped to sustain growth. Until very recently, the government's industrial policy relied on picking a few sectors and offering them generous export incentives—many through the SEZ regime. The decision as to which sector is promising primarily relies on growth rates of value added evaluated after the fact, in conjunction with certain targets for every sector. But such a policy exacerbates any type of production concentration by encouraging future growth and larger sectors that are already ahead of others, instead of creating incentives for innovation. The government should consider reducing its strategy of "picking winners" and instead focus on creating the right environment for all types of businesses to thrive.

How to do it? First is to withdraw some of the support to the Ready Made Garments sector, which has outlived its useful life. As a general principle, incentives for infant industries need to be time-bound. Special incentives, such as corporate income tax exemption or tax holidays for imported machinery, need to be removed. The longer they remain, the less likely it will be politically feasible for the government to remove them and to resist possible undue influence from garment factory owners. Even without these incentives, it is unlikely that the sector will lose its comparative advantage, as it has earned itself an excellent reputation. Second, identify the barriers to other productive sectors, both goods and services, formal and informal. Once they identify the barriers, it will be easier to provide solutions. In gathering better data and analyzing the evidence, some of the information externalities and coordination failures may be identified, and this itself will allow policy makers to determine the appropriate extent of intervention.

continued on the next page

Box 2.1 continued

Third, prioritize the elimination of anti-export bias against non-RMG exports to get traction on economic diversification. The trade policy regime and resulting tariff structure of Bangladesh is skewed toward import-substituting activities with a substantial anti-export bias and should be eliminated. RMG production exists as an insular "free trade" enclave. Fourth, government agencies that deal with investors and the foreign market must be reformed for a keener focus on promoting investment opportunities. Better coordination capabilities are required between private sector interests and government objectives. Finally, more has to be done to attract FDI, particularly the type that increases transfer of technology. FDI is critical for an export-oriented economy like Bangladesh, not just because of the capital it brings, but for the technology and knowledge transfer and job creation with skill development associated with such FDI. FDI, along with technology transfer and market access, is just as critical for economic diversification, particularly to exploit new product and market opportunities that would be difficult to acquire without partnership with well-established foreign companies."

Source: ADB. 2015. Bangladesh Consolidating Export-led Growth. Manila, Philippines

2.5　Conclusions and Policy Recommendations

This chapter examined the reasons for the low levels of private investment and entrepreneurship in Azerbaijan, and identified the most binding constraints to diversified growth and priority areas for reform. The growth diagnostics framework proposed by Hausmann, Rodrik, and Velasco (2005), a simple but powerful methodology for understanding the specific factors constraining growth and impeding sustainable economic development, was applied to Azerbaijan. It showed the following constraints:

Macroeconomic risks. These are binding constraints that need to be tackled in the short term. Azerbaijan's high dependence on oil for exports and government revenue made the economy extremely vulnerable to external shocks, as experienced during the 2014 oil price shock. The big falls in oil prices put tremendous pressure on the country's external balance, fiscal position, and bank balance sheets. Fiscal support to revive growth has yet to produce results. With limited capacity for expanding non-oil sectors, the depreciation of the manat since 2015 has led to rising inflation.

High cost of finance. This is caused by low domestic savings and insufficient local and foreign finance, and is another binding constraint on growth that needs to be tackled in the short term. High interest rates and a low share of bank financing in capital investments show that access to domestic savings is a problem, as is financial intermediation because of the wide spread between borrowing and lending rates. Azerbaijan's banks are acutely risk averse and mostly unwilling to grant credit even to potentially profitable projects. Firms, for their part, prefer using internal resources for their capital investment needs.

Gaps in infrastructure and public goods. These constraints to growth need to be tackled in the medium term. Azerbaijan has better infrastructure than comparator countries, although its logistic performance needs improving. For the country to make progress on its goal for economic diversification, as set out in the Strategic Road Maps, it needs to not only sustain investments in infrastructure but also ensure these investments are planned as a network of complementary assets. This will be especially important for expanding into agriculture, post-pandemic tourism, and manufacturing.

Market and coordination failures. Both are constraints to medium-term growth. The economy's low level of complexity and coordination failures mean there are few interdependent industries, making the production of more sophisticated goods and services difficult.

Low level of human capital. The lack of this could develop into a binding constraint for Azerbaijan's long-term economic development. The country has too few tertiary-educated graduates by international standards. Wages are generally much higher in the oil sector than in non-oil sectors, pointing to future difficulties in attracting workers to agriculture, tourism, and manufacturing.

To tackle these constraints, the following policy recommendations are offered:

Reduce macroeconomic risks. In order to secure sustainable and comprehensive diversification, macroeconomic stability needs to be supported and the stimulating role of macroeconomic policy strengthened. One of the four core targets of the Strategic Road Maps is to "strengthen fiscal sustainability and adopt a sustainable monetary policy." Here, the golden-rule approach on fiscal spending for oil revenue must be implemented and sustained in the long term and not be calibrated to short-term surges in oil prices. Changes in fiscal regulations since 2015, improvements in sovereign fund management, tighter monetary policies, and stricter exchange rate policies were major steps in reducing macroeconomic risk.

The government must ensure that fiscal policy is disciplined—and, to this end, that the rules on fiscal expenditure adopted in 2015 are implemented. The non-oil fiscal deficit and transfers from SOFAZ to the state budget must be kept at a sustainable level and free from the volatility that can affect oil revenue. A restrictive monetary policy aligned with a disciplined fiscal policy will enable full control of price stability. The next focus of monetary policy should be developing the financial system to facilitate the flow of loanable funds from savers to borrowers. Healthy financial institutions are needed to help maintain a flexible exchange rate regime, which will be important for mitigating oil price shocks.

Tackle the high cost of finance. The government has taken bold measures to solve major problems in the finance sector by, for example, devaluing the currency by 57% in 2015, closing troubled banks, restructuring state-run International Bank of Azerbaijan, and imposing new limits on dollar lending.[26] To further advance this agenda, the government could begin by reducing macro and micro risks in the real sector. Because economies are complex systems, an efficient financial system cannot be established and sustained without certain conditions prevailing in the broad economy. Achieving this requires a wide range of actions in the real sector, including increasing the protection of property rights and ending monopolies. Macroeconomic stability—manifested in exchange rate stability and sustainable government financing, for example—is the basic requirement of a healthy investment climate. In Azerbaijan, macroeconomic stability is particularly important for a disciplined fiscal policy on oil revenue. Investors operating in a credible, transparent, and competitive environment will carry less risk, and will therefore be able to tap finance with low interest rates.

As a next step, the government should start building on the gains it has made in reducing finance sector risk and restoring banking intermediation. A wide range of measures need to be implemented to achieve these objectives. The government should continue working on increasing the transparency and accountability of the country's financial intuitions. Credit to the private sector, which predominantly comes from banks, has sharply declined since 2015, and the share of bank credit in financing capital investments is abnormally low.

The level of NPLs is a concern and only slow progress was made in reducing it in 2016 and 2017. To make progress, better reporting by banks on their NPLs

---

[26] The Decree on "Additional Measures to Address the Problem Loans of Individuals in the Azerbaijan Republic" allowed to achieve significant results in addressing the problem loans. As a follow to this Decree signed by the Head of the State to address the problem loans, Financial Markets Supervisory Board developed a mechanism on covering the part of a principal amount that increased in AZN as a result of devaluation in foreign currency loans and identifying concessions that would be applied to interests and forfeited amount (penalty, fine).

and the management of these loans is needed, and all public sector NPLs need to be resolved. Legal systems for debt resolution, recovery, and restructuring, although in place, now need to be put into operation. A secondary market for distressed debt and a system for NPL sales needs to be set up. From 2014 to 2017, nonbank credit institutions contributed on average to only 3% of the total credit to the economy. Because of the urgent need to increase access to finance for non-oil sectors, developing Azerbaijan's nonbank credit institutions should be a priority. Measures that could advance this include the Financial Market Supervisory Authority drawing up a law on credit unions, and having these institutions covered by the Credit and Mortgage Guarantee Fund.[27] A financing facility should be set up to give nonbank credit institutions access to funding for lending to micro, small, and medium-sized enterprises in employment-intensive sectors, such as agriculture, manufacturing, and tourism.

Plan infrastructure as a network of complementary assets. Quality infrastructure is vital for attracting FDI and increasing productivity—and both are cross-cutting core targets of the Strategic Road Maps. The quality of Azerbaijan's infrastructure is not yet a binding constraint for an oil-led economy. But it will likely become one in the medium term because of aging infrastructure, a rising population demanding better transport services, and more goods being transported by land. Developing the agriculture sector as part of the economy's planned diversification implies prioritizing infrastructure investments in transport and irrigation. Farm-to-market roads and highways that link rural areas to urban agglomeration centers will be vital to get local produce into national and international market. Tackling the salinization of arable land will increase the production potential of many farms. Reforms are needed to improve the country's logistic performance, particularly for reducing the cost of importing and exporting to make these processes faster, and improving the tracking and tracing of shipments.

Incentives that go beyond subsidies are needed to attract investment and workers to the agriculture sector. Guaranteeing wages for farm workers that are comparable to the oil sector would be good start. Because of the vulnerable macroeconomic situation, it is imperative that agriculture policies are sustainable. For example, the Law of the Azerbaijan Republic on "Agricultural insurance" was adopted on 27 June 2019 to re-organize the mechanism on agricultural insurance. Agricultural Insurance Fund was set up as a follow up to implementation of the Law of the Azerbaijan Republic

---

27 Currently, work on legislation to regulate the credit unions and nonbank financial institutions is underway. FMSA is considering collaboration with Mortgage and Credit Guarantee Fund within the framework of a new legislation.

on "Agricultural insurance", dated 27 June 2018 (#1617-VQ) and the Decree #809 of the President of the Azerbaijan Republic on "Establishment of Agricultural Insurance Fund", dated 19 August 2019. In order to address the issues arising from the Decree of the President of the Azerbaijan Republic, a task force composed up representatives from FMSA, Ministries of Agriculture, Finance, Economy, and the Center for Economic Reforms Analysis and Communication was created. The group also benefited from support from TARSIM and the representatives from Turkish Ministry of Agriculture on 4-13 September 2019. The Fund will start its operations as of 1 January 2020. The government should conduct a review of its support to agriculture. This should be part of a strategy that links the country's main crops (for example, cotton) and high-value agriculture products (for example, grapes) to regional and global value chains in the context of the Strategic Road Map on the Production and Processing of Agricultural Products. Overarching policy reforms to unlock the full productive potential of these crops are necessary— for example, tying the Ministry of Agriculture's reforms targeting increases in the quality and quantity of grape harvests with the wine tourism campaigns of the Ministry of Tourism—and complementing these with reforms that make it easier to trade across borders.

Diversification into tourism in a post-pandemic scenario implies investing in non-transport-related infrastructure, particularly outside of Baku; for example, investments in improved drinking water in rural areas. The country is seeing a slow but continuous increase in tourist arrivals, although mostly in Baku and in part due to international events being hosted there. The successful efforts to achieve the targets of the Strategic Road Map on the Development of a Specialized Tourism Industry should continue.

Tackle market failures. Private investments and promotion of initiatives should be the key drivers of diversification. At the same time, current legal system needs to be adapted to meet the requirements of economic diversification. Strong, institutionalized and free competition can support development of a healthy business environment, which is key for diversification. A conducive business environment and highly skilled human capital can advance economic diversification. To this end, the government is targeting both in its Strategic Road Maps. But it is recommended that the following actions are also taken. Measures are needed to make it easier for new industries with export potential, especially firms specializing in the production of "nearby" goods, to do business. The government should take steps to close the gaps in economic activity where there is a lack of skilled workers. In addition, strengthening transformation of revenues to investment, increased financing through private and foreign direct investment, expansion of openness to foreign markets, as well as modernization of governance can play an important role in economic diversification and development. To complement the Strategic Road Maps, create an integrated industrial strategy and policy toward boosting the country's export potential. This will require that economic complexity and product space are examined to identify the industries and sectors where skills are most lacking.

Invest in human capital. Enhancing healthy and good quality human capital will secure diversification and a long-term sustainability of development. Because education is the cornerstone of sustainable and equitable economic development, it is vital that adequate investments are made in human capital. The government should continue to promote education at all levels and across all disciplines. Allocating ample resources for education would ensure that qualified people will be attracted to the teaching profession.

The Strategic Road Maps outline "investments across all pillars of education to support human capital formation and development." These include investments for modernizing technical and vocational education and training that are urgently needed to tackle skills mismatches in the labor market. The initial steps to achieve this are identified in the Strategic Road Map on Vocational Education and Training. But specific strategies are still needed for this. The labor force needs of the private sector and for a diversified economy must be taken into consideration in technical and vocational education and training, and other education curricula. The Strategic Road Maps call for investments that encourage the continual development of human capital, including "bringing primary vocation and secondary special education in line with requirements of the labor market" and for research and development.

The country's labor force needs to acquire soft skills in addition to the hard skills that can be acquired through education and training programs. Soft skills are the interpersonal and communication skills that relate to how a person interacts with others. They are particularly useful for high-level positions for creative thinking, decision-making, motivation, critical thinking, and conflict resolution. Soft skills are also useful for lower-level positions for problem-solving, work ethic, positivity, time management, flexibility, and teamwork.

Conduct regular progress assessments. It is important that Azerbaijan's performance against the indicators and targets in the Strategic Road Maps are regularly assessed. The Strategic Road Map on the National Economy Perspective and the road maps for the 11 main sectors of the economy provide the path toward sustainable economic development. The assessment should be done in an objective and transparent manner. To assess the progress being made, diversification and competitiveness indicators need to be formulated. The government's Center for Analysis and Communication of Economic Reforms is mandated to monitor and regularly report on the progress being made on the Strategic Road Maps.

References

ADB (Asian Development Bank). 2014. *Country Partnership Strategy: Azerbaijan, 2014–2018*. Manila.

———. 2019. *Country Partnership Strategy: Azerbaijan, 2019–2023*. Manila.

Aslanli, K., Z. Ismayil, R. Aghayev, and A. Mehtiyev. 2013. *Assessment of Economic and Export Diversification: Azerbaijan*. Revenue Watch Institute.

Azernews. 2018. Heydar Aliyev International Airport Serves 3.8 Million Passengers over Ten Months of 2018. https://www.azernews.az/travel/140818.html.

Bonilla-Chacin, M. E., G. Afandiyeva, and A. Suaya. 2018. Challenges on the Path to Universal Health Coverage: The Experience of Azerbaijan. *World Bank Working Paper*. No. 2018-01. Washington, DC: World Bank.

Calvo, S. 2006. *Applying the Growth Diagnostics Approach: The Case of Bolivia*. Washington, DC: World Bank.

Corden, W. M. 1971. *The Theory of Protection*. Oxford: Clarendon Press.

Deardorff, A. V. 1984. An Exposition and Exploration of Krueger's Trade Model. *Canadian Journal of Economics*. 5 (4). pp. 731–46.

ETF (European Training Foundation). 2015. Sector Skills Council of Azerbaijan: Reviewing Structures for Social Partnerships for Initial and Continuing Vocational Training. Turin.

Government of Azerbaijan, Ministry of Finance. 2018. Medium and Long-Term Debt Management Strategy for Debt Management of the Republic of Azerbaijan. Baku.

Hausmann, R., H. Hwang, and D. Rodrik. 2007. What You Export Matters. *Journal of Economic Growth*. 12 (1). pp. 1–25.

Hausmann, R., Rodrik, D. and A. Velasco. 2005. Growth Diagnostics. Cambridge, MA: John F. Kennedy School of Government, Harvard University.

———. 2006. Getting the Diagnosis Right: A New Approach to Economic Reform. *Finance and Development*. 43 (1). pp. 12–15.

Hausmann, R., and B. Klinger. 2006. Structural Transformation and Patterns of Comparative Advantage in the Product Space. *Working Paper*. No. 128. Cambridge, MA: Center for International Development, Harvard University.

Hausmann, R., B. Klinger, and R. Wagner. 2008. Doing Growth Diagnostics in Practice: A "Mindbook." *Working Paper*. No. 177. Cambridge, MA: Center for International Development, Harvard University.

Hidalgo, C., B. Klinger, A. Barabasi, and R. Hausmann. 2007. The Product Space Conditions the Development of Nations. *Science*. 317 (5837). pp. 482–87.

Ibrahimov, R. 2016. The Development of the Transport Sector in Azerbaijan: Implementation and Challenges. *Caucasus International*. 6 (1).

Krueger, A. O. 1977. *Growth, Distortions and Patterns of Trade Among Many Countries*. Princeton, NJ: International Finance Section.

Naceur, B., and B. Quillin. 2014. Determinants of Bank Spreads in Azerbaijan. *IMF Country Report*. No. 14/160. Washington, DC: International Monetary Fund.

Onder, H. 2013. *Azerbaijan: Inclusive Growth in a Resource-Rich Economy*. Washington, DC: World Bank.

WEF (World Economic Forum). 2013. *Global Competitiveness Report 2016–2017*. Geneva.

_____. 2018. *Global Competitiveness Report 2018*. Geneva.

World Bank. 2006. *Where Is the Wealth of Nations? Measuring Capital for the 21st Century*. Washington, DC.

_____. 2013. *Enterprise Survey: Azerbaijan Country Profile*. Washington, DC.

_____. 2015. *Azerbaijan Systematic Country Diagnostic*. Washington, DC.

_____. 2016. *Enhancing Financial Capability and Inclusion in Azerbaijan: A Demand-Side Assessment*. Washington, DC.

_____. 2018. *Doing Business 2018: Reforming to Create Jobs* . Washington, DC.

CHAPTER 3

Strengthening Human Capital

Human capital development is embedded in Azerbaijan's reform agenda. The Strategic Roadmaps on the National Economy Perspective and Main Sectors of the Economy recognize that human capital plays a key role in increasing labor productivity, sustainable economic growth, higher competitive capacity in manufacturing and services, and the country's integration into global markets. Numerous education system reforms have been undertaken since independence. An important gain from these reforms has been increased participation in primary and secondary education, especially since 2000. Despite this progress, challenges remain. These include low government spending on education, the poor quality of secondary and technical vocational education, low enrollment in tertiary education, and not enough skilled workers. Policy makers need to formulate new strategies to tackle the country's education challenges, since the supply of labor is projected to increase in the coming years. These strategies will also be needed to help the government diversify the economy and double national income (the target for this is less than a decade).

3.1 Demographic Trends and Labor Market Assessment

Demographic structure

Azerbaijan's population of 10 million is estimated to increase to 10.7 million by 2030 (Figure 3.1). The country has a low-age dependency ratio, with 29% of the population below 15 years and 6.8% above 65 (Table 3.1). Some 71% of the population is within the 15–64 working-age range—a share that is estimated to remain at that level until at least 2040. At the beginning of 2019, young people (25 or below) constituted 36.5% of the population, and that proportion is projected to grow in the coming years, posing a challenge to the government for job creation. With the population growing at an average rate of 1.2% a year, about 100,000 new jobs have to be created every year.

Figure 3.1: Population Composition and Dependency Ratio, 1990–2030

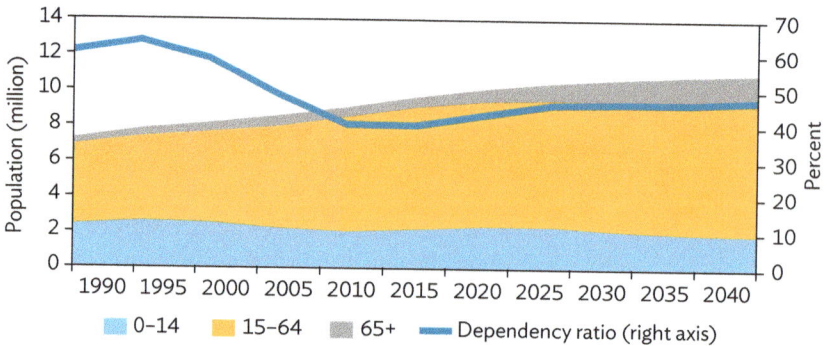

Notes: 1990–2010 population based on estimates, 2020–2030 based on medium variant projections as of 1 July of the year. Dependency ratio is the ratio of dependents—people younger than 15 years and older than 64—to the working-age population.
Source: United Nations. 2017. *World Population Prospects: The 2017 Revision*. New York.

Table 3.1: Total Population by Age Group, 2019

Age Group	Population ('000)	Population (%)
0–14	2,200.4	22.0
15–19	650.0	7.0
20–24	760.0	8.0
25–29	920.0	9.0
30–64	4,750.0	48.0
65+	680.0	7.0
Total	**9,960.4**	**100.0**

Note: Population projected from estimates using latest 2009 census.
Source: State Statistical Committee.

Migration is affecting Azerbaijan's demographic profile and economic performance. In general, migration affects a country's human resources in two ways: through a brain drain when skilled workers leave, and human capital enrichment when skilled workers return and are reintegrated into the labor market after gaining work experience or training abroad. UNDESA (2016) estimates the number of Azerbaijani emigrants at 1.15 million–1.28 million, about 14% of the population. Because there is no official registration system for labor migrants, information on their profiles is limited. But based on available data, a large majority live in other Commonwealth of Independent States, especially the Russian Federation, Kazakhstan, and Ukraine—and to a far lesser extent in Germany, Turkey, Israel, and the United States. Azerbaijan's labor migrants are predominantly male, ages 25–44, from rural areas, and working in crafts and professional services (ADB 2019a). Unemployment and low wages are the main factors for the high number of migrants moving to neighboring countries (Allahveranov and Huseynov 2013).

Migration affects local labor markets by its effect on the size and quality of a country's economically active population. Because of limited employment opportunities in Azerbaijan, migration has somewhat eased pressure on the country's labor market by absorbing the excess supply of labor. When the oil sector was booming, the country attracted inflows of foreign workers from neighboring countries. Most foreign labor migrants are men, with women comprising only 10%. Most foreign labor migrants are between 30 and 59 years old, and employed as skilled workers in the oil and construction industries (State Statistical Committee 2018a). In 2010, the government introduced quotas on foreign labor migration, putting a cap at 12,000 in 2013 and 2014 (Ministry of Labor and Social Protection of the Population 2017). The quota was lowered to 11,230 in 2015 in response to low labor demand during the economic slowdown. In 2016-2019, the quota continued to go down: 9,480 in 2016, 7,290 in 2017, 7,270 in 2018, and 6,815 in 2019.[1] While the number of foreign labor migrants is regulated, the strong demand for skilled workers shows there is a shortage of skilled local labor to work in the oil, mining, and construction industries.

Labor market trends and characteristics

A large proportion of Azerbaijan's population is working-age (15–64 years), and this segment has been growing by about 1%–2% since 2000. Table 3.2 shows the work force participation rate measured as the proportion of the economically active working-age population. The work force participation increased from 47% in 1995 to 54% in 2000 before declining to 52% in 2017. The work force employment rate followed a similar trend. Men's participation in the work force declined from the 1990s to 1998 while women's participation increased, but both have remained constant during the current decade (Figure 3.2). Throughout this period, men's participation rates were higher than women's, by 2–6 percentage points. The participation of young people (15–24 years) in the labor force, at 34.6%, is the lowest in the Central and

---

[1] The government expects the demand for skilled labor to be increasingly satisfied by the domestic human resources.

West Asia (ADB 2017). A large proportion of Azerbaijan's work force has a secondary education (70.4%), but only 16.4% have tertiary education and 5.5% have vocational education (Figure 3.3).

Table 3.2: Population and Work Force Overview, 1990–2017

Item	1990	1995	2000	2005	2010	2011	2012	2013	2014	2015	2016	2017
Total population ('000)	7,132	7,644	8,033	8,447	8,998	9,111	9,235	9,357	9,477	9,593	9,706	9,810
Working-age population ('000)	4,444	4,739	5,068	5,702	6,432	6,551	6,651	6,731	6,805	6,870	6,921	6,970
Total population (%)	62.3	62.0	63.1	67.5	71.5	71.9	72.0	71.9	71.8	71.6	71.3	71.1
Work force ('000)	3,703	3,641	4,370	4,380	4,587	4,626	4,688	4,758	4,841	4,915	5,013	5,074
Work force participation rate (%)	51.9	47.6	54.4	51.9	51.0	50.8	50.8	50.9	51.1	51.2	51.6	51.7

Notes: The working-age population comprises people older than 15 years or younger than 64. The labor force participation rate is the total labor force divided by total population. Data for Total population, Working-age population and Total population (%) are as of beginning of the period, while Labor force and Labor force participation reflect period end data.
Source: Asian Development Bank estimates based on State Statistical Committee. 2018a. *Labor Market Statistical Yearbook 2018*. Baku.

Figure 3.2: Work Force Size and Participation Rate by Gender, 1990–2017

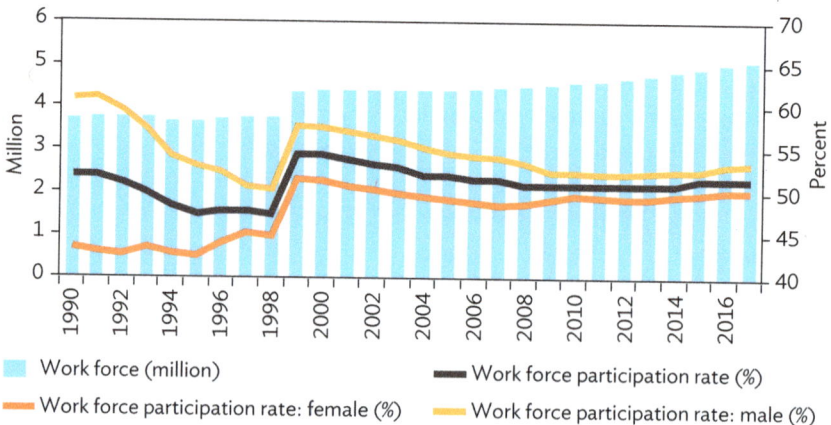

Work force (million) — Work force participation rate (%)
Work force participation rate: female (%) — Work force participation rate: male (%)

Note: Estimates are for the working-age population (15–64 years).
Source: Asian Development Bank estimates based on State Statistical Committee. 2018. *Labor Market Statistical Yearbook 2018*. Baku.

Figure 3.3: Labor Force by Age Group and Educational Attainment, 2017

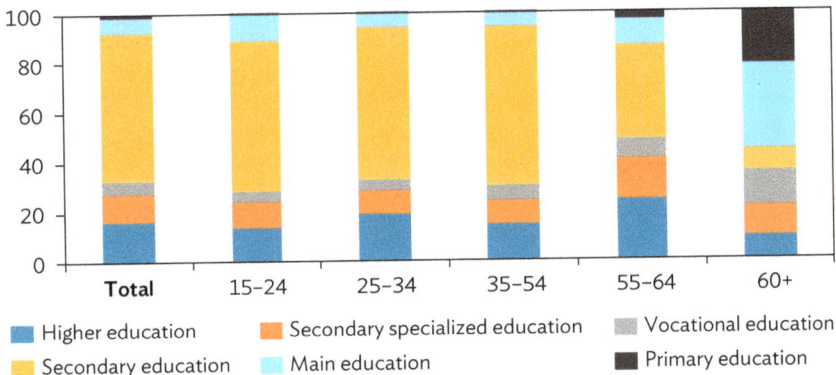

Legend:
- Higher education
- Secondary specialized education
- Vocational education
- Secondary education
- Main education
- Primary education

Source: State Statistical Committee. 2018. *Labor Market Statistical Yearbook 2018*. Baku.

A high proportion (63%) of the working-age population is employed (State Statistical Committee 2018a). The employment rate is 68% in rural areas and 59% in urban areas, reflecting differences in economic activity, such as the large share of the population working in agriculture. Men are more likely to be employed than women (67% compared with 59%). That said, more women than men work in agriculture, trade, education, health, and services; far more men than women work in oil and mining, construction, and public administration (Table 3.3).

The overall unemployment rate is low at 5%, but higher for women (5.9% versus 4.1%) and in urban areas (5.9 % versus 4%) (State Statistical Committee 2018a; Rahmanov, Qasimov, and Tahirova 2016). Among youth, the unemployment rate was 13.4% in 2015, and higher for women (15.8% versus 11.4%). High youth unemployment is due to several factors, including skills mismatches, weak labor market information and matching systems, and a small formal sector.[2] By educational attainment, the highest unemployment rate is among those with basic education (10%), followed by those with advanced education (5.8%) and intermediate education (4.5%).[3]

---

[2]   As part of the implementation of the Law on Unemployment Insurance, which entered in force on 1 January 2018, the government established the Unemployment Insurance Fund that supports self-employment of the unemployed. It enabled a 6.5-fold expansion of the government's self-employment program and engaged 7,200 unemployed. The self-employment program is expected to engage 10,000 people in 2019.

[3]   International Labour Organization Statistics. Employment by education. https://www.ilo.org/ilostat/faces/oracle/webcenter/portalapp/pagehierarchy/Page3.jspx?MBI_ID=11.

Table 3.3: Distribution of Employed by Sector, 2017
(%)

Sector	Total	Men	Women
Agriculture, forestry, and fishing	36.4	30.9	42.2
Mining	0.8	1.3	0.3
Manufacturing	5.2	6.6	3.6
Electricity, gas, and steam production, distribution, and supply	0.6	1.0	0.1
Water supply, waste treatment and disposal	0.6	0.8	0.4
Construction	7.2	12.5	1.5
Trade and repair of motor vehicles	14.6	11.2	18.4
Transportation and storage	4.2	7.3	0.8
Accommodation and food services	1.5	1.7	1.4
ICT	1.3	1.0	1.6
Finance and insurance	0.6	0.6	0.6
Real estate	1.8	2.2	1.4
Professional, scientific, and technical activities	1.5	1.8	1.2
Administrative and support services	1.2	1.4	1.0
Public administration, defense, social security	5.9	9.4	2.1
Education	7.8	4.1	11.9
Health and social work	3.9	1.8	6.2
Art, entertainment, and recreation	1.7	1.4	1.9
Other services	3.2	3.0	3.4
Total	**100.0**	**100.0**	**100.0**

ICT = information and communications technology.
Source: State Statistical Committee. 2018. *Labor Market Statistical Yearbook 2018.* Baku.

Azerbaijan has a large informal sector; its output was estimated at 31.5% of gross domestic product (GDP) in 2008 (Abdih and Medina 2013).[4] Informal employment is not ideal because jobs in this sector are not protected by legislation mandating wage rates and social security, as is the case with the formal sector and contracted jobs. Informal workers have fewer opportunities for training, and are vulnerable to exploitation from working longer hours and in hazardous conditions. To enable a more effective reduction of informal employment, in 2017 the government established a Commission on Regulation and Coordination of the Employment Relations (Presidential Decree No. 2760 dated 17 March 2017) and adopted an Action Plan on Prevention of Informal Employment (Presidential Decree No. 3287 dated 9 October 2017). As part of the implementation of the action plan, the government adopted the Law on Employment, which explicitly deals with informal employment. Azerbaijan has a high level of self-employment, estimated at 68.2% of the working-age population in 2018, the highest in the Commonwealth of Independent States.[5]

---

[4]   According to official statistics the share of informal economy in 2008 was 7.8%. In 2011, the informal economy contribution to GDP was 66.2% of GDP (Ibadoghlu 2018). In 2015, the shadow economy was 43.66% of GDP according to https://www.theglobaleconomy.com/Azerbaijan/shadow_economy/.

[5]   World Bank, World Development Indicators.

Economic growth and productive employment

Opportunities for decent employment will be vital for inclusive growth. This and the following two sections analyze the demand side of Azerbaijan's labor market and the factors that affect labor absorption capability. The country's real GDP per capita accelerated at an average rate of 14.9% a year from 2005 until 2010, which included the early years of oil boom, but slowed from 2010 to 2017, a period that covered the later years of the oil boom and the economic slowdown. Real GDP per capita is still relatively high at 14%.[6] Total labor productivity, as measured by GDP per employed worker, has increased markedly, rising from AZN545 ($617) in 1995 to AZN13,482 ($7,872) in 2017. This was largely driven by investments in oil and mining sector (Table 3.4).

Table 3.4: Gross Domestic Product per Capita and Labor Productivity, 1995–2017

Year	GDP/Pop (manat)	Oil GVA/Pop (manat)	Non-oil GVA/Pop (manat)	WAP/Pop (%)	LF/WAP (%)	Emp/LF (%)	GDP/Emp (manat)	Oil GVA/Oil Emp (manat)	Non-oil GVA/Non-oil Emp (manat)
1995	256	...	...	61.7	47.4	99.2	545	...	...
2000	548	170	379	62.8	54.1	88.2	1,148	41,359	799
2005	1,362	649	712	67.1	51.5	92.7	2,850	158,122	1,503
2010	4,372	2,254	2,118	71.0	50.7	94.4	9,145	558,389	4,468
2017	6,630	2,538	4,093	70.7	51.5	95.0	13,549	606,662	8,435

... = data not available, Emp = employed, GVA = gross value added, GDP = gross domestic product, LF = labor force, Pop = population, WAP = working-age population.
Note: GDP valued at basic prices.
Source: Estimates based on data from State Statistical Committee. https://www.stat.gov.az/ (accessed February 2019).

The decline in labor force participation and employment generally reflects limited job creation.[7] An analysis of the sectoral contribution to GDP and employment growth shows the oil industry—the biggest contributor to the economy's growth since 2000—did not generate enough jobs to accommodate the growth in the labor force (Table 3.5). Indeed, despite the oil industry's large contribution (40%) to total output, it employs about 1% of the labor force. Agriculture provides jobs to 37% of the labor force, but contributes 6% to GDP. The increase in the large share of labor working in agriculture during 1995–

---

[6] In accordance with official data, the real GDP per capita grew by 0.03% on average during 2010–2017. In 2017, it decreased by 0.8%, but grew by 0.5% in 2018.

[7] Since 2003, more than 2.2 million jobs were created and average wages increased 7.5 times. In the first quarter of 2019, 53,892 new jobs were created in the country: 85.4% in construction, 7.3% in trade and repair of vehicles, 5.2% in processing industry, 1.5% in agriculture, forestry, and fishery. Source: Ministry of Labor and Social Protection of Population 2017.

2000 may be because of limited employment opportunities in other sectors. Jobs are most concentrated in services, which has consistently absorbed about 50% of the share of employment since 2000.

Because Azerbaijan's labor force is still heavily engaged in agriculture, there is a need to improve farm productivity and move toward high value-added agricultural production through modernization and agribusinesses. At the same time, much of the rural labor force needs to transition from agriculture. It is essential that younger workers are provided with better education, skills, and training in higher-value nonfarm activities.

Table 3.5: Gross Domestic Product and Employment Structure, 1995–2017

Year	Shares of Major Sectors to GDP (%)				Employment Share (%)				Total Employed ('000 persons)
	Agriculture	Industry		Services	Agriculture	Industry		Services	
		Oil	Non-Oil			Oil	Non-Oil		
1995	27.5	23.0	10.6	38.9	30.8	1.2	13.7	54.3	3,613
2000	17.1	31.0	14.4	37.5	39.1	0.9	11.2	48.7	3,856
2005	9.9	47.7	15.9	26.5	38.7	0.9	11.6	48.8	4,062
2010	5.9	51.6	12.8	29.7	38.2	0.8	12.9	48.1	4,329
2017	6.1	38.5	15.0	40.4	36.4	0.9	13.5	49.3	4,822

GDP = gross domestic product.
Note: GDP valued at basic prices.
Source: Estimates based on data from State Statistical Committee. https://www.stat.gov.az/ (accessed February 2019).

Skills shortage and skills mismatches

Several studies discuss Azerbaijan's skills shortage and mismatches between the job skills wanted by the labor market and those actually available. The 2009 Business Environment and Enterprise Performance Survey by the European Bank for Reconstruction and Development and the World Bank ranked the skills and education of Azerbaijan's labor force as the sixth most important problem for doing business in the country, behind access to financing, foreign currency and tax regulations, inflation, and inefficient government bureaucracy (World Bank 2010).[8] No progress seems to have been made since then. The World Economic Forum's *Global Competitiveness Report 2017–2018* identified Azerbaijan's inadequately educated labor force as 6th out of 16 most problematic factors for doing business in the country (Figure 3.4). Employers encounter difficulties finding workers with the

---

[8]   According to Doing Business 2019 report results, Azerbaijan improved from 22nd spot to 1st based on the indicator of receiving loans.

required skills. The shortage is most pronounced for highly skilled positions (machine operators, professionals, technicians, and managers, for example) and job-specific technical skills and problem-solving skills that include soft skills, such as leadership, teamwork, and openness to experience (World Bank 2015a).[9] This situation suggests that employers not only value technical skills related to their specific job requirements but also soft skills, which are instilled and reinforced in learning institutions. The 2018 EU Business Climate Survey found that 37% of European Union companies that took part in the survey said the lack of a skilled labor force was among the unsatisfactory conditions that their businesses experienced in Azerbaijan (AHK and European Union 2018).

Figure 3.4: Most Problematic Factors for Doing Business, 2017

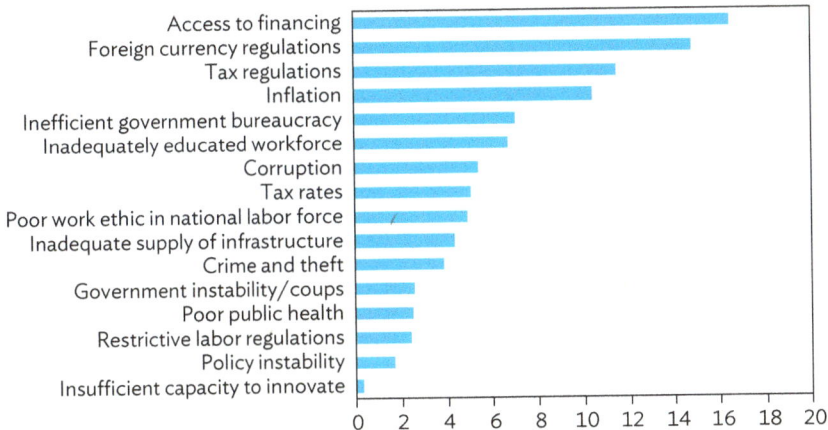

Source: World Economic Forum. 2017. *Global Competitiveness Report 2017–2018*. Geneva.

Before a policy response to the skills mismatch can be formulated, an accurate assessment of the problem is needed. Assessing this, however, is difficult because of the paucity of reliable data on both the supply and demand side of the labor market. Very few studies have attempted to examine in detail Azerbaijan's skills-mismatch problem; those that have typically encounter difficulties in getting information from employers, because of gaps in methodologies, lack of resources for collecting this information, and poor information and technology systems, as well as the large informal sector (ETF 2016).[10] Among the few studies on this issue are the World Bank's 2013 STEP

---

9   The STEP Employer Skills Survey used the International Standard Classification of Occupations, which classifies occupations in the following groups: (i) managers; (ii) professionals; (iii) technicians and associate professionals; (iv) clerical support workers; (v) service workers; (vi) sales workers; (vii) skilled agricultural, forestry, and fishery workers; (viii) construction, craft, and related trades workers; (ix) plant and machine operators, and assemblers and drivers; and (x) elementary occupations (World Bank 2015a).

10   Skills mismatches are hard to measure since there is no clear and established methodology in determining the type of skills needed for all types of jobs and occupations, hence the gap.

Employer Skills Survey, which show that employers find Azerbaijan's system for general education and technical and vocational education and training neither provides students with practical skills nor the up-to-date knowledge that meets the needs of the labor market.[11] The government decision in 2019 to set up a national observatory on labor market is expected to address the issue with the lack of reliable data on the supply and demand for skills.[12]

Using a framework for mapping occupations and tasks to the education and skills needed to perform them shows that a large share of Azerbaijan's labor force is engaged in low-skilled agriculture, and in both high- and low-skilled services (Table 3.6 and Figure 3.5). Because agriculture work typically involves the use of traditional and labor-intensive technologies, it is often considered a low-skilled occupation in which primary education is deemed adequate (Figure 3.6).

Table 3.6: Mapping Occupations and Tasks to Skills and Education

Occupation by Category	Tasks	Skills	Maximum Level of Education	Wage Ratio to Low-Skilled Occupations
High-skilled managerial	Problem solving, interpersonal, industry specific	Cognitive, noncognitive, technical	Tertiary	3.0
High-skilled professional/ technical (e.g., engineers, doctors, lawyers)	Problem solving, industry specific	Cognitive, technical	Tertiary	2.2
Middle-skilled routine (e.g., machine operators, drivers, clerks)	Routine, industry specific	Basic cognitive, basic technical	Secondary vocational	1.2
Middle-skilled nonroutine (e.g., services or sales)	Nonroutine, interpersonal, basic problem solving	Basic cognitive, noncognitive, basic technical	Secondary vocational/ general	1.6
Low-skilled (e.g., agriculture workers, cleaners, domestic helpers)	Physical, routine	Basic cognitive	Primary	1.0

Notes: ISCO-08 occupation groups at 1 digit: 1 = high-skilled managerial; 2, 3 = high-skilled professional/ technical;
4, 5, 6 = mid-skilled routine; 5, 6 = mid-skilled nonroutine; 9 = low skilled, except for 2-digit codes:
83 = mid-skilled nonroutine; 63 = low skilled.
Source: Adapted from Asian Development Bank. 2015. A Smarter Future: Skills, Education and Growth. Special chapter in Key Indicators for Asia and the Pacific 2015. Manila.

---

[11]   In this chapter, unless specified, vocational education and training refers to initial vocational education, specialized vocational education, and short-term training. To be consistent with the language of the Strategic Road Map on Vocational Education and Training, this chapter uses vocational education and training to cover the three types. Technical training is included in the sector road map.

[12]   Presidential Decree on the National Observatory on Labor Market and Social Protection Affairs no. 775, dated 4 July 2019. The observatory, whose statutory and institutional frameworks are yet to be finalized, will assess the demand for labor at regional and sector levels based on quantitative and qualitative parameters, and will, thus, contribute to a more effective supply side response."

Figure 3.5: Share of Employment by Sector, 2017

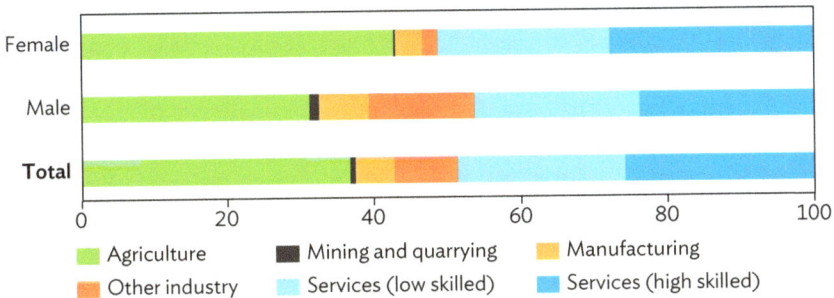

Notes: ISIC Rev 4 industry groups. Agriculture = 1.3; mining and quarrying = 5–9; manufacturing = 10–33; other industry = 35–43; services (low skilled) = 45–56, 94–99; services (high skilled) = 58–93.
Source: Authors' estimates using data from State Statistical Committee. 2018. *Labor Market Statistical Yearbook 2018*. Baku.

Figure 3.6: Employment by Occupation and Skills Category, 2017

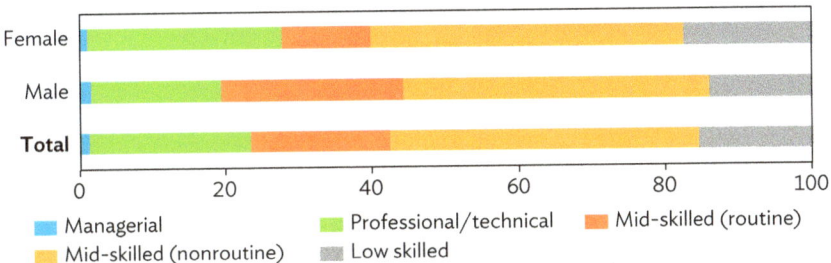

Notes: ISCO-08 occupations groups at 1 digit: 1 = high skilled managerial; 2, 3 = high-skilled professional/technical; 4, 5, 6 = mid-skilled routine; 5, 6 = mid-skilled nonroutine; 9 = low skilled, except for 2-digit codes: 83 = mid-skilled nonroutine; 63 = low skilled.
Source: Authors' estimates using data from the International Labour Organization's ILOSTAT (accessed 5 April 2019).

The level of under- or overqualified individuals shows the extent of the vertical skills mismatches (Table 3.7). While most of Azerbaijan's employed youth have completed secondary education, they are concentrated in high- and low-skilled services and manufacturing, where high-quality vocational or tertiary education is required (Figure 3.7). This indicates some level of vertical mismatch among the young, a demographic where there is high unemployment. In a survey on the employed ages 15–29, only 56% said they worked within their specialization or education qualification. The rest are either partly matched (7%) or not working within their specialization (37%) (State Statistical Committee 2016). A quarter of respondents said they were not using any knowledge or skills gained in education in their jobs, which points to a horizontal mismatch and a skills gap (Table 3.7).

Table 3.7: Types of Skills Mismatch

Types of Mismatch	Definition
Skills shortage	Demand (supply) for a particular type of skill exceeds the supply (demand) of people with that skill
Skills gap	Type or level of skills is different from that required to adequately perform the job
Vertical mismatch	The level of education or qualification is less or more than required
Horizontal mismatch	The type or field of education or skills is inappropriate for the job
Overeducation (undereducation)	Workers have more (less) years of education than the job requires
Overqualification (underqualification)	Workers hold a higher (lower) qualification than the job requires
Skills obsolescence	Skills previously used in a job are no longer required and/or skills have deteriorated over time

Source: International Labour Organization. 2014. *Skills Mismatch in Europe*. Statistics brief, September. Geneva.

Figure 3.7: Educational Attainment and Share of Employment by Sector for Employed Youth, 2018

a. Educational Attainment by Age Group

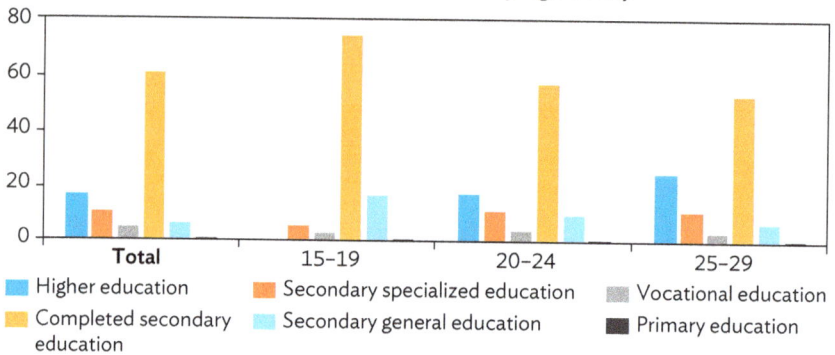

Higher education
Completed secondary education
Secondary specialized education
Secondary general education
Vocational education
Primary education

b. Share of Employment by Sector

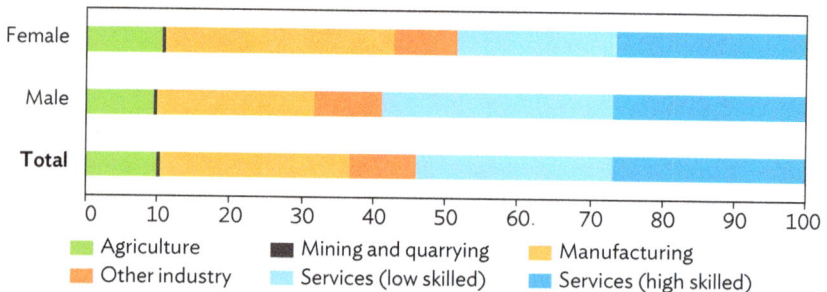

Agriculture
Other industry
Mining and quarrying
Services (low skilled)
Manufacturing
Services (high skilled)

Notes: ISIC Rev 4 industry groups. Agriculture = 1, 3; mining and quarrying = 59; manufacturing = 10–33; other industry = 35–43; services (low skilled) = 45–56, 94–99; services (high skilled) = 58–93.
Source: Authors' estimates using State Statistical Committee. 2018b. *Youth of Azerbaijan Statistical Yearbook*. Baku.

The skills gaps and mismatches clearly show the education system is failing to respond to the needs of the labor market. World Bank (2015b) notes that tertiary education colleges produce graduates in areas for which there is little demand, such as education, health, and oil-related manufacturing, and that there are not enough graduates to meet demand for labor in the services, agriculture, and non-oil related manufacturing sectors. EU Business Climate Surveys consistently underscore the need for further improvements to Azerbaijan's higher and vocational education systems to attract foreign investment (AHK and European Union 2016, 2017, 2018). The lack of a robust market information system is partly to blame for the mismatch, which also reflects weak links and cooperation between national and public bodies, and between industries and learning institutions (ETF 2015).

Azerbaijan has a young population, 40% of which is below 24. This is both a demographic dividend for the economy and a challenge for the government to provide the right kind of education and skills needed by the job market. A question related to this is whether the country has sufficient capacity, funds, and resources to prepare a growing labor force for productive employment. The following two sections analyze these challenges for education and skills development.

3.2   Challenges in Education

Low public spending on education

Government spending on education has long been low and it is on a declining trend, indicating its low prioritization. From a low 3.4% in 1998, education spending as percentage of GDP declined to 2.5% in 2018.[13] The share of education in total government spending fell from 19% in 1998 to 8% in 2018 (below the 12% average of countries in Europe and Central Asian (Figure 3.8).[14] For higher education, while spending increased from AZN150 million ($190 million) in 2011 to AZN160 million ($92 million) in 2017, the number of students increased from 120,000 to 153,000 over the same period, resulting in spending per student falling from AZN1,250 ($1,583)

---

[13]   In 2019, education spending as percentage of GDP increased to 2.9%. In 2020, education spending is expected to increase by 38% compared to 2019, to reach 3.8% of GDP.

[14]   In 2019, the share of education in the state budget rose to 9.1%. In 2020, this share is expected to further increase to 11.7%.

to AZN1,046 ($607) (State Statistical Committee 2018c).[15] More than half of government spending on education goes to general education (Table 3.8 and Figure 3.9). Insufficiency of state educational expenditures negatively affect the opportunities to receive education and the quality of education. Limited access to education means families must dedicate a significant portion of their household budget for education, which disadvantages those on low-income. A poor-quality education affects students' performance, contributing to low educational outcomes.

Figure 3.8: Education Spending in Azerbaijan and Europe and Central Asia, 1998–2018

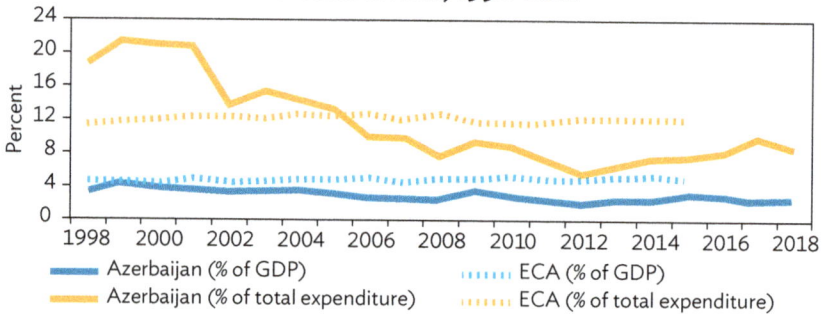

ECA = Europe and Central Asia, GDP= gross domestic product.
Source: World Bank, World Development Indicators Database; and State Statistical Committee.

Table 3.8: Education Spending Breakdown, 2018

Level of Education	Manat (million)	Percentage
Education total	**2,043.99**	**100.0**
Preschool education	175.31	8.6
General education	1,082.16	52.9
Initial vocational education	27.98	1.6
Secondary specialized education	41.30	2.0
Higher education	42.72	2.1
Additional education	3.74	0.2
Other institutions and activities	670.78	32.8

Source: Ministry of Finance.

---

[15] Since 2010, allocation of state budget to the higher education institutions is based on the per capita financing approach, which was introduced through the Presidential Decree No. 220, dated 10 February 2010. Higher educational institutions have become financially autonomous, may generate and freely spend own-generated funds, and set merit-based staff salaries. Paid educational services are exempt from the value added tax. Students from eligible vulnerable groups (e.g., internally displaced people, orphans, disabled people, children of war or military service veterans) are eligible for state budget to cover their educational expenses and to receive stipends from the government. In 2019, there were 17,120 students from vulnerable groups, whose education cost was covered from the budget. In 2019, the number of university student places receiving stipends from the state budget (subject to successful performance) was increased by 16,000. The share of higher education students receiving stipends is envisaged to rise from 45% in 2019–2020 academic year to at least 50% at the beginning of 2020-2021 academic year. In 2019, the government raised the student stipends by an average of 20%.

Figure 3.9: Share of Higher Education and Vocational Education and Training Spending in Total State Education Spending, 2014–2018

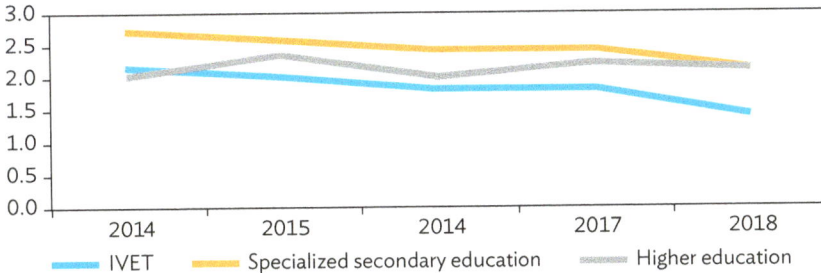

IVET = initial vocational education.
Source: Ministry of Finance.

Poor-quality secondary education

Azerbaijan has a high literacy rate, at 99.9% in 2017. Its ranking on the education index of the UNDP's Human Development Index has increased since 1995, and is within the midrange of other countries in the region (Figure 3.10). Access to basic education is close to universal, with a completion rate of 89% for lower secondary education and a gross enrollment rate in primary schools close to 100 percent in 2017. But student performance has not improved, going by the latest available Programme for International Student Assessment test results for Azerbaijan for 15-year-olds, conducted in 2009.[16] Azerbaijan ranked 64th among 65 countries in reading, 63rd out of 65 in science, and 45th out of 65 in mathematics (OECD 2010).[17]

The quality of secondary education is a determining factor for admission to higher education. In 2015, 24% of Azerbaijan's university admission applicants got the lowest score of 0–100, while 20% got a score of 100–200 (State Student Admission Commission 2015). In 2018, the number of university admission applicants, who scored 0-200 points, decreased by 28% (compared to 2014); the number of those who scored more than 600 points increased by 81.3%; and the number of those who scored more 500 points increased by 51.5%.[18]

---

[16] Azerbaijan participated in the Programme for International Student Assessment in 2006, 2009, and 2018.

[17] Note that in the 2016 Progress in International Reading Literacy Study (PIRLS) for fourth graders, Azerbaijan scored 472 and ranked 39 out of 50 countries. Compared with the PIRLS done in 2011, the reading skills in the 2016 PIRLS increased by 10 points and the number of students performing at the "outstanding" and "high" levels increased by 2 times.

[18] Based on the new regulations, decision on university admission is based on the sum of score received from the final examination at school and the score received from university admission examination. The examination tests include open- and closed-ended questions.

Figure 3.10: Education Index Azerbaijan and Selected Countries, 2017

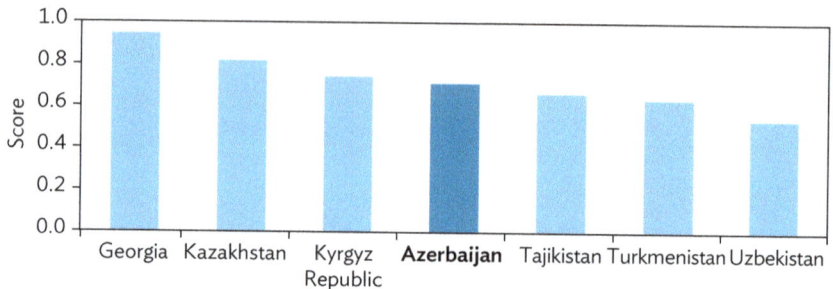

Note: The education index is measured by combining average adult years of schooling and expected years of schooling for children, each receiving 50% weighting.
Source: UNDP. Education index. http://www.hdr.undp.org/en/indicators/103706#.

The minimum entry requirement of the national university exam is frequently lowered to allow the targeted number of students to enter universities. The dismal exam results show that the quality of secondary education was inadequate to prepare students for university.

Low participation in preschool and tertiary education

Although the goal of universal access to education has been largely achieved at the primary and secondary level, the gross enrollment ratio in preschool and tertiary education has long been considerably lower than the average for Europe and Central Asia. The reasons are low access and the high cost of sending children to school at these levels.

Azerbaijan's gross enrollment ratio in 2017 was 36% for preschool, compared with an average of 75% in Europe and Central Asia. The benefits of early childhood education and care are widely recognized for their contribution to improving children's cognitive abilities and socio-emotional development, thereby laying the foundations for skills development. Children in preschool enable their mothers to go to work. (ADB 2015; OECD 2017). Reforms are underway to tackle the low participation of children ages 5–6 in preschool education, and efforts by the government in this area have increased the coverage of preschool education, from 24% in 2015 to 65% in 2017 and 84.2% in 2019 (Ministry of Education 2018).[19] The government is targeting 90% coverage by 2020 (through the school readiness groups initiative).

---

[19] Raising preschool coverage occurs mainly through setting up school readiness groups for 5-6-year-old children at the public general education schools (Decision of the Cabinet of Ministers on "Organization of school readiness of children", no. 271 dated 11 July 2016). In 2019, AZN233,8 million was allocated for preschool education (33.4% more than in 2018).

Tertiary education enrollment in Azerbaijan, at 27%, is considered low compared with rates in other countries in Europe and Central Asia (average 68%).[20] Only about 30% of secondary school graduates get into university in Azerbaijan. This is because of the highly centralized state quota allocation system in which the government arbitrarily sets student admission quotas for all programs in public and private universities regardless of whether they are subsidized by the state or self-financed (Aliyev 2011). In the 2015/16 academic year, admission rate at 81% was lower than the quota set by the government for that year (Table 3.9).[21] During 2015–2019, the number of students admitted in higher education increased by 21% and exceeded 44,000 in 2019. University admissions are done through an entrance exam administered by the State Student Admission Commission. Secondary school students from public schools in rural areas and from poor households who cannot afford the high cost of private tutoring to prepare for these exams are at a disadvantage. University tuition fees, ranging from AZN1,300 ($1,269) to AZN4,800 ($4,685) a year, based on 2015 fees, are expensive for poorer households. These rates are 2–3 times higher than the tuition fees in universities in the neighboring country of Turkey. The only students who qualify for state support are those who passed the admissions exam with high grades; a small number of scholarships are awarded to outstanding applicants and for study in universities abroad.[22] For the 2015/16 academic year, only 36.8% of those admitted to universities were state funded (Table 3.9).

Another barrier to access to tertiary education is the geographical concentration of higher education institutions in Baku. Of the country's 51 public and private universities, 42 are in Baku—and some 78% of students going on to higher education are allocated places to these colleges through quotas.[23] This and the higher cost of tertiary education (tuition and living expenses) severely disadvantages students from rural areas wanting higher education. Azerbaijan's universities also have a reputation for low quality; one manifestation of this is the increase in Azerbaijani students attending higher education in Turkey, which has increased since 2015 (Clayton 2019). Getting

---

[20] According to the Ministry of Education, the enrollment rate in higher and specialized secondary educational institutions is 41%.

[21] The government sets quota for admission every year, but the admission rate is even lower than the quota due to low scores.

[22] The State Program on the Education of Azerbaijani Youth Abroad 2007–2015, which provides financial assistance to Azerbaijani students for study abroad, was suspended in 2015 when there was a sharp downturn in the economy. This program, which followed the moto of turning the black gold to human capital, was supported by the State Oil Fund of Azerbaijan. It enabled 3,558 Azerbaijanis to study in the prestigious higher educational institutions in 32 countries around the world.

[23] In the 2019-2020 academic year, admissions to higher educational institutions in the regions modestly increased by 2.4% (2,955 people) compared with the 2015-2016 academic year. In 2019, the share of the regional higher education institutions in the total number of students admitted to the country's higher education institutions was 25%.

Table 3.9: Admission Quota to Universities by Specialty and Education Institutions, 2015/16 Academic Year

Specialized Subjects	Admission Quota	Admitted		Admission (%)	
		Total	State Funded	Total	State Funded
Mathematics, physics, engineering, architecture, design	12,131	10,044	5,108	82.8	50.9
Economics, management, international relations, regional studies, sociology, geography	11,672	9,002	1,923	77.1	21.4
Humanities and pedagogic	9,534	8,209	2,559	86.1	31.2
Medicine, chemistry, biology, agrarian and psychology	3,139	2,405	1,328	76.6	55.2
Art, music, and sport	2,355	2,039	734	86.6	36.0
Total	**38,831**	**31,699**	**11,652**	**81.6**	**36.8**
Education Institutions					
State	32,277	28,383	11,037	87.9	38.9
Private	6,554	3,316	615	50.6	18.5
Total	**38,831**	**31,699**	**11,652**	**81.6**	**36.8**

Source: State Student Admission Commission. 2015. Digest of Education Statistics in Testing and Admissions. Baku.

into universities in Turkey is considered easier than getting into universities in Azerbaijan. Applicants only need to take the SAT used for US college admissions or a similar Turkish test, both of which are less time consuming and require less knowledge of the subjects.

3.3   Challenges in Skills Development

Low government funding for vocational training and education

The vocational education and training system is insufficiently funded from the national budget, one of several challenges the system faces. Government funding for the improvement of logistical support for vocational education and training schools and colleges started only in 2008. At that time, most of these schools and colleges had outdated courses and aging facilities (UNESCO-

UNVECOC 2013).[24] The share of vocational education and training spending in total education spending is low and declining, from 2.1% in 2014 to 1.4% in 2018 (Table 3.9).

Enrollment in vocational education and training is persistently low, with only 5% of enrolled students in 2018 in initial vocation education or specialized secondary schools (Table 3.10).[25] The reason seems to be the unattractiveness of vocational education and training on grounds of quality and relevance. Because of this, there is a shortage of qualified workers with the skills and knowledge required to meet the needs of the labor market. With only 30% of secondary school graduates admitted to universities yearly, and less than 30% in specialized secondary and vocational education, the rest of secondary school graduates enter the labor market without tertiary education or vocational education qualifications or skills (ETF 2017). The informal education system covers vocational training for the unemployed, and for training and retraining employees of organizations, companies, and agencies. Statistical State Committee data show that participation in professional training among public sector employees has declined since 2012 (Table 3.11). In the private sector, only 20% of firms provide training for their employees (13% of small, 26% of medium, and 44% of large firms). This is nearly half the average in Europe and Central Asia.[26] The State Employment Services provides professional training for the unemployed, but fewer people are doing this training, reflecting a similar trend for professional training for public sector workers (Table 3.12).

Poor institutional links for data gathering

The links between concerned government agencies need to be strengthened to be able to properly project Azerbaijan's skills needs. Data gathered through the current mechanisms of skills-needs assessments are in different formats and used by various stakeholders for different purposes. Different agencies work in parallel and communication channels among them are weak, impeding synergies from being formed. The main institutions involved in data collection and the analysis of labor market trends and skills needs are the following:

---

[24] After independence, the vocation education and training system was neglected and reprioritized only in 2006 when education reforms were initiated. A year later, a presidential decree approved funding for vocational education and training.

[25] The number of the state budget funded admission places in the vocation education institutions increased from 11,600 in 2018-2019 school year to 11,960 in the 2019-2020 school year. The increase was mainly because of additional places in the technology and service professions.

[26] World Bank, World Development Indicators.

Table 3.10: Distribution of Enrolled Students by Education Level, 2010–2017
(number of students)

Students	2010/11 SY	2011/12 SY	2012/13 SY	2013/14 SY	2014/15 SY	2015/16 SY	2016/17 SY
Total	**1,545,586**	**1,517,912**	**1,517,055**	**1,533,053**	**1,566,286**	**1,595,452**	**1,701,043**
General education centers (grades 1–11, includes primary, basic, and secondary)	1,324,564	1,291,317	1,284,853	1,289,272	1,322,182	1,353,309	1,461,748
Initial vocational educational centers and vocational centers	27,330	28,993	30,664	29,234	25,414	24,482	23,814
Specialized secondary educational centers	53,451	54,456	55,954	63,273	60,478	56,427	51,702
Higher education centers	140,241	143,146	145,584	151,274	158,212	161,234	163,779

SY = school year.
Source: State Statistical Committee. 2018. *Education, Science and Culture Statistical Yearbook 2017.* Baku; and Ministry of Education.

Table 3.11: Professional Training of Labor Force, 2012–2017
(number of workers)

Item	2012	2013	2014	2015	2016	2017
Passed professional training	7,745	6,849	6,914	7,453	4,815	4,502
Retrained	1,877	2,610	2,687	4,029	681	1,180
Improved professional qualification	7,358	3,333	4,136	3,888	11,147	7,102
Graduated from total number of workers who passed professional training and improved qualification	**15,103**	**10,182**	**11,050**	**11,341**	**15,962**	**11,604**
in enterprise	3,845	2,297	4,091	4,164	7,324	2,117
in a foreign country	112	103	49	33	28	119
in educational institutions	197	148	1,695	4,002	1,344	3,838
advanced training institutes	...	...	86	218	607	441
training courses	...	...	5,129	2,924	6,659	5,089
women	735	479	665	440	751	488

... = not available.
Sources: State Statistical Committee. 2018. *Labor market statistical yearbook, 2017.* Baku; and Ministry of Education.

- The State Statistical Committee collects mainly quantitative and qualitative data, but this is limited to revisions to titles of occupations. It carries out quarterly and yearly labor force surveys.

- The Ministry of Labor and Social Protection of the Population's State Employment Services collects labor market data from its regional offices. But this covers only state-owned enterprises, and analysis is limited to registered unemployment. Regional labor market forecasts for the short term and a 1-year horizon are made on the basis of these data. The ministry's Scientific and Research Center for Labor and Social Problems develops skills-anticipation models and methods as part of its activities. The methodologies used cover horizons of up to 3 years, and the data is used by the State Employment Services.

- The Ministry of Economy publishes forecasts of macroeconomic indicators for the coming year and the following 3 years. These forecasts include employment indicators for general employment and economic areas. The ministry's Institute of Education collects information on skills needs categorized by professions and curricula.

Table 3.12: Vocational Education and Training for the Unemployed

Year	Total	First Trained	Retrained	Upgrading of Qualification
Total				
2012	4,464	3,922	273	269
2013	4,329	3,957	142	230
2014	3,786	3,459	4	323
2015	4,147	3,697	52	398
2016	3,352	2,908	33	411
2017	3,561	3,154	109	298
Women				
2012	2,122	1,757	221	144
2013	2,067	1,810	104	153
2014	1,755	1,550	1	204
2015	1,707	1,462	25	220
2016	1,490	1,189	21	280
2017	1,826	1,574	62	190

Sources: State Statistical Committee. 2018. Labor market statistical year book. Baku; and Ministry of Education.

3.4 Review of Policies and Programs

Since independence, Azerbaijan's education policies have been characterized by three periods: postindependence, comprising the regression (1991–1994) and reform (1995–2003) years; the oil boom (2004–2014);

and the economic slowdown from 2015. Policy documents supporting skills development and labor productivity reflect the period in which they were introduced.

During the late Soviet period and early years of independence, war with the separatist Nagorno-Karabakh region and a recession caused Azerbaijan's education system to deteriorate until a series of laws were passed that aided the sector's recovery. In 1991, the Law on the Restoration of the Azerbaijani Alphabet with Latin Graphics replaced the Cyrillic script with a modified Latin script. The 1992 Education Law established the basic principles of a state policy that ensures the right to education and the general terms for regulating various aspects of education. The law was amended from time to time, eventually becoming the New Education Law in 2009. Notable features of this law were clarifying the role and authority of the Ministry of Education and replacing the single-level university degree with bachelor's degrees and master's degrees. Presidential decrees were issued in 1998 on a Program for Education Reform and in 2000 on Improving the Education System (ADB 2004).[27]

Azerbaijan took a major step toward a European-level education system by becoming a full member of the Bologna Process in 2005. This is a series of interministerial agreements between European governments that ensure comparability in standards and the quality of higher education qualifications. A 2007 presidential decree on a State Program on the Education of Azerbaijan Youth Abroad 2007–2015 aimed to meet the need for highly qualified specialists to help make the economy more competitive.[28] Under the program, Azerbaijani students were sent to universities in Australia, Germany, Malaysia, the People's Republic of China, the Republic of Korea, Singapore, the United Kingdom, and the United States, among other countries. Over the program, 3,000 students went to universities in these countries. The 2013 presidential decree on a State Strategy for the Development of Education is aimed at promoting a competitive business environment by identifying human resource needs for training and management.[29] Under this decree, satellite universities of prominent foreign universities and colleges were established in Azerbaijan and international double diploma programs were set up.

The main objective of education reforms since the slowdown in 2015 has been to further increase the quality of education, and to strengthen the link between education and employment. The main policy documents supporting

---

[27] Presidential Decrees No. 295, latest reform dated May 22, 2009, and No. 349, dated 13 June 2000.

[28] Presidential Decree No. 2090, dated 16 April 2007.

[29] Presidential Decree No. 13, dated 24 October 2013.

skills development and labor productivity on national and sector levels are the Strategic Road Maps, the State Strategy for the Development of Education and Action Plan for Implementation, the State Program on Azerbaijani Youth 2017–2021, and the Employment Strategy 2019–2030. These are discussed in the following section.

Policies supporting skills development and labor productivity

The four core targets of the Strategic Road Map on the National Economy Perspective include developing human capital, which will be essential for Azerbaijan to achieve a competitive, inclusive, and sustainable economy. This road map outlines a two-pronged approach for supporting human capital development—improving the quality of education at all levels, and investing in research and development in areas that can increase labor productivity. To underscore the importance of skills development, the Strategic Road Maps include a sector road map for vocational education and training.[30]

This outlines a short-term vision (2016–2020) for piloting new vocational education and training schools and colleges. It also aims to optimize existing institutions by recruiting highly qualified teachers,[31] and overhauling the vocational education and training curricula and standards to respond to labor market needs.[32] The long-term vision to 2025 for this road map is to have fully functional vocational education and training schools and colleges that continue to match labor market needs and that forge close partnerships with the private sector. Beyond 2025, the road map aspires to have a competitive and globally recognized vocational education and training system. Human capital development components were embedded in the other sector road maps, as follows:

- The Strategic Road Map on the Production Consumer Goods in Small and Medium Enterprises underscores the importance of financial literacy and business management skills for entrepreneurs. This includes studying

---

[30] The Strategic Road Map on the Development of Logistics and Trade does not specifically prioritize skills development, but it sees this sector as an opportunity to create decent jobs for young workers.

[31] In 2018, the salaries of the primary vocational educational training institutions' staff, who passed the knowledge and skill assessment, increased by 2 times on average (Presidential Decree No. 3579 dated 17 January 2018). To support to students studying in vocational educational institutions, in 2019 the government increase their monthly stipends from AZN38 to AZN50, or by 31.6% (Presidential Decree No. 961 dated 14 February 2019).

[32] The government has adopted several policy measures to implement the agenda of the strategic road map on vocational education and training. Among such measures are adoption of (i) normative rules on financing of state vocational educational institutions (Decision of the Cabinet of Ministers No. 561, dated 22 December 2018); (ii) a sample charter of public vocational educational institutions (Decision of the Cabinet of Ministers No. 65, dated 26 February 2019); (iii) the state standards of vocational education (Decision of the Cabinet of Ministers No. 85, dated 11 March 2019); and (iv) the average student density indicators for vocational educational institutions (Decision of the Cabinet of Ministers No. 86, dated 11 March 2019).

the labor market needs of small and medium-sized enterprises (SMEs) and accelerating the implementation of international best practices for these firms. This sector road map emphasizes the need for coordination between vocational education and training systems and SMEs, and for ensuring lifelong-learning opportunities for SME workers. It gives special attention to expanding economic opportunities to women entrepreneurs.[33]

- The Strategic Road Map on the Development of Heavy Industry and Machine-Building envisages calibrating vocational education and training programs with the specific labor needs of heavy industry. The skills needed for the oil and mining industry, metallurgy, and developing new defense products are identified under this sector road map. It also envisages adopting Germany's dual system of study that combines apprenticeship in a company and vocational education and training into one course.

- The Strategic Road Map on the Development of a Specialized Tourism Industry focuses on education and training through investment in education programs, increasing the number of vocational education and training and higher education graduates with work experience, and bringing the local tourism industry up to international standards. Interventions to achieve this include setting up regional tourism vocational education and training schools and colleges and drawing up occupational standards and curricula, including master of business administration programs in tourism and the certification of tour guides.

- The Strategic Road Map on the Development of Financial Services prioritizes increasing the capacities and capabilities of the Financial Markets Supervisory Authority and Central Bank of Azerbaijan through training, certification programs, and higher education programs. The road map also aims to increase awareness on financial services and consumer rights.

- The Strategic Road Map on the Development of Telecommunication and Information Technologies aims to increase information and communication technology knowledge and skills. The sector road map plans a skills-needs analysis to reform digital education systems.

- The Strategic Road Map on the Development of Communal Services (Electricity and Heat Energy, Water and Gas) plans to establish qualifications and courses for the communal services sector, and manuals and methodological tools for education institutions and research centers.

---

[33] Developments in this area include FMSA-organized training courses in Baku, Ganja, Lankaran, Nakhchivan, Shamakhi, and Guba for organizations operating in the financial sector on various topics, broad awareness activities on financial literacy for securities market and competitions on trade simulation with securities.

The State Strategy for the Development of Education and Action Plan for Implementation, approved in 2013 and 2015, respectively, aim to set curricula to the needs of the labor market and national development goals.[34] The strategy aims to create competency-based education, develop innovative learning methods and technologies, set up public policy administration systems that adhere to transparent regulation mechanisms, promote public and private sector partnerships, and create new mechanisms for education funding. The main achievements of the strategy so far are the Diagnostic Assessment of Teachers on General Education,[35] new curricula in general education, improving education infrastructure, and the approval, in 2018, of the National Qualifications Framework for lifelong learning.

The Second State Program on Azerbaijani Youth 2016–2021, approved in 2017, is a continuation of the first 2011–2015 program. The second program has a special focus on the education and employment of youth, including skills development, career guidance, and entrepreneurship. The program aims to develop employment opportunities for young people, and increase awareness on occupational and professional career choices. Both state programs are only in a framework format, lack detailed activities and indicators, and do not have expenditure plans.

The Employment Strategy 2019–2030 is designed to carry out pro-employment macroeconomic policy and support for micro, small, and medium-sized enterprises; improve the legislative framework and institutional structure of the labor market; and build labor force skills.[36] The strategy also aims to improve labor standards, increase the coverage and efficiency of labor market programs, and integrate target groups into the labor market.[37] Long-term aims include preventing informal labor and developing a labor market

---

[34] State Strategy on Development of Education in the Republic of Azerbaijan, adopted through a Presidential Decree No. 13 dated 24 October 2013. Action Plan on Implementation of the State Strategy on development of education in the Republic of Azerbaijan, adopted through the Presidential Decree No. 995 dated 19 January 2015.

[35] A diagnostic assessment was conducted for teachers in general education institutions in Baku but who had not taken certification and licensing exams or had taken these exams and failed. The assessment was also conducted for teachers who changed their workplace or were newly hired by the Ministry of Education.

[36] To encourage formal employment, in 2018 the government adopted measures aimed at streamlining the taxation, social insurance, coordination and data management systems. For example, a simplified income tax rate of 2% was introduced for individual self-employed people; employment coordination committees were established at local level; phased rollout of mandatory health insurance is expected to be completed in 2020; and unified and inter-agency-integrated electronic platforms on the registry of employed people and on informal employment monitoring were designed.

[37] One of the targets of the employment strategy that at least 20% of the jobseekers, who applied for support from the state employment service, get engaged in professional training programs. By promoting delivery of professional training through the state employment service of the Ministry of Labor and Social Protection of Population, the vocational education facilities under the Ministry of Education, and the accredited private education institutions, the government intends to increase the number of unemployed engaged in professional training to 10,000-15,000.

monitoring and forecasting system. The strategy is a continuation of the first Employment Strategy 2006–2015 to provide productive employment and to fully utilize labor resources. Both strategies have a holistic approach to skills development and increasing labor productivity, unlike the other labor policy plans and strategies currently in place.

Areas where education policy can be improved

The Strategic Road Maps mainly focus on vocational education and training to provide the economy with skilled workers for less complex products and services. The economy, however, also needs technicians and professionals for higher value and more complex products and services. A holistic view to developing skills to increase labor productivity across sectors would be a better approach for the strategic development of human capital than the current fragmented approach. This means looking at how to meet labor market needs through a combination of higher education and vocational education and training strategies, and not just through vocational education and training alone. It also means identifying learning tracks for higher education and vocational education and training, while creating nodes where education pathways can freely intersect. A holistic approach to developing skills would also improve the nexus of education-science-industry. In this regard, the in-country dual university diploma initiative of the government adopted in 2018 is an encouraging development that can efficiently facilitate knowledge transfer from reputable higher institutions abroad.[38]

A decentralized and private-sector-led approach to vocational education and training and skills development is important because it will make training both regionally relevant and responsive to the private sector's labor needs. Vocational education and training is still largely organized by state authorities, and this approach is upheld in the Strategic Road Maps. Continuing with a centralized approach will make it harder to close the gap between the worlds of education and work. Allowing the private sector to provide vocational education and training services, and introducing policy flexibility in some regulations, could bring the labor demands of the market closer to current and future labor supply.

A more systematic approach is needed for upgrading skills and for the compatibility of education standards. The Strategic Road Map on Vocational Education and Training proposes creating a mechanism to admit vocational

---

[38] State Program on improving international competitiveness of higher educational system in the Republic of Azerbaijan in 2019–2023, approved by Presidential Decree No. 711, dated 16 November 2018.

education and training graduates with high grades to higher education institutions without them having to take an entrance exam. A systemic approach for this would be to introduce progression pathways within the curricula. For example, progression pathways envisioned in the sector road map traverse only a track from vocational education and training toward the higher education track. In reality, however, education pathways could also lead to the reverse—that is, a track from higher education toward the vocational education and training track. In this regard, the quality assurance of skills through certification is a critical component of the sector road map. Yet the specific procedure to link this to formal education and training is still missing. Also, while the sector road map has a few quality control measures, their compatibility with each other is unclear.

Early achievements in education reform

Data from the Center for Analysis of Economic Reforms and Communication show that 33% of the Strategic Road Map on Vocational Education and Training was completely implemented as of January 2019, 12% partly implemented, and 55% yet to be implemented. As one of the sector road map's short-term objectives, the State Agency on Vocational Education was set up in April 2016 under the Ministry of Education to help focus the vocational education system on the needs of the labor market. To enable better response to the skills need of the private sector, the agency (including several vocation educational institutions) have signed memoranda of understanding with about 120 employer organizations. The network of vocational educational institutions has been rationalized, and renovation and reconstruction of the 4 out of 10 pilot vocation educational pilot institutions is ongoing. Progress on the implementation of the sector road map is slow because of the inadequate financing and prioritization of vocational education and training as part of the education sector's budget, and failure to fully resettle internally displaced persons living in vocational educational institutions.

Another step toward optimizing the components of vocational education was the June 2018 Law on Vocational Education, which defines the main legal, organizational, and economic structure of the country's vocational education system.[39] The law provides for a three-tier vocational education system of

---

[39] The Strategic Road Map on Vocational Education and Training defines component optimization in actions 1.1.2 and 1.1.3, priority 1.1, and strategic target 1. Component optimization is viewed as the "aim to rationalize educational institutions, terminate or temporarily suspend the operation of some vocational education institutions if necessary, as well as identify new initial vocation education institutions to be built." The optimization process involves "terminating the 'operation of unpromising educational institutions and the temporary suspension of operation of some educational institutions at the area of which it might be possible to build new vocational education institutions in future.'"

initial, technical, and higher technical vocational education. Under the law, the quality of 113 vocational education and training schools and colleges (including three training centers for teachers) operating in 2016 were evaluated. These were gradually streamlined and brought down to 82 as of January 2019 (ADB 2019b). The law is inclusive in that it exempts vulnerable groups in need of special social protection from paying for vocational education in schools and colleges (Azernews 2019). Licenses will be granted under the law to vocational education schools and colleges to certify new professions and encourage the development of new training modules for professions (Report AZ 2018).

The classification system of vocational education has been improved to meet the needs of the labor market and projected labor market trends.[40] More than 20 new qualifications have been added to the classification system. In 2019, the government approved the new state standards of vocational education. In January 2019, the Ministry of Labor and Social Protection of the Population reported that 350 occupational and training standards, including 52 occupational profiles and 63 specialty standards, were formulated for tourism, manufacturing, construction, energy, agriculture, transport, and services. These standards are being used by many firms.

The Strategic Road Map on Vocational Education and Training includes a draft document outlining performance indicators for vocational education and training in schools and colleges. These include measurable indicators on their training and staff capacities, and income. They also include indicators for student participation and absenteeism, academic achievement, employment levels of graduates, satisfaction of employers with graduates, and the level of cooperation between vocational education and training schools and colleges with employers.

Vocational training courses based on 86 traditional and 58 modern-module training programs are provided in regional vocational training schools and colleges for the unemployed and jobseekers by the employment services of Baku, cities in the Nakhchivan Autonomous Republic, and the Goychay district. Each center can train 1,000–1,500 students a year, and these schools and colleges meet the requirements for training technical professions. More regional vocational education schools and colleges are set to be established in other regions.

---

[40] The current vocational education and training specializations in Azerbaijan are derived from the *Classification of Worker Occupations and Common Tariff Qualifications Reference* book that determines the structure for the classification of specializations in vocational education (DVV International 2008).

Training material on 35 modules were developed and modules in 10 professions are under preparation. In September 2018, seven module textbooks for "fruit specialists" and "vegetable specialists" were prepared under the British Council's Development of New Occupations in Agricultural Vocational Education Project, cofunded by BP PLC and its partners.

A new strategy to respond to the skills needed to expand into health tourism was adopted by the government at the end of 2018. The Action Plan for the Development of Health Tourism 2018–2020 was not at the time of writing fully adopted because of reforms at the Ministry of Culture and Tourism and the establishment of the State Tourism Agency. The ministry plans a program to develop culinary tourism, focused on Azerbaijan's cuisine and the country's ancient history (Trend News Agency 2018).

3.5 Conclusions and Policy Recommendations

The government is striving to redress the lack of formal vocational education and training qualifications for most of the working-age population through education reforms. It hopes that embedding human capital development in the Strategic Road Maps will fix the mismatch in qualifications for skills and increase non-oil labor productivity. The main policies for this prioritize improving skills, particularly for finding decent jobs for young people. The Strategic Road Map on Vocational Education and Training has a more clearly defined focus than the Strategic Road Maps on skills development that outlines strategies for improving the country's vocational education and training system. The sector road map wants to create a positive new image for vocational education and training, and increase the attractiveness of this type of education to get more applicants for skills certification.

Early gains have been made in implementing the sector road map. The government should now allow policy space for stakeholders in the education system to adjust to policies in the sector road map—and to contribute to streamlining these policies. To this end, the diagnostic of Azerbaijan's human capital and skills development strategy leads to the following policy recommendations:

Strengthen the institutional set-up on education and skills development

Consider drawing up an overarching strategy on skills development to reflect the medium- and long-term needs of the economy. This strategy should be developed with the objective of preparing Azerbaijan's education and labor market for the impact of the Fourth Industrial Revolution.

To ensure institutional support for skills development, the Strategic Road Map on Vocational Education and Training needs to be sufficiently financed to be able to improve the infrastructure for vocational education and training, and to raise occupational standards. This can be promoted by prioritizing the implementation measures in the sector road map during the preparation of the education sector strategic plan as part of the medium-term expenditure framework process.[41]

Skills development needs to be institutionalized as an essential step for building human capital regardless of professional orientation. Education systems could examine introducing education pathways on the basis of professional orientation and simple vocational education and training skills for children in school that are as young as those in grades 6–9. Youth career guidance and counselling services, and education fairs targeting vocational education and training and higher education students (ages 15 to 24), could widen the service they provide by going beyond information on job options to include trends in labor market supply and demand. Apprenticeships and on-the-job training opportunities could be promoted by providing soft loans to apprentices and tax incentives for employers. The curricula for vocational education and training and higher education should be aligned with occupational standards and needed labor market skills and professions. Against this background, it is also recommended that the new classification of vocational education as stipulated in the Vocational Education Law be implemented; the new classification covers initial vocational education, technical vocational education, and higher technical vocational education.

Monitoring and evaluating the intermediate results will help determine whether education reforms are moving in the right direction. To do this, better data collection is needed, especially for on-the-job training opportunities and the skills needed in the private sector and for emerging occupations. Data also need to be collected on the variables that are useful for empirical analysis, such as skills and qualifications or proxies of both. The joint analysis and monitoring of education performance results and labor productivity measures by the

---

41   Decision of the Cabinet of Ministers No. 571, dated 28 December 2018.

State Statistical Committee, the Center for Analysis and Communication of Economic Reforms, the State Agency on Vocational Education, and the Ministry of Labor and Social Protection of the Population will be useful for collecting this data.

A system that can anticipate skills needs could be set up by using the data gathered. To do this, it is recommended that research on skills be aligned with the Ministry of Economy's forecasts for macroeconomic indicators. Labor market demand and supply could also be analyzed both quantitatively and qualitatively.

Refine policy frameworks for skills development

There are areas where the frameworks in policy documents on skills development could be strengthened. The Strategic Road Map on Vocational Education and Training could emphasize the importance of coordination among stakeholders in skills development to make progress on this sector road map. This would initially entail drawing on the convening power of the state until stakeholder interaction gains momentum. For vocational education and training services, it is recommended that more autonomy to providers be granted and to allow the private sector to provide vocational education and training services to help align these services to labor market requirements.

Strengthening the link between vocational education and training and higher education by institutionalizing education progression pathways between the two will be important not only for students but also for improving both types of education. Here, better quality assurance and ensuring the interoperability of standards in skills development will be vital to simplify the recognition of nonformal and informal learning to formal education and training.

It is also recommended that the preparation and approval of an action plan for the implementation of the National Employment Strategy 2019–2030 be accelerated by prioritizing roundtable discussions with stakeholders to identify activities and timelines. The Ministry of Labor and Social Protection of the Population is encouraged to bring the action plan forward.

References

Abdih, Y., and L. Medina. 2013. Measuring the Informal Economy in the Caucasus and Central Asia. *IMF Working Paper*. No. 13/137. Washington, DC: International Monetary Fund.

Allahveranov, A. and E. Huseynov. 2013. *Costs and Benefits of Labour Mobility between the EU and Eastern Partnership Partner Countries: Azerbaijan Country Study*. Brussels: European Commission.

Aliyev, R. 2011. Azerbaijan: How Equitable Is Access to Higher Education? *Khazar Journal of Humanities and Social Sciences*. 14.

ADB (Asian Development Bank). 2004. *Educational Reforms in Countries in Transition*. Manila. http://www.pitt.edu/~weidman/2004-educ-reforms-countries.pdf.

————— 2015. A Smarter Future: Skills, Education and Growth. Special chapter in *Key Indicators for Asia and the Pacific 2015*. Manila.

—————. 2017. *Emergent Themes for Education and Skills Development for Inclusive Jobs in Central and West Asia*. Manila.

—————. 2019a. *Good Jobs for Inclusive Growth in Central Asia and the South Caucasus*. ADB Regional Report. Manila.

—————. 2019b. *Azerbaijan: Country Digital Development Overview*. Manila.

Azernews. 2019. These Persons to Be Exempt from Tuition Fees in Azerbaijan. May 20. https://www.azernews.az/travel/140818.html.

Clayton. 2019. Azerbaijani Students Increasingly Drawn to Turkey. Eurasianet. April 11. https://eurasianet.org/azerbaijani-students-increasingly-drawn-to-turkey.

DVV International. 2008. *Vocational Education and Training in the South Caucasus: On the Road from Survival to Efficient Functioning of National Systems*. Bonn: DVV International.

(ETF) European Training Foundation. 2015. *Sector Skills Council in Azerbaijan: Reviewing Structures for Social Partnerships for Initial and Continuing Vocational Training*. Torino, Italy.

—————. 2016. Torino Process 2016–2017. Azerbaijan Working Paper. Torino, Italy.

—————. 2017. *Education, Training and Employment Development 2017*. Torino, Italy

AHK and EU. (German-Azerbaijani Chamber of Commerce and European Union). 2016. *EU Business Climate Survey Azerbaijan Report 2016: Perceptions of EU Businesses Active in Azerbaijan*. Baku.

_____. 2017. *EU Business Climate Report Azerbaijan 2017: Perceptions of EU Businesses Active in Azerbaijan*. Baku.

_____. 2018. *EU Business Climate Report Azerbaijan 2018: Perceptions of EU Businesses Active in Azerbaijan*. Baku.

Ibadoghlu, G. 2012. The Shadow Economy in Azerbaijan: Size and Causes (January 01, 2012). Available at SSRN: https://ssrn.com/abstract=3103392

ILO (International Labour Organization). 2014. Skills Mismatch in Europe. Statistics brief, September. Geneva.

Ministry of Education. 2017 *Annual Report*. Baku.

Ministry of Labor and Social Protection of the Population. 2017. Statistics on Quota by 2010–2017. Baku.

OECD (Organisation for Economic Co-operation and Development). 2010. *Programme for International Student Assessment 2009 Results*. Executive summary. Paris.

_____. 2017. *Starting Strong 2017: Key OECD Indicators on Early Childhood Education and Care*. Paris.

Rahmanov, Qasimov, and Tahirova. 2016. *The Labor Market in Azerbaijan*. Leibniz Information Centre for Economics, German National Library of Economics, Kiel und Hamburg.

Report AZ. 2018. Milli Majlis Approves Draft Law "On Vocational Education." April 24. https://report.az/en/milli-majlis/milli-majlis-approves-draft-law-on-vocational-education/.

State Statistical Committee. 2016. *Youth of Azerbaijan Statistical Bulletin*. Baku.

_____. 2018a. *Labor Market Statistical Yearbook* 2018. Baku.

_____. 2018b. *Youth of Azerbaijan Statistical Yearbook*. Baku.

_____. 2018c. *Education, Science and Culture in Azerbaijan Statistical Yearbook*. Baku

State Student Admission Commission. 2015. *Digest of Education Statistics in Testing and Admissions: Report for the Academic Year of 2014–2015*. Baku.

Trend News Agency. 2018. Azerbaijan Eyes to Actively Develop Gastronomic Tourism. August 27.

UNDESA (United Nations Department of Economics and Social Affairs). 2016. *International Migration Report 2015*. New York.

UNESCO-UNEVOC, International Centre for Technical and Vocational Education and Training. 2013. World TVET Database: Azerbaijan. Bonn.

United Nations. 2017. *World Population Prospects: The 2017 Revision*. New York.

World Bank. 2010. *BEEPS At-a-Glance 2008: Azerbaijan*. Washington, DC.

———. 2015a. *Demand for Skills: Main Results of the Azerbaijan STEP Employer Survey*. Washington, DC.

———. 2015b. *Azerbaijan Systematic Diagnostic. South Caucasus Country Management Unit, Europe and Central Asia*. Washington, DC.

WEF (World Economic Forum). 2017. *Global Competitiveness Report 2017–2018*. Geneva.

CHAPTER 4

Enhancing Infrastructure for Economic Diversification and Competitiveness

Azerbaijan has made solid economic gains since independence in 1991. The economic difficulties during the early years of independence and the country's transition to a market economy were rapidly overcome. From 2000 to 2009, gross domestic product (GDP) grew at a remarkably high average yearly rate of 16.1%. Heavy investment in the oil sector and the 2006–2014 oil-price boom vaulted Azerbaijan into upper-middle-income status. That high growth, however, began to dissipate as oil prices fell in 2014, causing the country's oil production to plateau. Since 2010, GDP growth has dwindled to low single digits. The economic thinking in the Strategic Road Maps on the National Economy Perspective and Main Sectors of the Economy (Strategic Road Maps) centers on stepping up efforts to diversify the economy, spur competitiveness, and increase resilience to external shocks, especially to the volatility of oil prices and production.

Enhancing infrastructure will be vital for advancing economic diversification and intergenerational equity in Azerbaijan. The experience of resource-dependent economies globally shows that expanding and raising the quality of infrastructure is an essential component of economic diversification and structural transformation strategies (Sebastian and Steinbuks 2017). Removing infrastructure bottlenecks reduces the cost of doing business and fosters private sector development. Doing this will help integrate Azerbaijan with the regional and global economy, and so promote the growth of non-oil tradable sectors.

A large body of research shows that infrastructure is a major driver of inclusive growth in developing countries. Infrastructure development is particularly important for strategies to diversify the economies of resource-dependent developing countries such as Azerbaijan. And the argument for enhancing infrastructure is stronger in this context. Moreover, the intergenerational transfer of resource rents is best achieved by investing a defined part of these rents in physical and human capital.

Azerbaijan has maintained a consistently high level of fiscal support for infrastructure for which it deserves credit. Since independence, three factors have shaped its infrastructure investments. The first is maintaining the capital stock inherited from the former Soviet Union. The second is developing the country's north–south and east–west transport corridors and oil and gas pipelines to take advantage of its geographic location. This has become more important since Azerbaijan became a major hydrocarbon exporter. The third factor is the need to provide a critical mass of basic public infrastructure. In addition to these factors, newer economic challenges will affect infrastructure development. These are:

- **Hard budget constraints.** Under the rules-based transfer of resource rents to the state budget, the infrastructure plan must be set within a medium-term fiscal framework, as must sector strategic plans to ensure fiscal sustainability and alignment with the national and sector priorities.[1]

- **Economic diversification.** The infrastructure that will be vital for supporting economic diversification—that is, developing non-oil sectors, including agriculture and tourism in a post COVID-19 scenario—must be carefully identified, cohesively planned, and prioritized for inclusion in the state investment program.

- **Human capital.** Azerbaijan will need to make sizable investments in social infrastructure in addition to meeting its basic public infrastructure needs, the Strategic Road Maps' objectives to 2025, and the aspirational vision beyond 2025. Social infrastructure includes facilities for health and education, and for developing skills and entrepreneurship.

4.1 Infrastructure Vital to the Development Blueprint

Azerbaijan has set out a bold new development vision and strategies to achieve the ambitious aspirations of the Strategic Road Maps. Enhancing the country's infrastructure and promoting its sustainability are a critical part of this development blueprint. Because infrastructure development is finance-intensive, a sizable portion of national resources will be needed for this effort. Using infrastructure to help diversify the economy will require institutions and policies to be overhauled for them to be able to plan the right type of infrastructure, to procure and build infrastructure efficiently, and to

---

[1]   Presidential Decree No. 235, dated 24 August 2018; Decision of the Cabinet of Ministers No. 571, dated 28 December 2018.

ensure its sustainable operation. With the country's shift in strategic priorities toward accelerating diversified development and sustainable macroeconomic management, the planning, budgeting, and implementation of infrastructure projects will become more complex. The following areas will need to be strengthened to be able to invest more efficiently and smartly in infrastructure:

- **Public investment management systems.** It will be important to shift the focus from spending levels alone to the robustness of institutional frameworks for making infrastructure investment decisions. The new focus should also be on rigorous ex ante project appraisals; the quality of the management, implementation, and evaluation of projects; and efficient public procurement. These factors could have big impacts on the return on infrastructure investments and their growth dividends. For the best economic benefits, infrastructure must be planned as a network of complementary assets, services, and policies.[2] Missing links in this network will make it difficult to achieve the desired objectives of infrastructure projects. Ensuring there are no missing links requires a program for planning, implementing, monitoring and evaluating infrastructure on a consolidated public sector basis.[3]

- **Public utility regulation.** The sustainable maintenance of infrastructure assets, and providing infrastructure services at the desired level, will require tariff and institutional reforms at the sector level and for individual utilities.

- **Private sector participation**. The government will continue to play the dominant role in providing infrastructure. But private sector participation in some sectors will help improve the overall efficiency of infrastructure services and have spillover benefits for the economy from the modern technologies, and the skills and practices, that the private sector can bring. The government could consider divesting from the state-owned-enterprise (SOE) sector and using public–private partnerships (PPPs) as the main mode for financing public infrastructure and services.

The current level of spending on infrastructure in Azerbaijan must be sustained. The quality and composition of that spending will be increasingly important for achieving the objective of diversified economic development. To this end, it will be essential to raise the quality of institutions and policies that guide infrastructure investments. The Strategic Road Maps include reform

---

[2]   National priorities and not the availability of funds should guide the choice of projects.

[3]   The State Investment Program is developed annually and submitted to Parliament along with the annual state budget bill. The program includes investment projects (infrastructure and non-infrastructure) that are financed or supported by the state budget. A consolidated public investment program would reflect—regardless of the funding source—infrastructure investments made by the central government, the Nakhchivan Autonomous Republic, local administrations, SOEs, the State Oil Fund of Azerbaijan Republic, and PPPs.

directions and plans for infrastructure development. As a single reference point for state agencies and private investors, the authorities could consider a unified whole-of-government framework for infrastructure policies and an infrastructure implementation plan covering the following cross-sector pillars of infrastructure development:

- **Coordinated delivery.** This refers to the robustness of the institutional and policy framework for arriving at a consolidated public investment program, a medium-term fiscal program for predictable funding, rigorous ex ante project appraisal, efficient project management, monitoring and evaluation, and rules-based public procurement.

- **Sustainable investments.** This refers to asset management systems, predictable funding, effective policies and institutions to maintain infrastructure assets over their economic life, and to realize the targeted economic and financial returns of these assets.

- **Independent and effective regulation.** This is to ensure that reliable and high-quality infrastructure services are delivered at competitive prices, and equal treatment among market participants.

- **Private sector investment**. This relates to the definition of the rationale and scope of private investment, ensuring predictability of government policies, and having a road map for sustainably increasing private sector participation.[4]

Infrastructure refers to the basic structures that facilitate and support economic activity. Infrastructure is an indispensable input for economic production, and it is highly complementary to other more conventional inputs, such as labor and non-infrastructure capital.[5] This chapter focuses on core infrastructure—transport, power, telecommunications, and water supply and sanitation.[6] It briefly examines infrastructure in terms of the requirements of Azerbaijan's three tradable sectors—agriculture, manufacturing, and tourism. Because of the government's policy priority on skills development, the chapter

---

[4]   Investment in infrastructure is a long-term commitment. Policies that form a critical basis for investment decisions by the private sector must remain unchanged over the long-term or change in a predictable and inclusive manner.

[5]   Three key characteristics distinguish infrastructure from other types of capital. First, infrastructure often requires large investments in the form of capital-intensive projects that tend to be "natural monopolies." In other words, it is deemed more cost-effective for services to be provided by a single entity. Second, infrastructure projects tend to have significant up-front costs, but the benefits or returns accrue over very long periods (often many decades), posing a problem for the private sector to finance and build infrastructure. Third, infrastructure investments have the potential to generate positive externalities, so that a project's social return can exceed the private returns it would generate for the operator. This can lead to the under-provision of needed investments. For these reasons, infrastructure has historically been provided by the public sector, PPPs, and regulated private entities (IMF 2014).

[6]   This definition is consistent with the Asian Development Bank's practice. See ADB (2017a).

also examines the facilities and structures for delivering social services for technical and vocational education and training sector.[7]

Following standard practice, three dimensions—quantity, quality, and access— are used for measuring infrastructure performance to give a snapshot of the state of and recent developments in Azerbaijan's core infrastructure (Klein 2014; World Bank 2017).[8] This albeit subjective of assessment of the quality of Azerbaijan's infrastructure comes from the World Economic Forum's *Global Competitiveness Report 2017–2018*. Other data used in this assessment came from the State Statistical Committee and international databases, including those of the Organisation for Economic Co-operation and Development and the World Bank's World Development Indicators. The assessment of Azerbaijan's infrastructure was compared using the same metrics with those used for comparator countries. While these are mostly from the group of former Soviet Union countries, Georgia and Kazakhstan were used as much as possible because of their immediate geographical proximity to Azerbaijan.

The assessment pulls together data from multiple sources to estimate Azerbaijan's infrastructure investments in recent years and to assess its future investment needs. To put the numbers in context and for comparison purposes, absolute amounts are given as shares of GDP. Because of severe data constraints and the use of multiple sources, the estimates must be treated as approximations, and they were used to derive mostly directional conclusions.

The aim of this chapter is not to be prescriptive but rather to lay out broad contours for Azerbaijan's future infrastructure development. The chapter uses international indices and the literature to provide a global context to the assessment and recommendations to enhance the country's infrastructure to diversify its economy and make it more competitive, while being mindful of specific country contexts.

4.2 Infrastructure Development: Taking Stock

The quality of Azerbaijan's core infrastructure has improved significantly because of sustained high investment. The *Global Competitiveness Report 2017–2018* ranks the country higher on infrastructure indicators than other countries in the Commonwealth of Independent States. Even so, significant infrastructure constraints remain to be overcome, and institutional and policy

---

[7]   While not always as capital-intensive as core infrastructure, social infrastructure is also associated with large up-front costs and significant positive externalities. Social infrastructure is included in the scope of the Law on the Implementation of Special Financing for Investment Projects in Connection with Construction and Infrastructure Facilities (Law No. 177-VQ, dated 15 March 2016).

[8]   See Appendix III on the diagnostic approach in Klein (2014).

reforms need to be put in place to support the acceleration and sustainability of economic diversification.

This section reviews the achievements made in infrastructure development; the major infrastructure constraints; needed infrastructure reforms; and the infrastructure requirements for advancing agriculture, manufacturing, and tourism. The main findings of this review are:

- Heavy capital investments are needed for replacing and modernizing infrastructure assets, including in irrigation, power (generation, transmission, distribution), rail transport, and water and sanitation. Assets that are beyond their useful life can significantly disrupt operations and affect efficiency.
- The focus on road infrastructure has been on maintaining assets rather than expanding the network. A review is needed of whether the road network, particularly regional and rural connector roads, is adequate for supporting the development of agriculture, manufacturing, and tourism after the impact of COVID-19.
- Access to water and sanitation, and information and communication technology (ICT) services, has generally increased. But a huge gap remains between access to these services in Baku compared with other parts of the country. Fixed internet speed and internet coverage varies significantly between urban and rural areas and are below comparator countries in the region; this is mainly because of the reliance on old copper landline connections.
- The international connectivity of the broadband network must be upgraded and the national broadband network expanded, including through private sector participation. Better ICT infrastructure would help increase Azerbaijan's competitiveness, especially in manufacturing and tourism; improve digital connectivity for the country's industrial parks; and help computer and digital companies (the high productivity end of ICT sector) to grow.
- Diversifying the economy into new sectors and the structural transformation needed to do this will require new skills. Building these skills is a priority, and will require the active participation of industry, and new training facilities, methods, curricula, and certification systems.

Inland transport system

Roads carry over 80% of Azerbaijan's total passenger traffic and over 60% of freight; railways carry the rest. The country has two major international transport corridors: the east–west corridor connecting Baku to the border with Georgia, and the north–south corridor connecting the Russian Federation's border with Iran's border through Baku.

The government has invested heavily in inland transport, with the biggest share of spending going on the two corridors (Figures 4.1 and 4.2). Public spending in inland transport from the state budget totaled AZN17.5 billion ($10.26 billion) during 2003–2017, and this would have been much higher on a consolidated public sector basis. Road transport was the major beneficiary of spending from the state budget in this period, receiving nearly 75% of aggregate spending. Inland transport features prominently in the government's plan to position Azerbaijan as a major transit and trade hub. As a result, Azerbaijan's transport infrastructure scores well: in the quality of overall infrastructure, it ranks 26 out of 137 countries (WEF 2017). It is also now in a favorable position to capture new opportunities for regional cooperation and integration in the realization of the Belt and Road initiative (ADB 2019). The success of efforts to upgrade and expand inland transport will be vital for achieving this goal, and for developing agriculture, manufacturing, and revitalizing tourism after the pandemic. There is, however, insufficient clarity on the government's plans for this because an overall transport sector road map is lacking, as are assessments of connectivity needs in the individual sector road maps.

Figure 4.1: Inland Transport Infrastructure Investment as a Percentage of Gross Domestic Product, 2012–2016

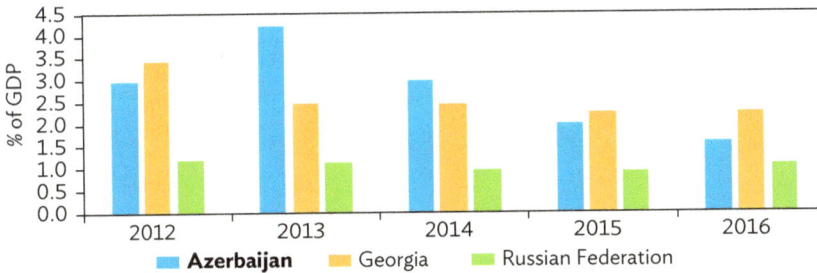

Source: OECD.Stat (accessed August 2018).

Figure 4.2: Inland Transport Infrastructure Investment, in Current Dollar per Inhabitant, 2012–2016

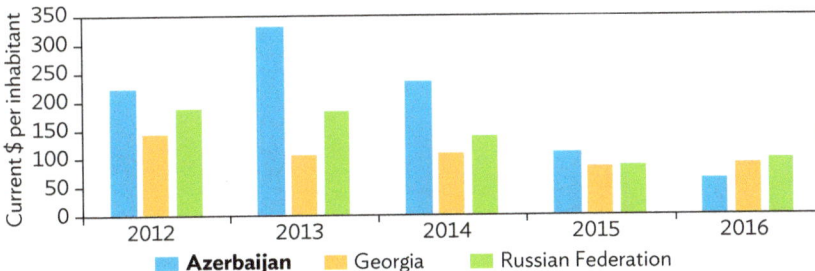

Source: OECD.Stat (accessed August 2018).

Road transport

As Figures 4.3 and 4.4 show, sizable public investments have been made in road transport. The quality of road infrastructure is better than in comparator countries but many roads in Azerbaijan are nevertheless in poor condition. Figure 4.5 makes the comparison with Georgia and the Russian Federation. Maintaining rather than expanding capital stock was the focus of past investments. State Statistical Committee data show that from 2000 to 2017 Azerbaijan's nonurban road network increased by only 1.4%, from 18,759 kilometers to 19,016 kilometers. Road density has remained stagnant, and

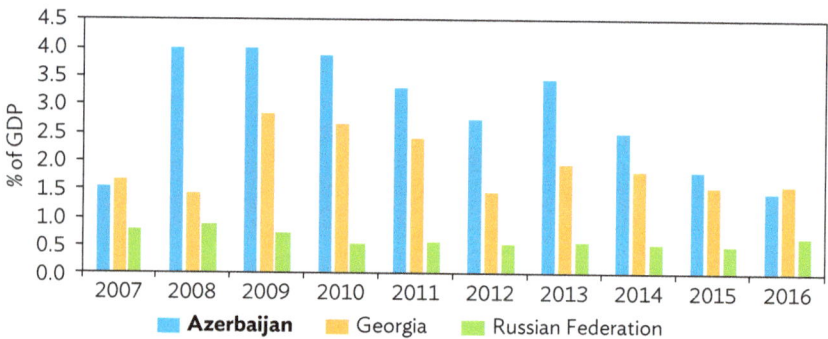

Figure 4.3: Road Infrastructure Investment as a Percentage of Gross Domestic Product, 2007–2016

Source: OECD.Stat.

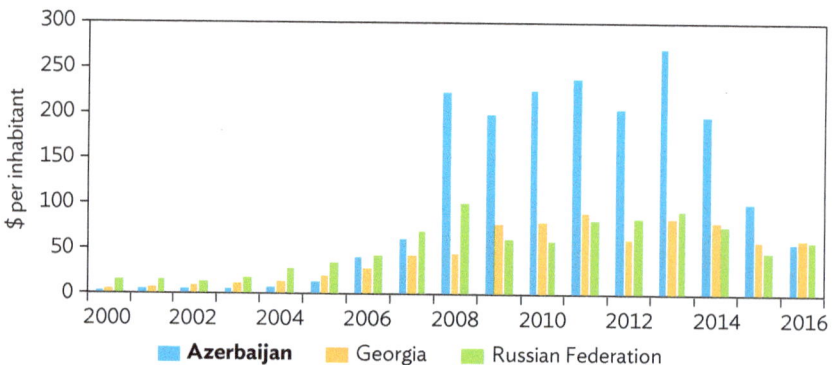

Figure 4.4: Road Infrastructure Investment, in Dollar per Inhabitant, 2002–2016

Source: OECD.Stat.

is lower than in Georgia and Turkey (Figure 4.6). From 2003 to 2017, public spending on connector roads, which connect rural habitations known as *kend* to each other and to markets and regional roads, was just AZN1 billion ($586,424), according to the Ministry of Finance. Only 67% of Azerbaijan's population lives within 2 kilometers of an all-weather road, compared with 82% for Georgia, 94% for Indonesia, and 97% for the People's Republic of China (World Bank 2014).[9]

Figure 4.5: Road Quality, 2013–2017

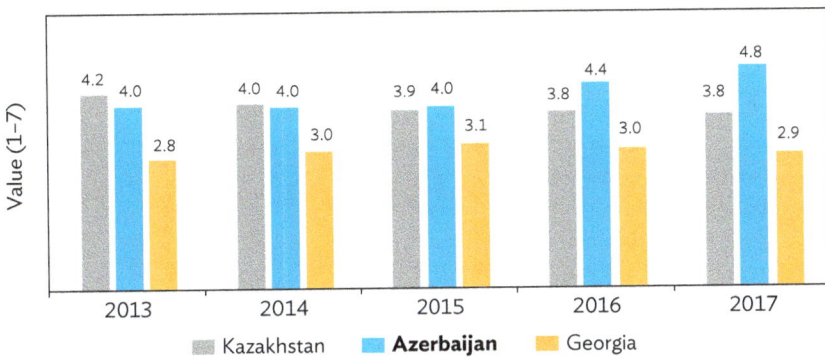

Note: 1 = worst, 7 = best.
Source: World Economic Forum.

Figure 4.6: Road Density, 2003–2011

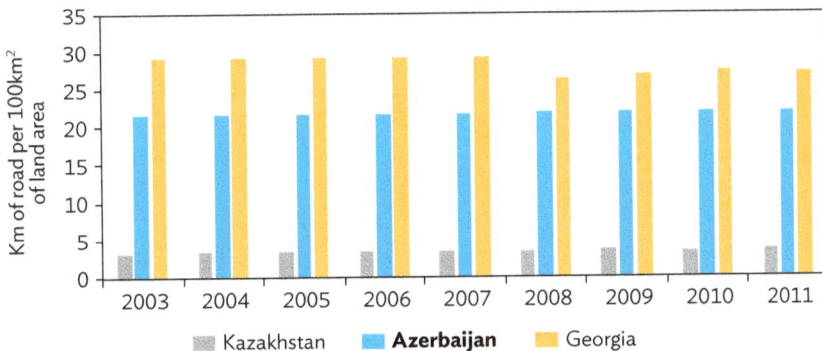

Km= kilometer.
Source: World Bank, World Development Indicators Database.

[9] It is not possible to assess Azerbaijan's all-weather roads that connect rural habitations to each other and to markets and warehouses from the available official data. The government has invested in gravel roads for villages through the World Bank–supported Azerbaijan Rural Investment Program. The pilot program has reportedly upgraded about 95 kilometers of connector roads linking villages to markets.

The road infrastructure that Azerbaijan inherited from the former Soviet Union has not posed a binding constraint to oil-driven economic growth since the start of the 2000s. Diversified economic development, led by agriculture, manufacturing, and a revitalized tourism sector post COVID-19, will be connectivity-intensive. For each of these sectors, connectivity infrastructure will be essential for developing value chains. For agriculture, paved roads need to connect farms to markets and warehouses, and these to agri-parks, and these to the nearest logistics infrastructure. Hinterland connectivity will be vital for reaping broader economic benefits from Azerbaijan being at the crossroads of rapidly expanding international transit and trade routes.

Rail network

Azerbaijan's rail network is more extensive than that of Georgia, Kazakhstan, Turkey, and Uzbekistan (Figure 4.7).[10] Substantial investments have been made in maintaining and upgrading Azerbaijan's rail infrastructure to link the country's main economic centers to neighboring countries (Figure 4.8). Since 2000, the government invested nearly AZN2.5 billion ($1.5 billion) in modernizing the rail network along the two main international transit routes (north–south and east–west), and significant new investment is planned. In September 2017, the fully modernized Baku–Tbilisi–Kars railway opened, providing a rail link to Turkey and Europe. The ongoing reconstruction of the railways between Baku and the Russian border and between Baku and Astara on the Iranian border will allow continuous railway connectivity along the "South Silk Road" corridor. In addition, a new port is being developed in Alat to replace the port of Baku (65 kilometers to the north). This new port could potentially stimulate trade beyond oil and gas. The ferry rail terminal for this port opened in 2014, enabling a direct link between Central Asia and the Black Sea, and the roll-on roll-off terminal opened in January 2018 (ADB 2019).

The competitiveness of rail compared with road transport has steadily declined. Only 50% of the network is electrified (Figure 4.9), and the substations that supply power from the grid are in poor condition. The volume of freight and passenger traffic carried by rail has nearly halved in absolute terms since 2000 (Figure 4.10). The main causes for the loss of competitiveness are (i) aging rolling stock of which a sizable share is beyond its useful life; (ii) a steady decline in track quality; (iii) low labor productivity in railway services;[11] and (iv) the severe institutional and financial problems facing Azerbaijan

[10]   Kazakhstan is steadily expanding its freight and passenger business.

[11]   Labor productivity at Azerbaijan's Railways is 260,000 traffic units per operating employee—low for a freight-dominated railway. This is 40% less than in Georgia and a fraction of Kazakhstan's level (3.2 million traffic units per operating employee) (ADB 2017b). Traffic units are passenger kilometers plus net ton-kilometers.

Figure 4.7: Density of Rail Lines, 2000–2015

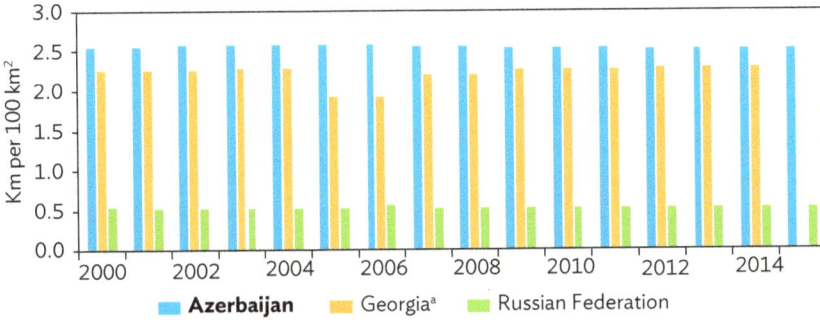

km = kilometer.
a No data for Georgia for 2015.
Source: OECD.Stat.

Figure 4.8: Rail Infrastructure Investment, 2007–2016

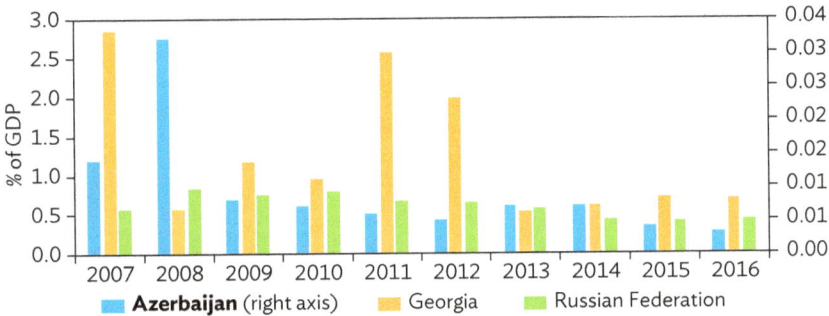

GDP = gross domestic product.
Source: OECD.Stat.

Figure 4.9: Share of Electrified Rail Lines in Total Rail Network, 2000–2015

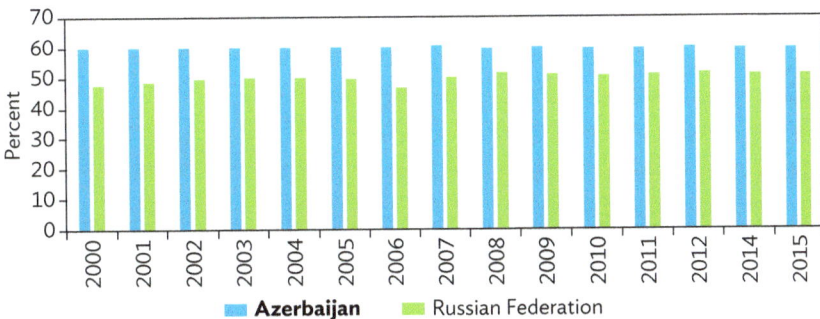

Source: OECD.Stat.

Figure 4.10: Rail Line Coverage and Traffic Volume Azerbaijan and Kazakhstan, 2008–2016

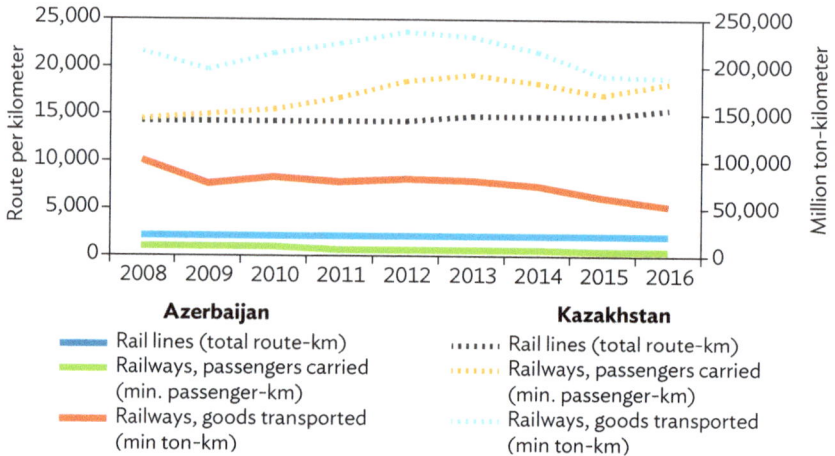

Km = kilometers.
Source: World Bank, World Development Indicators Database.

Railways, which builds, operates, and maintains the rail infrastructure.[12] The railways need modernizing at many levels, including the skills of technical personnel; assets, including signaling, track, and rolling stock; and Azerbaijan Railways itself.

Electricity

Figure 4.11 shows electricity consumption per capita over 2003–2014, with consumption since 2010 increasing by on average 7.8% a year. Transmission and distribution losses are high because of operational inefficiencies and aging infrastructure—more than half the distribution lines are older than 45 years.[13] These losses have, however, declined since 2009 because of capital investments and operational improvements, but remain high compared with other countries in the region.

Since 2010, the growth in electricity consumption has outpaced growth in generation capacity (Figure 4.12). While the reserve margin in generation capacity is above the norm of 25%, it is forecast to fall to 14% by 2020. To

---

[12] Azerbaijan Railways reports directly to the Cabinet of Ministers. The President has authority over the appointment of the company's chair and deputy chair, and any reorganization. The Board of Directors comprises the chair, first deputy chair, four deputy chairs, and the director of Nakhichevan Railways. Other than a few industrial railways operating within their own plants, Azerbaijan Railways is the only rail operator of both passenger and freight services.

[13] The three largest natural-gas-fired thermal power stations meet more than half of the country's power demand. Long distances between generation and load centers require a backbone of transmission lines.

counter this, capital investment in the power sector needs to be significantly increased to build new generation capacity, diversify the country's energy portfolio, and replace aging transmission and distribution equipment. Sector reforms, meanwhile, need to be vigorously implemented.

Figure 4.11: Electric Power Consumption, 2003–2014

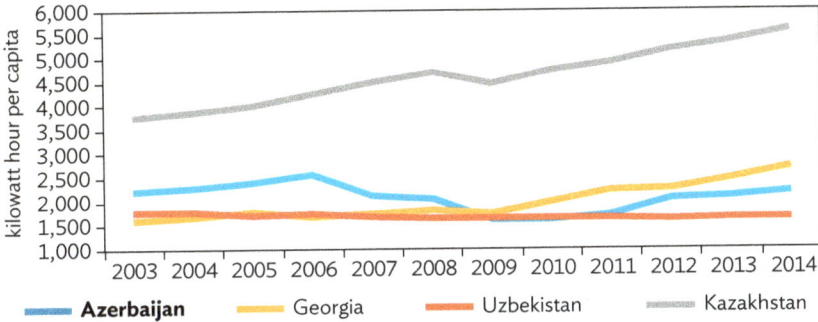

Source: World Bank, World Development Indicators Database.

Figure 4.12: Electricity Capacity, 1992–2015

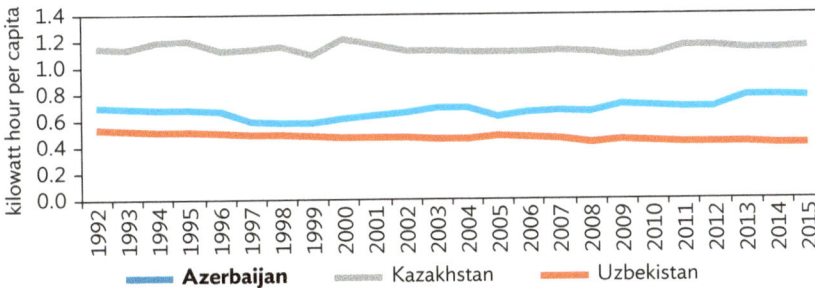

Source: US Energy Information Administration; and World Bank, World Development Indicators Database.

Water supply and sanitation

Azerbaijan falls far behind comparator countries in access to basic drinking water and sanitation services (Figures 4.13 and 4.14). Although this is improving, much more needs to be done. Large disparities exist between access to basic drinking water and sanitation services in rural and urban areas (Figures 4.15–4.18). The Asian Development Bank (ADB) estimates that 78% of Baku's population has access to basic drinking water and sanitation services, compared with only 32% of the population in urban areas outside the capital and 36% of the rural population.

Figure 4.13: Access to Basic Drinking Water Services, 2003–2015

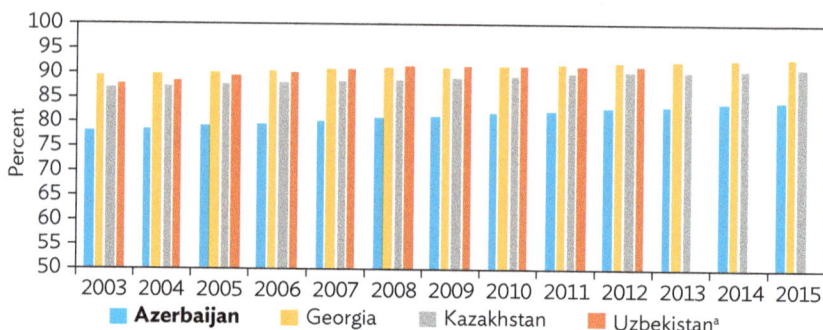

- Azerbaijan   Georgia   Kazakhstan   Uzbekistan[a]

[a] Data for Uzbekistan are available only for 2003–2012.
Source: World Bank, World Development Indicators Database.

Figure 4.14: Access to Basic Sanitation Services, 2003–2015

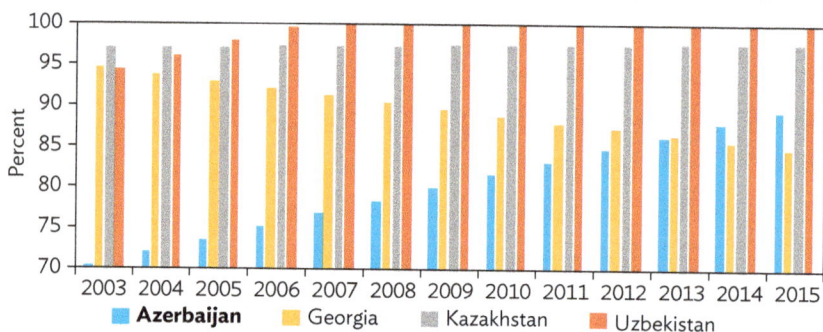

- Azerbaijan   Georgia   Kazakhstan   Uzbekistan

Source: World Bank, World Development Indicators Database.

Figure 4.15: Urban Access to Basic Drinking Water Services, 2003–2015

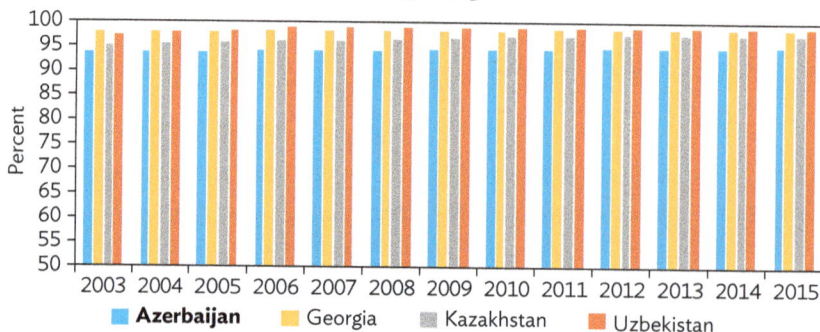

- Azerbaijan   Georgia   Kazakhstan   Uzbekistan

Source: World Bank, World Development Indicators Database.

Figure 4.16: Rural Access to Basic Drinking Water Services, 2003–2015

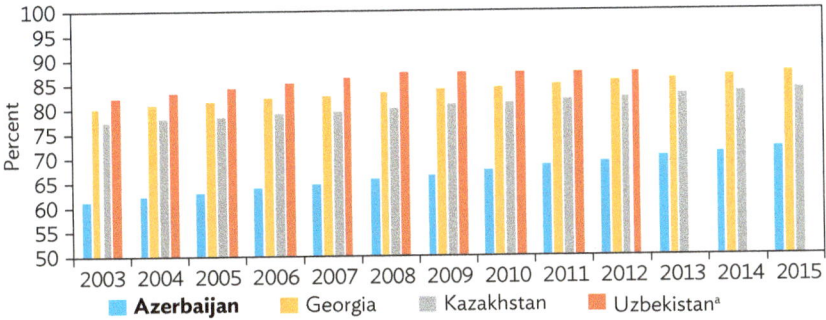

ᵃ Data for Uzbekistan are available only for 2003–2012.
Source: World Bank, World Development Indicators Database.

Figure 4.17: Urban Access to Basic Sanitation Services, 2003–2015

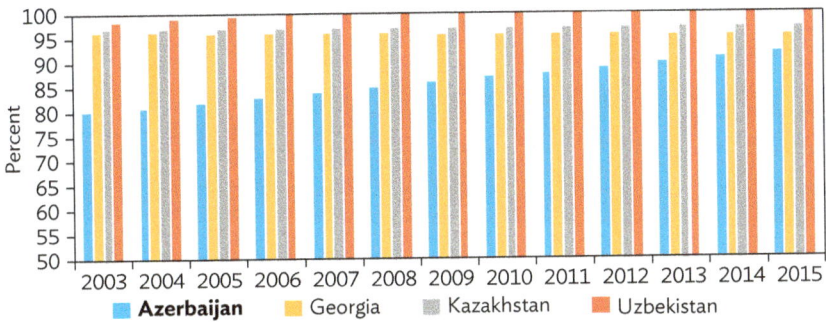

Source: World Bank, World Development Indicators Database.

Figure 4.18: Rural Access to Basic Sanitation Services, 2003–2015

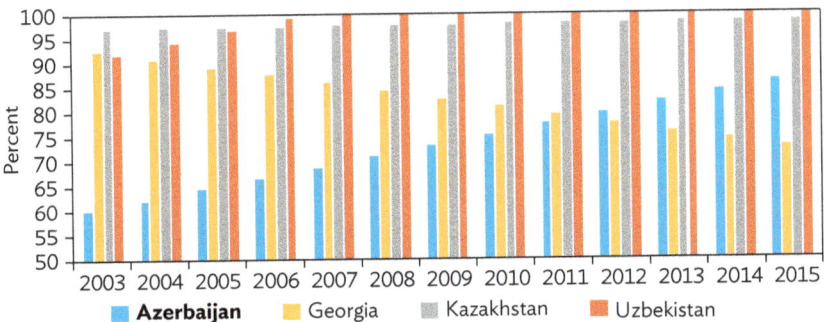

Source: World Bank, World Development Indicators Database.

Technical and commercial losses from water and sanitation services, though declining, are still noticeably above the 10% norm mainly because of the outdated infrastructure. Despite a recent upgrade, the sewerage system is still below the optimal level. The agenda for building an efficient and effective water supply and sanitation system includes (i) capital investment for infrastructure modernization and increasing access outside Baku—most funding for this may still have to come from the national budget; (ii) a strategy for optimal tariffs for water and sanitation services, which could include lifeline tariffs for low-income customers; and (iii) substantial reforms in the sector's SOE Azersu, an open joint stock company.

Information and communication technology

Azerbaijan is putting a strong emphasis on developing the ICT sector.[14] The government aims to turn the country into an information communications technology hub for the Caucasus region. This vision is articulated in the Strategic Road Map on the Development of Telecommunication and Information Technologies. This outlines three key strategies and 10 priorities for achieving this by 2020 (Table 4.1). The cost of implementing this sector road map is estimated at AZN586.6 million ($344 million). Funding sources are identified as the government, private sector (including foreign investment), and bilateral and multilateral partners. Implementing the sector road map will be essential for tackling shortcomings in the ICT sector that are constraining the development of a digital economy.

The ICT sector generated revenue of AZN958.7 million ($600.7 million) in 2016, or 1.6% of GDP (2.4% of non-oil GDP).[15] Although the sector has grown since 2010, the rate of growth has been less than the overall economy and consequently its share of GDP has declined (Figure 4.19). Telecommunication services accounted for 88% of total sector revenue, suggesting that Azerbaijan has yet to exploit its hard infrastructure through a vibrant computer and information services industry. The value added of the ICT sector, which includes publishing, broadcasting, telecommunications, and computer and information services, made up 1.6% of GDP, less than comparator countries with available data, and significantly smaller than the European Union—and notably Bulgaria and Romania (Figure 4.20). The low and stagnant contribution of ICT to GDP, and the dominance of telecommunications in the sector, is a big challenge for the government to realize its vision for ICT revenues to surpass those of oil. Employment in ICT was 61,700 in 2017, an increase of 11% since 2010, with the sector accounting for 1.3% of total employment.

---

[14] The discussion in this section draws from ADB. Forthcoming. *Azerbaijan: Country Digital Development Overview*. Manila.

[15] For a detailed breakdown, see Value Added in the ICT Sector in the State Statistical Committee's website https://www.azstat.org/MESearch/search?departament=24&lang=en.

Table 4.1: Targets and Priorities of the Strategic Road Map on the Development of Telecommunication and Information Technologies

Strategic Target	Priorities
1. Improve governance structures and strengthen ICT	1.1. Set up an independent regulatory body 1.2. Liberalize the telecommunications market 1.3. Increase mobile infrastructure investments
2. Increase productivity and operational efficiency of the business environment	2.1. Extend digital payments 2.2. Extend technology-based operations for businesses 2.3. Upgrade the use of technology in education by involving businesses in this process 2.4. Improve the electronic systems of government institutions 2.5. Increase knowledge and skills in ICT sector; use ICT in the education system
3. Digitize government and the social environment	3.1. Improve the information systems of government institutions 3.2. Create an end-to-end integrated e-health infrastructure

ICT = information and communication technology.
Source: Strategic Road Map on the Development of Telecommunication and Information Technologies.

Figure 4.19: Information and Communication Technology Sector's Share of Gross Domestic Product, 2010–2016

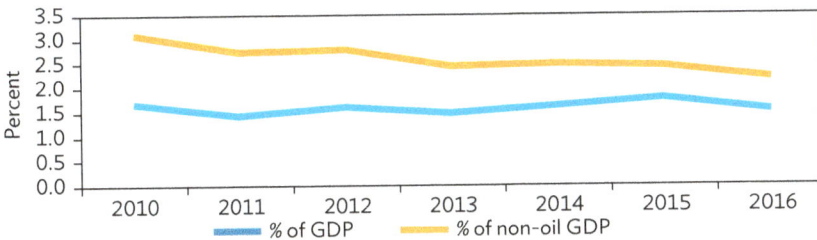

GDP= gross domestic product.
Source: State Statistical Committee and Eurostat.

Figure 4.20: Azerbaijan's Information and Communication Technology Sector Value Added Compared with Several European Union Countries, 2016

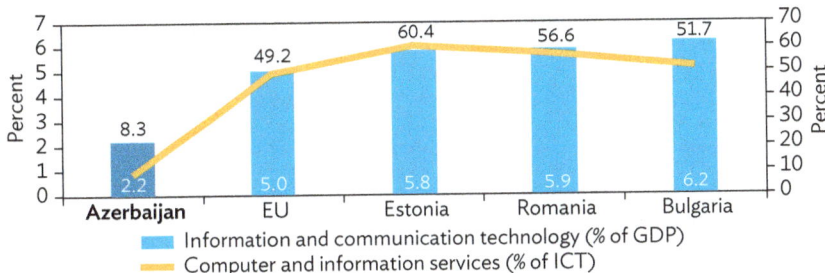

GDP = gross domestic product, ICT = information and communication technology.
Source: State Statistical Committee and Eurostat.

Azerbaijan has steadily improved its ranking and score for technological readiness on the Global Competitiveness Index. In 2013, it launched its first telecommunications satellite, Azerspace-1.[16] Mobile high-speed broadband connectivity services have significantly improved, and mobile broadband prices are more affordable than fixed broadband. The price of a monthly fixed broadband basket is equivalent to 1.1% of per capita income and a mobile broadband package (at least 1 gigabyte per month) to 0.5% of per capita income.

3G mobile coverage is at 96% of the population, and 4G long-term evolution (4G LTE) covers about two-fifths of the population. Although 4G LTE coverage is widely available in urban areas, it is limited in rural ones. It is also only used at the 1,800-megahertz frequency that does not have as wide coverage as lower frequencies, resulting in higher investment costs in dispersed and rural regions. The Strategic Road Map on the Development of Telecommunication and Information Technologies proposes allocating lower frequencies to expand 4G LTE coverage.

Azerbaijan's digital divide is also characterized by urban–rural differences in wired broadband penetration. In 2017, 63% of urban households had access to fixed internet compared with 43% for rural households. The digital divide is also apparent among different regions; for instance, fixed broadband penetration in Absheron is 72% compared with 42% in Guba-Khachmaz.[17] These gaps are because of shortages of fixed infrastructure and lower levels of digital literacy in rural areas.[18]

Azerbaijan's average fixed internet download speed was 14 megabits per second (Mbps) in July 2018, well below Kazakhstan (28 Mbps) and the Russian Federation (38 Mbps). Mobile download speeds were 24 Mbps, faster than Kazakhstan (22 Mbps) and the Russian Federation (18 Mbps), but slower than Georgia (29 Mbps) and Turkey (34 Mbps).[19] Azerbaijan compensates

[16] Its service area includes countries in Europe, the Caucasus, Central Asia, the Middle East, and Africa. The satellite provides services including digital television, data transmission, VSAT multi-service networks, and government communications. The Azerspace-1 project cost AZN669 million ($392.3 million), with revenue from the operation of Azerspace-1 so far totaling AZN123 million ($72 million) (Azernews 2018).

[17] Fixed telephone network services are mainly provided by two government-owned operators: Aztelekom LLC and Baku Telephone Communications LLC. Aztelekom operates nationwide except in Baku and the Nakhchivan Autonomous Republic. Baku Telephone operates in the capital. Given this geographic split, consumers have no choice of fixed-line operators.

[18] Although Azerbaijan has some 40 internet service providers (ISPs), the two fixed-line operators control last-mile wired access to households, and ISPs need to enter into agreements with them. The two fixed-line operators also provide internet service using their own ISPs.

[19] Three private companies offer GSM, 3G, and 4G mobile services: Bakcell LLC, the oldest, founded 1994; Azercell Telecom LLC, founded in 1996 and owned by Turkcell LLC of Turkey; and Azerfon LLC, launched in 2007 under the Nar Mobile brand.

for low fixed speeds with higher mobile ones. The country's high proportion of relatively low speed copper wire fixed broadband connections and limited infrastructure competition in fixed broadband strongly impact internet speeds.

Azerbaijan is far from intercontinental fiber optic submarine cable systems, and there is limited wholesale competition for providing internet in the country.[20] This has resulted in low international internet capacity: in 2016, this was 34 kilobits per second of international bandwidth per internet user, the lowest of the four comparator countries in Figure 4.21 and less than half the world average.

Figure 4.21: International Internet Bandwidth per Internet User, 2016

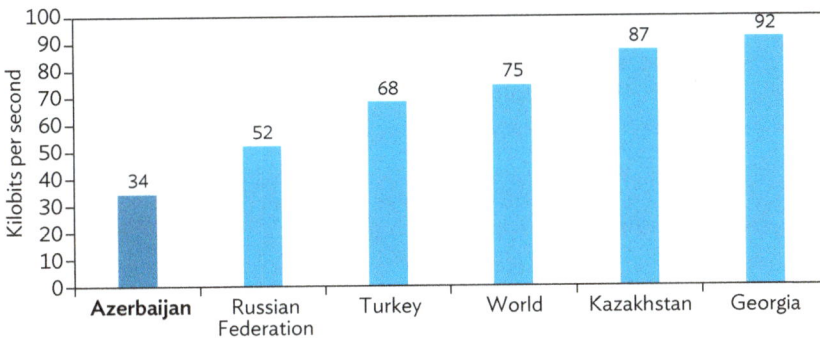

Source: International Telecommunication Union.

Developing ICT will have significant spillover benefits on other sectors, particularly education, health, logistics, and tourism. It will also increase overall economic efficiency and thus international competitiveness. The ICT sector accounts for a relatively low level of value added. Computer and information services that leverage the huge investment in infrastructure make up just 7% of the ICT sector's revenue compared with over half in countries with growing digital economies. Just as diversifying the economy is essential, so is diversifying the ICT sector. This can be done by strengthening the computer services industry and its capacity to develop software, mobile apps, and e-commerce platforms. The following areas also warrant attention to improve ICT services:

- Better spectrum management policies and capital investment to bridge the digital divide

---

[20] Only two companies are licensed to connect international internet traffic, Delta Telecom LLC and AzerTelecom LLC.

- Reducing market concentration and improving the competitiveness of ICT services

- Allowing independent ICT regulation for market formation and development, transparency in tariff setting, and independent pricing and allocation of spectrum

Allowing independent ICT regulation would create confidence among industry participants by showing that they are being treated equally. Better ICT regulation would also help attract foreign direct investment to the sector, which would help upgrade technologies.

Agriculture

Although the share of agriculture in GDP has fallen significantly over the years, and is at about 6%, the sector still accounts for nearly two-fifths of employment. The aging Soviet-era infrastructure—principally irrigation and drainage, power, and transport—that still services the sector urgently needs upgrading to meet the needs of a diversified and growing economy, and to create quality jobs.[21]

The main thrust of the Strategic Road Map on the Production and Processing of Agricultural Products is to foster greater commercialization of farming and increase value addition by integrating all aspects of agriculture value chains.[22] Globally, several countries have spatially bound value chain initiatives, such as agri-parks, agri-corridors, and agri-clusters.[23] Agri-parks help expand the productive capacity of the agriculture sector. Going by international experience, successful value chain interventions need robust links between farmers, markets, and agri-processing facilities; and farm aggregation (this is particularly important for Azerbaijan, where most farms are small). Successful interventions also typically cover multiple value chains, and can be used to promote spatial synergies within value chains.[24]

---

[21] According to the agriculture products road map, 81.5% of irrigation canals, 77% of the collector-drainage network, and 72% of hydrotechnical facilities that are in use were once owned by Soviet-era farmers, collective farms, and agricultural businesses. Large-scale interventions will be required to upgrade them.

[22] Similar previous government efforts have not succeeded. According to agriculture products road map, weak agri-industrial integration has resulted in the poor development of regional clusters across the country. It would be useful to evaluate the past efforts to derive lessons.

[23] The Food and Agriculture Organization of the United Nations's report The State of Food and Agriculture 2017 contains a comprehensive analysis of these initiatives and recommendations on how to promote various types of agriculture value chains.

[24] The Azerbaijan Agricultural Insurance Fund was established to re-organize the mechanism on agricultural insurance. In order to address the issues arising from the Decree of the President of the Azerbaijan Republic, a task force composed up representatives from FMSA, Ministries of Agriculture, Finance, Economy, and the Center for Economic Reforms Analysis and Communication was created. The group also worked together with TARSIM and the representatives from Turkish Ministry of Agriculture on 4-13 September 2019. The Fund will start its operations as of 1 January 2020.

To implement a successful agri-park strategy, Azerbaijan must carefully consider the institutional, infrastructure, and skills requirements that will be needed for this.

- **Institutions.** Successful agri-parks depend on the integration of interrelated policies, public goods, and services with scattered institutional responsibilities. To avoid coordination failures, an umbrella institutional framework that integrates the delivery of all public policies, goods, and services for agri-parks should be considered.[25]

- **Infrastructure.** Bottlenecks in irrigation systems, markets, power supply, transport, and storage and warehousing (including cold chain) need to be systematically identified and measures taken to remove them. Infrastructure development is vital for the success of agri-parks. Where multiple value chains are integrated in a cluster, the infrastructure for reaping synergies from spatial integration will need to be developed.[26]

- **Skills.** Small-scale agri-business entrepreneurs and farmers need to gain new skills to participate in or cooperate with enterprises residing in agri-parks. Farmers will need to acquire knowledge of training on technology adoption, compliance with quality standards and certification requirements, and basic logistics management. And agri-enterprises, for their part, need to acquire basic business skills, management skills, and skills for logistics management; and to be able comply with quality standards and certification requirements.

Manufacturing

Robust growth is needed in manufacturing and other non-oil sectors for the country to avoid the middle-income trap. Research by Ricardo Hausman and Cesar Hidalgo shows that building knowledge and capabilities for manufacture goods can help put a country on the path to prosperity. Increasing prosperity is associated with a country moving up the product complexity ladder and shifting to more sophisticated industrial processes. Country experiences also show that developing a manufacturing industry can have huge spillover benefits for the growth of a knowledge economy, which in turn improves a country's international competitiveness.

Developing a manufacturing industry requires action on several fronts. Since 2010, Deloitte Touche Tohmatsu Limited has conducted a yearly assessment of the manufacturing competitiveness of various countries

---

[25] In the context of an agri-park development, farmers and agri-business entrepreneurs would have to bear the cost of coordination failures.

[26] One benefit of an agri-park strategy is that it allows for the spatial and value chain-based targeting of infrastructure investments.

using a set of 40 indicators.[27] Applying these indicators to manufacturing infrastructure in Azerbaijan shows that action in the following areas should improve the competitiveness of the country's emerging manufacturing industry:

- The quality, availability, and productivity of the workforce, particularly scientists, engineers, researchers, and skilled workers; industry-driven training and vocational education programs; manpower planning; incentives; and institutions for research and development.

- The quality and efficiency of the electricity grid and ITC network infrastructure—investments to improve and modernize both are needed.

- Access to quality airports, roads, railroads, and ports—these are basic elements of a logistics system to make the movement of people and goods easier, and will drive productivity improvements and therefore competitiveness.

- Setting up free trade zones, industrial clusters, and agri-parks—in-country and regional connectivity infrastructure will be a key logistical requirement.

Tourism

Prior to the COVID-19 pandemic, tourism has been growing in Azerbaijan and the government has been taking decisive steps to promote the sector. However, travel restrictions and public health concerns due to COVID-19 has strongly and adversely affected the tourism industry in the country. This makes the country's noble efforts to develop the tourism industry even more relevant and as important as ever. [28] The devaluation of the manat in 2015 increased the country's price competitiveness as a tourist destination. In 2017, Azerbaijan made the second biggest advance in the rankings of the World Economic Forum's Travel and Tourism Competitiveness Index, rising 13 places to rank 71st among 146 countries. The Strategic Road Map on the Development of a Specialized Tourism Industry points out that Azerbaijan has huge untapped tourism potential. Baku is the main tourist destination, but the scope is considerable to develop tourism in other parts of the country. That said, Azerbaijan faces stiff competition from its neighbors. The Russian Federation and Georgia rank higher than Azerbaijan on the Travel and Tourism Competitiveness Index. Among the countries of the former Soviet Union, Estonia, Latvia, and Lithuania have emerged as the most attractive tourist destinations.

---

[27] Deloitte Touche Tohmatsu's 2016 assessment, its most recent, does not rank Azerbaijan.

[28] The assessment in this section is based on WEF (2017).

Improvements in the following infrastructure areas would help Azerbaijan further increase its competitiveness as a tourist destination:

- **Transport.** Improving the quality and coverage of air transport, ground transport, and port infrastructure. The scores on these indicators in the Travel and Tourism Competitiveness Index are low; improving them will involve building an integrated transport infrastructure network and logistics system around the country's most popular tourist sites.

- **ICT readiness**. Here, Azerbaijan already scores highly, but increasing broadband penetration across the country and international connectivity will further improve the competitiveness of its tourist destinations.

- **Solid waste management.** Infrastructure for this and solid waste management control systems are needed along the Caspian shore as part of measures to promote the country as a beach destination to expand its tourism offerings beyond historical sites and a culinary experience.

- **Water supply and sanitation infrastructure**. This is another area requiring attention for diversifying tourism beyond Baku.

Technical and vocational education and training

A 2017 global survey ranked Azerbaijan low on the availability of skilled employees, but high for technical and vocational education and training (TVET) (UNDP 2017).[29] According to the 2013 Enterprise Survey by the European Bank for Reconstruction and Development and the World Bank, 63% of Azerbaijan's production workers were unskilled, compared with 22% in Europe and Central Asia (World Bank 2015). The share of workers offered formal training in Azerbaijan was 13.5%, compared with 55.8% in Europe and Central Asia. Inadequate qualifications are a major constraint to the supply side of the labor market, and people entering the labor market often lack the skills to be employed in the private sector.

Azerbaijan has a young and growing population—a strategic and necessary resource without which diversifying and modernizing the economy would be more difficult. This resource needs to be converted into productive human capital, which will require education and training. Success in achieving the objectives of diversifying and modernizing the economy will depend on the availability of business, professional, and technical skills in the labor market. To help meet this need, it is important to identify and address short-, medium- and long-term skill gaps—and not to delay in plugging them before

---

[29] Out of 131 countries surveyed, Azerbaijan ranked 60th on the composite index, 105th on availability of skilled employees, and 11th on TVET.

they become binding constraints. The country faces a huge challenge to strengthen its TVET system covering soft and physical infrastructure.[30] The physical infrastructure needs to do this are significant. For example, out of 30 TVET centers in Baku, more than 20 require significant rehabilitation and modernization, as do most TVET facilities outside the capital. According to the Ministry of Education, the government has initiated significant reforms and infrastructure improvements to its TVET centers in accordance with the Strategic Road Map and the Road Map on Vocational Education and Training.

4.3   Public Investment in Infrastructure

Taking advantage of fiscal support from the booming oil sector, Azerbaijan has significantly increased public investment in infrastructure, building on the capital stock it inherited from the former Soviet Union.[31] From 2003 to 2017, infrastructure spending from the state budget was nearly AZN40 billion ($20.6 billion) or 6.6% of GDP excluding the oil and gas sector.[32] This would have been higher on a consolidated public sector basis, though data on this are not readily available. SOEs were a major contributor to public infrastructure investment, particularly in electricity, oil and gas, transport, and water and sanitation. The International Monetary Fund (IMF) estimates this was 20.3% of GDP in 2013, 15.3% in 2014, and 16.3% in 2015 (IMF 2016).[33] The IMF estimates this tapered off in later years.[34] These estimates indicate that the government nevertheless made significant infrastructure investments from 2003 to 2017.[35]

With the push to diversify sources of growth and spur competitiveness, the momentum in building and upgrading infrastructure will need to be sustained. The Strategic Road Map on the National Economy Perspective and most sector road maps give estimates of the economy's investment needs, of which most are implicitly for infrastructure. An estimated AZN12 billion ($7 billion) will be needed until 2020 to meet the country's infrastructure

---

[30] FAO (2017) has a chapter on skills development that includes a discussion on the soft aspects of education and skills training.

[31] For the discussion in this section, infrastructure excludes oil and gas extraction and export infrastructure. The section uses data from multiple sources, because of the lack of readily available official data. The estimates are approximations, which reflect orders of magnitude, and are used to draw qualitative conclusions.

[32] GDP data are from the State Statistical Committee database.

[33] IMF (2016) is the latest publicly available Article IV report for Azerbaijan.

[34] On average, infrastructure investment is estimated at 70% of the State Investment Program.

[35] Negligible private investments have been made in infrastructure other than in oil and gas.

needs, excluding the oil and gas sector.[36] This translates to infrastructure investments of nearly 4.7% of GDP from both the public and private sector.[37]

The government expects there will be greater participation in infrastructure from the private sector. But private investments so far have been negligible outside the oil and gas sector. Major institutional and policy reforms will be needed to attract private sector investment in infrastructure, and this is discussed in detail later in the chapter. That said, it will probably be too much to expect a substantial engagement from the private sector in the medium term.

The following are further observations on Azerbaijan's infrastructure needs:

- The government expects infrastructure needs to be lower than levels in the past. It takes the view that major infrastructure—specifically airports, highways, and ports—is already in place. This emerged from discussions between the Country Diagnostic Study's team with the government at which it was also explained that infrastructure needs identified in the sector road maps will be reviewed as national and sector investment programs are drawn up.

- The infrastructure needed to position agriculture, manufacturing, and tourism as leading growth sectors are not identified in the sector road maps. At the time of writing, line ministries were still assessing this for their investment programs. Hence, the required investments could be greater than those given in the sector road maps.

- ADB estimates the infrastructure investment needs for upper-middle-income countries for 2016–2030 at 4.9% of GDP a year (ADB 2017a). ADB's estimates are for long-term averages, which means medium-term needs would be higher. While these estimates are not specific to Azerbaijan, they give an indication of the spending levels that will be needed. Azerbaijan-specific estimates suggest this will need to be as high as 11.6% of GDP a year during 2018–2020: 75% in transport, 16% in electricity, 6% in ICT, and 3% in water supply and sanitation (EBRD 2017).

In terms of the fiscal space for infrastructure investment, the State Investment Program for 2019 is expected to be AZN3 billion ($1.76 billion)—AZN3.5 billion ($2.0 billion). This excludes the oil and gas sector and includes expected disbursements from development partners. At about 70% of the

---

[36] This figure was arrived at by aggregating estimated investment amounts in the sector road maps wherever investment estimates were reflected in the Strategic Road Maps.

[37] Underlying GDP figures are projections from IMF (2016). These figures, however, are dated. GDP for 2017 and projected GDP for 2018–2020 are likely to be higher. Thus, the estimate of investment needs as a share of GDP is likely to be even lower.

program, infrastructure investment from the state budget is expected to be AZN2.1 billion ($1.23 billion)—AZN2.5 billion ($1.76 billion) or about 3.0% of GDP, according to the Ministry of Finance.[38]

The IMF, under its recommended fiscal rules, estimates that optimal public investment is 15%–18% of total government revenue (IMF 2016).[39] Using the IMF's projections for total government revenue for Azerbaijan, the optimal public investment can be estimated at 6%–7% of GDP.

4.4 Institutional Reforms for Smart Public Investments

The government uses resource rents to make many types of public investments—and these have undoubtedly raised the economy's productive potential. It is clear from economic trends, however, that these investments have not translated into sustained productivity growth in tradable sectors, including agriculture and manufacturing. Economic growth usually involves structural economic transformation in which labor moves to the most productive sectors. In the case of Azerbaijan, the growing dominance of oil caused labor to move to sectors producing nontradables, the demand for which has grown along with income from oil. As envisioned in the Strategic Road Maps, a key objective of infrastructure investment is to ensure this transformation includes labor moving to tradable sectors other than oil, and that these sectors can be made more competitive if infrastructure weaknesses are removed.

To achieve this objective, more cohesive national infrastructure planning is needed that treats infrastructure as a network of complementary assets, services, and policies. An uncoordinated, agency-driven approach to infrastructure investment will not help achieve diversified economic development. A nationally coordinated infrastructure investment plan will therefore be necessary to ensure the individual links in a network are put in place to achieve national objectives. An institutional approach will promote the efficient allocation of public investment across geography (spatial planning), sectors (sector planning), and projects (cost–benefit analysis). The broader institutional contexts in which investment decisions are arrived at—and the quality of project selection, management, implementation, and evaluation— will play a big role in determining the return on infrastructure investments and their contribution to growth.

---

[38] Nominal GDP for 2019 is assumed at AZN75.0 billion ($44 billion) and GDP in 2017 at AZN 70.1 billion ($41 billion).

[39] Box 4 in IMF (2016) details the underlying assumptions and methodology.

The following are the essential building blocks, presented in sequence, for putting in place a robust public investment management system:

(i)   An agency-level investment program and project proposals.

(ii)   A national development plan and a results framework for the plan; this is the first test against which the proposed programs and projects are screened.

(iii)   A consolidated public sector infrastructure program is drawn up on the completion of steps (i) and (ii).

(iv)   The second test is determining availability of budgetary resources at two levels. The first level is the medium-term expenditure framework on which the consolidated public investment program must be anchored. This is so that annual budgets make adequate provision for planned sector capital spending and recurrent expenditure for the operation and maintenance of existing assets. The second level is the annual budget cycle, with which the selection and appraisal of individual projects need to be tightly linked to ensure that projects are allocated sufficient finance.

(v)   The next level of screening involves the appraisal of individual projects for economic and financial viability, technical design, the capacity of the implementing agency to handle the project, and social and environmental safeguards.

(vi)   The monitoring of projects during implementation; this is needed to ensure they are implemented on time and within budget.

(vii)   Project evaluations once the project has been completed.

(viii) A new public procurement legal and institutional framework for greater transparency and efficiency, reducing corruption, and promoting value for money.[40]

An IMF survey ranked Azerbaijan 43rd out of 71 countries on the strength of its public institutions and processes for public investment management (IMF 2012). The survey covered 17 indicators grouped into four stages of the public investment management cycle: (i) strategic guidance anchored on national development plans and project appraisals, (ii) project selection,

---

[40] At the time of writing a draft of a new public procurement law was being reviewed by the Cabinet of Ministers. The new law is intended to address weaknesses in public procurement. The draft includes provisions on (i) introducing e-procurement and setting up an integrated online procurement portal, (ii) developing a common registry of contracts and a blacklist of suppliers, contractors, and consultants, (iii) introducing electronic bidding, (iv) preparing and submitting procurement plans, (v) the passage of a code of conduct for officials involved in public procurement; (vi) the application of framework agreements and competitive dialogue procedures; (vii) improving how complaints are reviewed and handled, and (viii) the involvement of small and medium-sized enterprises in public procurement. As soon as the law is enacted, a presidential decree is expected to be issued on the institutional set-up of public procurement, including the creation of an oversight agency for public procurement.

(iii) project implementation, and (iv) project evaluation and audits. Azerbaijan urgently needs to put in place public institutions and improve the processes for the efficient management of public investments. For instance, the Ministry of Economy's 2009 Instructions for the Evaluation, Appraisal and Monitoring of Projects have yet to be adopted. Box 4.1 explains how the Philippines set up its institutional framework for its upstream public investment management for infrastructure planning, project selection, appraisal, and budgeting.

Box 4.1: Upstream Public Investment Management in the Philippines

The Philippines has relatively strong national planning and project selection systems that are under the leadership of the National Economic and Development Authority.

The public investment program contains a rolling list of medium-term priority programs and projects to be implemented by the government and its national agencies, state-owned enterprises, and government financial institutions. These are chosen for the contribution they can make to achieving the social goals in the Philippine Development Plan, a 6-year national plan, and its results framework.

The public investment program is used to tighten links between planning, programming, budgeting, and monitoring and evaluation, and is the basis for allocating budget resources for priority programs and projects for review by the Investment Coordination Committee (ICC). The ICC consists of the secretary of finance, as chair; the National Economic and Development Authority's director general, as cochair; and the executive secretary, the secretaries of agriculture, trade and industry, and budget and management; and the governor of the Central Bank of the Philippines.

The ICC (i) evaluates the fiscal, monetary, and balance of payments implications of major national projects, and makes regular recommendations to the President of the Philippines on the timetable for their implementation; (ii) advises the President on the country's domestic and foreign borrowings program; and (iii) submits a status report of the fiscal, monetary, and balance-of-payments implications of major national projects. The ICC is assisted by a group of experts that appraise project documents submitted by government agencies for the committee's approval. The ICC's recommendations are submitted to a board chaired by the President.

Government programs and projects costing above ₱2.5 billion ($47 million) are required to undergo ICC's approval process. All public–private partnership projects require ICC approval before proceeding with bidding, as do projects involving government borrowing. The ICC appraises projects in the context of

continued on the next page

Box 4.1 continued

sector plans and geographical strategies for their economic and financial viability, and their technical, economic, financial, social, and institutional impact. The ICC also reviews the proposed sources and terms of financing for projects. ICC approval is a prerequisite for including a project in the medium-term budget, and for negotiations with creditors.

A Three-Year Rolling Infrastructure Program (TRIP) is part of public investment management in the Philippines. This is drawn up annually to build a pipeline of strategic and other projects needed to sustain inclusive economic growth. TRIP synchronizes the government's infrastructure planning, programming, budgeting and execution processes, both at the oversight and implementing agency level. TRIP indicates the type and size of budgetary resources needed by projects. These include resources for resettlement plans, developing feasibility studies, right-of-way acquisition, detailed engineering designs, and construction and reconstruction expenses. TRIP's objective is to ensure that well developed and readily implementable projects are queued for the budget, and that a more rigorous program and project appraisal system is put in place.

These measures aim to ensure that infrastructure programs and projects make a positive contribution to economic growth and social welfare objectives, and do so in an integrated way to ensure the largest possible convergence among infrastructure programs and projects in different sectors (for example, roads, rail, and airports).

TRIP covers all nationally-funded infrastructure projects irrespective of cost and financing source—for example, whether foreign-assisted or locally funded projects—based on the synchronized planning, programming and budgeting process of the government, including public–private partnership projects.

Source: Komatsuzaki, T. 2016. *Improving Public Infrastructure in the Philippines. IMF Working Paper.* WP/16/39. Washington, DC: International Monetary Fund. For information on the National Economic and Development Authority, see http://www.neda.gov.ph/.

4.5 Pricing Infrastructure Services, Infrastructure Maintenance, and Economic Regulations for Infrastructure

The delivery of infrastructure services has two stages. The first is the investment stage, which creates a network of infrastructure assets. The previous section highlighted the need for Azerbaijan to undertake institutional reforms to increase the efficiency of public investment management to create this network. In the second stage, the network is made available to users. Infrastructure investments catalyze diversified development through the sustainable use of these assets over their planned economic life. The second stage also involves institutional and pricing reforms. A detailed discussion of these reforms for each sector and utility in Azerbaijan is beyond the scope of this chapter. But three broad areas—the pricing of infrastructure services, infrastructure maintenance, and economic regulation—are briefly considered. And because SOEs are major providers of infrastructure services, their reforms are relevant for the infrastructure sector.

Pricing infrastructure services

Most infrastructure services have traditionally been regarded as public goods and have therefore either not been priced or could not be priced. Over time, however, the categories of what constitute public goods have been shrinking globally. Economic and technology developments are making it possible to put restrictions on the use of certain types of infrastructure services (the excludability criterion). Scarcity of fiscal resources has also made this necessary in some countries. The negative externalities often associated with the use of public goods, such as congested roads and pollution, have also contributed to the pricing of infrastructure services. There are therefore intermediate stages between pure public goods (free use) and private goods (market pricing).

In Azerbaijan, the provision of gas, power, transport, and water and sanitation, among other infrastructure services, has been improving, and income per capita has risen rapidly. Because of this, it is both economically necessary and socially feasible (indeed justifiable) to price a growing list of infrastructure services. The global experience on this is rich and the government can draw on this.[41] Many countries successfully use differentiated pricing or price discrimination so that economically weaker households are not excluded from basic infrastructure services.[42] Utilities in many countries have effectively used pricing signals to manage the demand–supply balance; for example, time-of-day tariffs for electricity. In Azerbaijan it will be important to ensure that tariff reform, which is urgently needed, becomes an integral part of infrastructure planning.[43]

---

[41] ADB and other international financial institutions have worked with client governments on pricing reforms at the sector and subsector levels; for example, road and rail transport, power, and water and sanitation.

[42] In many countries, utilities charge so-called lifeline tariffs for economically weaker households, allowing them to meet their basic needs, usually in power, sanitation, and water, at affordable rates. Lifeline tariffs are a way to address equity concerns and improve service efficiency.

[43] It may not yet be possible for Azerbaijan to rely solely on user fees to fully fund infrastructure services. But to avoid wasteful investments, cost-covering prices are an appropriate benchmark to assess consumer demand for carrying out a cost–benefit analysis on a project.

In Azerbaijan and other market economies, prices act as important signals for the efficient allocation of productive factors and drive producers or providers of infrastructure services toward the efficient provision of these services. It is therefore worth making the effort to provide as many infrastructure services as possible at market-clearing prices. Where the government determines that certain sections of the population should receive services at below-market prices (in other words, subsidized), these should be explicitly funded through the state budget.

Azerbaijan has already embarked on pricing reforms in several infrastructure sectors. Azerbaijan Railways subsidizes passenger traffic and absorbs this cost through the prices of its freight services. It may well be a valid government objective to subsidize passenger traffic. But this subsidy must be funded through the state budget to allow the railways to price its freight services on a cost basis, thereby improving the competitiveness of rail freight services compared with road transport. Other utilities, notably electricity, gas, and urban transport, have initiated pricing reforms, including differentiated tariffs.

Infrastructure maintenance

Infrastructure usually has a long economic life. Maintaining these assets is essential for their sustainability. Roads that are built to last for decades may rapidly degrade because of a lack of routine maintenance. And because roads have maximum load limits, overloading will damage them, make maintenance more expensive, and reduce their economic life.[44] Financial and institutional factors determine the quality of infrastructure maintenance, and the two are often interlinked. This chapter has already suggested that Azerbaijan link its infrastructure program with its medium-term fiscal program so that an adequate budget is earmarked early for maintaining infrastructure assets. Pricing infrastructure services ease the budget burden, and it is crucial to do this if service providers fund maintenance from their own sources, as Azerbaijan Railways does.

Conducive institutional mechanisms and processes are important for maintaining infrastructure. These are inadequate in Azerbaijan's road transport sector, where institutional reforms are urgently needed. The sector has a sizable maintenance budget that is neither efficiently allocated nor effectively used, because of the absence of a coherent institutional structure and systems

---

[44] The motorway that connects Baku to the border with the Russian Federation has been severely degraded since its reconstruction, which involved sizable capital spending.

for road asset management. The government recognizes this and has initiated reforms to strengthen road maintenance. These include:

- **Road maintenance**. Several motorway maintenance units have been set up as limited liability companies under service agreements with the State Agency of Azerbaijan Automobile Roads for routine and emergency maintenance. A proposal has been made to pilot a performance-based maintenance contract for the routine and periodic maintenance for a regional road. The proposal for the pilot has been developed with an initial focus on eliminating the maintenance backlog on regional and local roads. These initiatives should be promptly implemented to raise the efficiency and effectiveness of the country's sizable road maintenance fund.

- **Vehicle axle loads**. In 2015, the Cabinet of Ministers adopted an important decision on installing electronic scales and chips for measuring the weight and mass parameters of heavy and large vehicles. It will be important to show that the weight measurement stations set up for this are continuing to function efficiently. It will also be also important to increase the number of stations on all motorways and regional roads, and to publicly release the monitoring reports on the vehicle-weight control system.

- **Tolling.** The government intends to introduce tolling on the new motorway connecting the Russian Federation's border with Iran's border through Baku.[45] It is envisaged that, in the initial phase, toll roads will be managed by the State Agency on Automobile Roads, with the potential future participation of the private sector for operating selected segments of the north–south road corridor. To make this initiative a success, it will be necessary to strengthen the policy, financial management, and institutional arrangements to promote the right level of tariff setting, fund flow, and the use of the collected funds for road maintenance.[46]

The maintenance of the country's railway assets has also suffered from institutional impediments. This is a problem because poor maintenance slows train speeds, which diminishes the development and public service roles of

---

[45] The introduction of the tolling system, however, faced delays due to gaps in the sector legal framework that required time to be addressed. For instance, in November 2017, the government adopted amendments to the Law on Automobile Roads detailing tolling arrangements. On 20 July 2018, the Cabinet of Ministers adopted the Resolution on Toll Road Signage and Information Provision. The introduction of the tolling arrangement was also affected by the economic slowdown in 2015–2016 that followed the oil price shock, causing the government to focus on restoring macroeconomic stability and tackle problems in the banking sector.

[46] A gradual approach to this is being pursued mainly because of social considerations. In 2014, the government commissioned a demand (willingness to pay) analysis for tolling on one section of the new motorway. In 2018, the government introduced tolling on the M3 Alat–Astara (Iran border), and approved the construction of the Baku–Guba toll road (Russian Federation border) from the state budget.

the railways. The government and Azerbaijan Railways are in the process of instituting far-reaching reforms to improve the maintenance of rail assets (ADB 2017b).

Economic regulation

Economies of scale and network effects can result in natural monopolies, which are often infrastructure service providers. Azerbaijan Railways is such a monopoly, as are the agencies that own and operate the country's roads and ports. Over time, contestable markets will be the best way to provide infrastructure services, and to improve service quality. For now, however, independent economic regulation will be needed to balance the interests of consumers and infrastructure providers by setting tariffs, and to deliver decent services at competitive prices. Azerbaijan could learn from the extensive global experience on regulatory issues for infrastructure on which considerable research has been done.

An overarching objective of economic regulation should be to create incentives and penalties that replicate as far as possible a service as if it was being delivered in a competitive market. As Azerbaijan undertakes tariff reforms and seeks private investment in infrastructure, it would have to move away from administratively determined prices of infrastructure services to credible independent regulators. The government needs to pass legislation for legal and contractual frameworks—within which economic regulation would be embedded—for infrastructure services, and to set out organizational and procedural arrangements for regulators. Setting up of the Tariff Council and a standalone regulator for the power sector are welcome, albeit initial, steps. As a case in point, the public transport system in Baku and other cities would benefit from periodic fare revisions arrived at through independent regulation. Box 4.2 provides an example of the long overdue increase in fares for public bus services in Baku and other cities that was eventually implemented in 2018. The delay in fare increases was due to the lack of an agreed mechanism for revising fares for city bus services between the public and private sector that shared the provision of these services.

Box 4.2: Increasing Fares on Public City Buses

In July 2018, the Tariff Council approved a 50% flat increase in fares on public bus services in Baku and other cities, and between the country's cities. The increase was long overdue. In Baku, for example, fares were last increased in 2007 for the city bus service, in 2011 for the metropolitan service, and in 2013 for the intercity service.[a]

The cost of providing these services obviously increased over these periods, requiring significant fare increases for full cost recovery. When both public and private sectors are engaged in providing an infrastructure service, as was the case for Baku's public city buses, economic regulation, such as an agreed mechanism for fare revision, ensures equal treatment between the two. The impact of the lack of such a mechanism resulted in delays in fare revisions that eroded the profitability of private bus operators.

Although public bus fares should be revised to reflect changes in the cost of providing services, this needs to be done on a predetermined schedule; for example, quarterly, six-monthly, or yearly. An agreed mechanism for revising fares that considers the structure of inputs, standard input price indices, and data sources is also needed. Doing this will increase the transparency and predictability in decisions on public bus fares and infrastructure tariffs more generally—outcomes that are essential for effective and independent regulation.

[a] Center for Economic and Social Development. 2018. *An Analysis of The Costs and Benefits of Increasing Baku's Public Transportation Tariffs.* Baku.

4.6 Private Sector Participation

Private investment in Azerbaijan's non-oil infrastructure has focused on ICT. From 1996 to 2014, this totaled AZN4.26 billion ($2.5 billion), of which ICT accounted for AZN3.6 billion ($2.1 billion). Power distribution accounted for the rest.[47] All the ICT projects were merchant arrangements done through the sector's legal framework. Beyond oil, the public sector is the dominant player in infrastructure, funding most investment and managing and operating most infrastructure assets. There has also been private investment in waste-to-energy, health, and tourism projects that have PPP features.[48] These projects, however, have been on-off undertakings done on the basis of the legal framework of the concerned sectors.

---

[47] All closed electricity private participation in infrastructure projects were eventually canceled. In 2001, a 10-year management and lease contract was concluded for the city of Imishli's water supply system, but there is no available information on the size of the investment. The source for this and private investment in power distribution comes from the World Bank's Private Participation in Infrastructure Database (country snapshot for Azerbaijan).

[48] American Chamber of Commerce in Azerbaijan. 2019. *Impact Azerbaijan.* 33. pp. 19–22 and 27–29.

To raise the level of private investment in economic and social public infrastructure, Parliament, in March 2016, passed the Law on Implementation of Special Financing for Investment Projects for Construction and Infrastructure Facilities.[49] This cross-sector legal framework envisages private participation in infrastructure through the build-operate-transfer (BOT) modality. This involves private investors being paid back by facility users, the government, or both. In May 2017, the Ministry of Finance approved rules on the definition of state budget support and guarantees for BOT projects.[50] Given the novelty of the BOT model for the public and private sectors, its rollout has yet to happen. The standard bidding documents and template contracts for BOTs have also not yet been drawn up. The issues related to the definition of the bidding consortium, the role and liability of the special purpose vehicle in the BOT contract, the ownership of the project during the BOT contract and how it is taxed, the step-in rights of lenders, the form and term of both the government and private partner performance undertaking during facility operation, and the return of the facility to the government at the end of the BOT contract have to be clarified. In addition, the respective roles of the government proponent agency and the Ministry of Economy as the BOT authority during project implementation need further clarification in the BOT and related sector legal frameworks.

The 2016 law envisages using solicited proposals for procuring infrastructure projects, with the concession term not exceeding 49 years. The private sponsor is expected to put up at least 20% of a project's financing. BOT projects are eligible for government guarantees. The initiation, preparation, and implementation of BOT projects are the responsibility of line ministries or SOEs. The Ministry of Economy is the authorized body responsible for approving a project's prefeasibility study; project procurement, with the participation of the concerned government agency and the Ministry of Finance; contract award; and overseeing implementation. The Ministry of Economy's public investment department performs these functions. The ministry seeks the Ministry of Finance's concurrence on draft BOT contracts before signing a concession agreement with the private sponsor.

Azerbaijan Investment Company, set up in 2006 by presidential decree, may share the risk capital (equity) of privately funded infrastructure projects.[51] The company manages state investments in regional development, and its main purpose is to support the development of the non-oil sector through

---

[49] Law No. 177-VQ, dated 15 March 2016, and Presidential Decree No. 867, dated 20 April 2016.

[50] Decision of the Ministry of Finance No. Q-06, dated 22 May 2017.

[51] Presidential Decree No. 1395, dated 30 March 2006, on additional measures to promote investment activity. Azerbaijan Investment Company's charter capital is about AZN500 million ($293.2 million).

termed equity injections along with local and foreign coinvestors in greenfield and brownfield projects. It is also responsible for managing industrial sites in locations where the state has established certain facilities and services, such as infrastructure, office space, and discounted public services and utilities for SMEs.

The development of PPPs in Azerbaijan for all types of modalities (not just BOTs) is among the priority measures of Strategic Road Map for the Production of Consumer Goods in Small and Medium Enterprises. In 2017, the government established the Agency for the Development of Small and Medium Sized-Enterprises, a legal entity under the Ministry of Economy.[52] A PPP development center is supposed to be established under the agency to promote PPPs, including involving SMEs in these partnerships. The government has drafted a concept paper for developing PPPs, and a vision and policy statement on PPPs to be put into effect by presidential decree. These are all important steps for increasing private investment in infrastructure in a pragmatic and sustainable way. At the same time, two questions are pertinent to ask on Azerbaijan's efforts to increase private sector participation in infrastructure. Should the country be doing this at all given size of the economy and given the availability of sizable financial resources from oil and gas revenues and associated savings? And, if the answer is yes, which parts of the infrastructure value chain should private sector participation be sought?

It is difficult to make the case for the private delivery of public infrastructure assets and services in Azerbaijan purely on financial grounds. The government does not face severe credit constraints and could sustainably fund reasonable levels of infrastructure spending from its own resources. The decision to go for some form of private participation in infrastructure will therefore need to be made on the basis of the efficiency of the underlying incentive regime and not on financial considerations alone. Even on grounds of efficiency, the case for private participation is less straightforward for natural monopolies. In the event of a nonperforming infrastructure PPP, the government may find it more difficult to replace a private concessionaire than a service provider that is an SOE.

A strong rationale for private participation in infrastructure in Azerbaijan is that it would bring modern management and accounting practices, know-how, and above all frontier technologies. These will be useful for the economy, which is trying to modernize and diversify. The private sector, particularly

---

[52] Presidential Decree No. 1771, dated 28 December 2017.

foreign investors, is the best vehicle to tap into these benefits.[53] For every infrastructure project for which private participation is proposed, the question must be asked: will this bring more efficient investment and operations? If there is potential for efficiency gains, there is a strong case for bringing in a private investor. A further consideration is the potential spillover benefits (positive externalities) to the broader economy by adopting modern technologies and best international practices from private sector participation. So, it is necessary to assess ex ante the potential value addition of a private investor coming in on a public infrastructure project.

It is important to note that the choice is often not between full private or state ownership. The global experience with PPPs is enormous and ranges across many types of partnership arrangements, ranging from the government having majority ownership to the private sector having majority ownership. PPPs seek to leverage the best that both public and private sectors offer. The underlying objective is to pass as much commercial risk as possible to the private partner and to give that partner the appropriate incentives to perform well.

To achieve efficiency and welfare gains from private participation in public infrastructure projects using the rationale just described, the first layer of decision-making involves unbundling natural monopolies so that segments that can be opened to competition are separated from those that do not lend themselves to price competition.[54] Countries in developing Asia have tried numerous approaches to calibrating price formation processes to maximize efficiency and welfare gains, albeit with varying degrees of success. The following areas seem relevant for deciding on further steps for private participation in public infrastructure in Azerbaijan:[55]

- **Toll roads and solid waste management.** Price competition happens when concessions are auctioned to the lowest bidders through transparent bidding processes. Concessionaires then have the incentive to improve the quality of operations and maintenance of toll roads and solid waste management facilities to maximize profits. Concession contracts should set out minimum service standards.

---

[53] The government proposes to offer attractive tax and nontax concessions to foreign private sector investors in the Alat Free Trade Zone. Getting access to modern technology, management, and accounting practices were cited by the government as the main justification for the tax breaks.

[54] It is beyond the scope of this chapter to make specific proposals for doing this since this would require extensive sector analytical work.

[55] In these areas, coordination costs may exist between the provider of physical infrastructure and the operator. These need to be recognized, and mechanisms devised to minimize these costs.

- **Rail freight.** Although the ownership of rail infrastructure is a natural monopoly, the ownership and operation of rolling stock is not because there is potential competition from road transport. At least some competition in rail freight, even if it is small, could be created by licensing a limited number of private freight service providers.

- **Power generation**. Developing countries in Asia have shown the feasibility of functioning competitive markets for private producers, sellers, and traders.[56]

- **Airports.** In many countries, airports are owned, operated, and maintained by the private sector. Because airport customers are commercial airlines it is easier to set prices for airport services on a cost-plus basis. As Azerbaijan tries to position itself as a major tourist destination in the region, handing over the operation and maintenance of its airports, which were all built by public funds, to the private sector could potentially not only bring efficiency gains but also spillover benefits from modern airport management practices.

- **Ports.** Similar considerations apply to Azerbaijan's ports as for its airports. In general, the logistics sector provides an excellent opportunity to enhance operational efficiencies through greater private sector participation. And as noted earlier, efficient logistics services will be needed to support the development of tourism particularly after the COVID-19 pandemic.

- **Social infrastructure.** In Azerbaijan, there is tremendous scope for PPPs to build and operate modern health and education infrastructure given growing demand, the availability of idle state land and assets in these sectors, and the interest of the private sector to expand into longer-term assets. In education, such projects would help the country attain modern skills, management practices, and technologies. The technical assistance provided by ADB for a BOT project for student accommodation in two Baku universities highlights a proactive approach to catalyze private investment in social infrastructure.[57]

The economic thinking that underpins the Strategic Road Map on the National Economy Perspective envisions the private sector as the main driver of economic development in Azerbaijan. One of the road map's strategic targets

---

[56]   Azerbaijan's privatization of three brownfield power generation assets on a rehabilitate-operate-and transfer basis was later canceled.

[57]   This project is financed from subproject 4 of ADB's regional technical assistance project Strengthening Project Preparation Capacity in Asia and the Pacific—Supporting Preparation of Infrastructure Projects with Private Sector Participation in Asia and the Pacific (TA-9292 REG).

is for a clear path to be laid out for moving from the developmental state model to private sector-led development. For infrastructure, it would be prudent to adopt a step-by-step approach that builds on the demonstrated benefits of and lessons learned from the private delivery of public infrastructure assets and services, the commercialization and broader reforms of SOEs, and the strengthened economic regulation of public utilities. For sustainable economic development, it will be better for Azerbaijan to have credible and beneficial private participation.

4.7 Conclusions and Policy Recommendations

Azerbaijan has made impressive socioeconomic gains since independence. Poverty has declined to single-digit levels and the country has reached upper-middle-income status. It has leveraged its considerable hydrocarbon resources and favorable terms of trade not only to sustain infrastructure inherited from the former Soviet Union but also to upgrade and modernize infrastructure. As a result, Azerbaijan's global competitiveness has greatly improved. At the same time, the dominance of the hydrocarbon sector has been growing, as has economy's dependence on sector. To reduce this, the policy focus is shifting to the sustainable use of resource rents and accelerating the economy's diversification.

This chapter's assessment of the country's infrastructure performance and its infrastructure investment needs highlighted the importance of interventions and policy reforms in four main areas. The first is ensuring adequate resources to sustain and enhance infrastructure. For planning purposes, infrastructure investment of 6%–7% of GDP may be needed in the medium-term for this. While SOEs and the private sector will contribute, most investments may have to be funded from the state budget.

The second is having an effective institutional set-up to strategically manage infrastructure. A case can be made for an interministerial organizational structure that is well coordinated to draw up (i) a consolidated public sector infrastructure program for planning infrastructure as a network of complementary assets, services, and policies; (ii) a medium-term fiscal framework to ensure there is predictable funding for planned capital investment and maintaining existing assets; (iii) rigorous ex ante project appraisals, robust project management, and monitoring and evaluation; and (iv) rules-based and transparent public procurement of goods and services.

The third is having a cohesive policy framework for infrastructure, because various policies currently relate to infrastructure development. This chapter focused on (i) independent and effective regulations to ensure infrastructure services are delivered at competitive prices and equal treatment for all market participants; (ii) tariff reforms, which are underway in varying degrees in most infrastructure industries and articulated in the sector road maps; and (iii) asset management systems for maintaining infrastructure assets over their long economic life. Policies in all these areas need to be cohesively planned, implemented, and evaluated; and be guided by a set of key principles and strategic directions applicable to the entire infrastructure sector.

The fourth area is a gradual and value-for-money-focused approach to private participation in infrastructure. The Strategic Road Maps envision the greater participation of private actors in the infrastructure sector. Besides being an additional source of capital, private sector participation would boost efficiency and help bring much-needed modern technologies, skills, and management practices to the provision of public infrastructure. Because infrastructure investment is essentially long-term in nature, this means that durable and predictable policies (for example, tax policies), and independent and effective regulatory oversight, will be prerequisites for attracting private investment. This chapter suggests a step-by-step approach for Azerbaijan to increase private participation in public infrastructure, an iterative process that will build on successes and adjust policies, processes, and expectations as lessons from this experience are learned.

Establishing an effective institutional framework to strategically manage infrastructure, ensuring cohesiveness of the policy framework, and following the value-for-money-focused approach to private participation in infrastructure will be critical to ensure that infrastructure funds are well spent.

References

ADB (Asian Development Bank). Forthcoming. *Azerbaijan: Country Digital Development Overview*. Manila.

———. 2017a. *Meeting Asia's Infrastructure Needs*. Manila.

———. 2017b. *Report and Recommendation of the President to the Board of Directors on Proposed Loans, Technical Assistance Grant, and Administration of Loan to the Republic of Azerbaijan for the Railway Sector Development Program*. Manila. https://www.adb.org/sites/default/files/linked-documents/48386-004-ssa.pdf.

American Chamber of Commerce in Azerbaijan. 2019. *Impact Azerbaijan*. 33. Baku.

Azernews. 2018. Azerbaijan to Launch Third Satellite. 23 December.

Center for Economic and Social Development. 2018. *An Analysis of The Costs and Benefits of Increasing Baku's Public Transportation Tariffs*. Baku. http://cesd.az/new/wp-content/uploads/ 2018/08 /CESD-Research-Paper-Inreasing-Transportation-Taarifs-in-Azerbaijan.pdf.

EBRD (European Bank for Reconstruction and Development). 2017. *Transition Report 2017–18*. London.

FAO (Food and Agriculture Organization of the United Nations). 2017. *The State of Food and Agriculture 2017*. Rome.

IMF (International Monetary Fund). 2012. *Investing in Public Investment: An Index of Public Investment Efficiency*. Washington, DC.

———. 2014. *World Economic Outlook: Legacies, Clouds, Uncertainties*. Washington, DC.

———. 2016. *Republic of Azerbaijan Staff Report for the 2016 Article IV Consultation*. Washington, DC.

Klein, M. 2014. Infrastructure Policy: Basic Design Options. *Policy Research Working Paper*. No. 6274. Washington, DC: World Bank.

Komatsuzaki, T. 2016. Improving Public Infrastructure in the Philippines. *Working Paper*. WP/16/39. Washington, DC: International Monetary Fund.

Sebastian, F. P., and J. Steinbuks. 2017. Public Infrastructure and Structural Transformation. *Policy Research Paper*. No. 8285. Washington, DC: World Bank.

UNDP (United Nations Development Programme). 2017. Global Knowledge Index. New York. http://knowledge4all.com.

World Bank. 2014. *Diversified Development: Making the Most of Natural Resources in Eurasia*. Washington, DC.

———. 2015. *Azerbaijan: Systematic Country Diagnostic*. Washington, DC.

———. 2017. *Africa's Pulse*. April. Washington, DC.

WEF (World Economic Forum). 2017. *Travel and Tourism Competitiveness Report 2017*. Geneva. http://www3.weforum.org/docs/WEF_TTCR_2017_web_0401.pdf.

CHAPTER 5

Transforming State-Owned Enterprises into Engines of Growth

This chapter examines the factors that have led to the underperformance and inefficiency of Azerbaijan's state-owned enterprises (SOEs). This analysis is needed to show how SOEs could be transformed into engines of economic growth and diversification.

The economic significance of SOEs has declined since 1995, reflecting the reduced role of the state in the economy (Figure 5.1). Even so, SOEs continue to be critical economic and social players in Azerbaijan. As of January 2018, there were 10,565 national SOEs and 1,706 municipal state firms (10.3% of all registered firms).[1] SOEs have dominant positions in power, gas distribution, roads, rail, ports, air transport, water supply and sanitation, and telecommunication. In aggregate, the contribution of Azerbaijan's SOEs to GDP at 17.7% of GDP in 2014–2016 is the second largest among the countries in Europe and Central Asia shown in Figure 5.2.

Figure 5.1: Share of the State in Employment and Output, 1995 and 2018

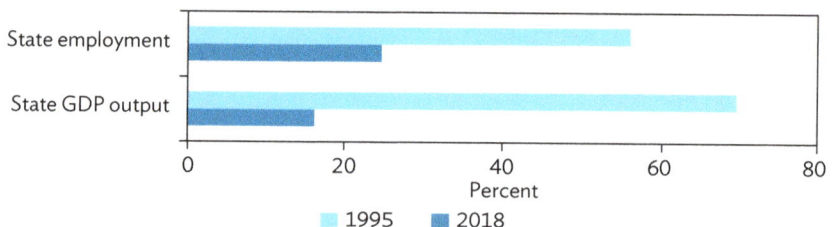

GDP = gross domestic product.
Source: State Statistical Committee.

---

[1] There are four legal forms of SOEs in Azerbaijan: joint stock companies, limited liability companies, public legal entities, and SOEs with a special legal form. The latter type includes the production associations and the State Oil Fund of Azerbaijan Republic.

Figure 5.2: Contribution of SOEs to Gross Domestic Product in Azerbaijan and Selected Countries , 2014–2016

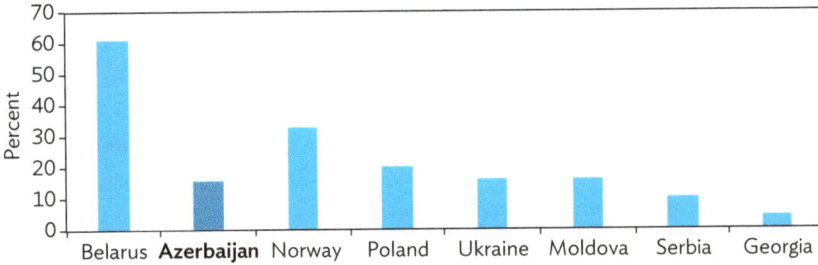

SOE = state-owned enterprise.
Source: World Bank. 2017. *Republic of Azerbaijan: Corporate Governance and Ownership of State-Owned Enterprises*. Technical note. Washington, DC.

State Oil Fund of Azerbaijan Republic (SOCAR), a quasi-government company with a specific regulatory framework, plays an especially important role in the economy. In 2017, SOCAR and the whole public sector (inclusive of SOCAR) contributed to 16.2% of GDP. SOCAR's tax payments made up 9.2% of the 2017 state budget's revenue, and its total revenue was 5.6 times larger than the state budget's. In the finance sector, majority state-owned International Bank of Azerbaijan accounts for 35% of sector assets.

The large contribution that Azerbaijan's SOEs makes to GDP and employment not only show their economic importance but also explain the risks they pose to the economy. Because many of the country's SOEs depend on budget subsidies, they are ultimately vulnerable to swings in global oil prices given the budget's dependence on oil revenue. This situation requires interventions to raise the sector's efficiency and sustainability.

5.1   Oil Shock Exposes SOE Weaknesses

The sharp fall in global oil prices in 2014 and devaluations in the manat in 2015 put Azerbaijan's unsustainable dependency on oil and the inefficiency of its SOE sector into a harsh light. The fall in oil prices led to the need for increased transfers from the State Oil Fund of Azerbaijan Republic (SOFAZ) to fund government spending and build up foreign exchange reserves. From the SOE sector's perspective, the oil boom of 2004–2014 allowed SOCAR to offset the underperformance of major SOEs in the non-oil sector. But the fall in global oil prices, aggravated by Azerbaijan's lower oil production, significantly impaired the government's capacity to provide budget support to SOEs.

To illustrate this, Figure 5.3 shows the revenue performance of SOCAR, International Bank of Azerbaijan, and Azersu during the oil boom and during the economic slowdown after the fall in oil prices. Azersu's continual losses required budget support during 2012–2016. The same became necessary for International Bank of Azerbaijan in 2015 and 2016. From the perspective of the state as owner, SOCAR's profits before the fall in oil prices helped offset the losses of Azersu and International Bank of Azerbaijan. Ideally, all SOEs in the state's portfolio need to be profitable and none should be continually making losses. McKinsey & Company was selected in the bidding to support the process of developing a new business model and strategy for preparation of Azerbaijan International Bank for privatization. The Company started to work on it as of January, 2019 and the document has already been finalized. In the recovery process, a total of toxic assets in amount of AZN14.9 billion was envisaged to be transferred to Agrarcredit. As of end of the Quarter 3, 99% of toxic assets were already transferred. The transfer of remaining assets (as of 30 September 2019 AZN164.6 million) were not finalized due to failure of non-resident borrowers to agree with restructuring process, lack of documents in credit files, expiration of the loan claim period, etc. Currently, the quality of assets is satisfactory. According to the information as of 30 September 2019, 8% of loans constituted overdue loans and 6% made up inactive loans in total credit portfolios. The status of liquidity is stable. Instant liquidity ratio constitutes 53.5% (as of 30 September 2019). Currently, the bank operates with profits and restored its capital status. Thus, the total profit of the bank constituted AZN323 million as of 30 September 2019. As for the aggregate capital adequacy ratio and scope, they make up 35% and AZN1.3 billion, respectively.

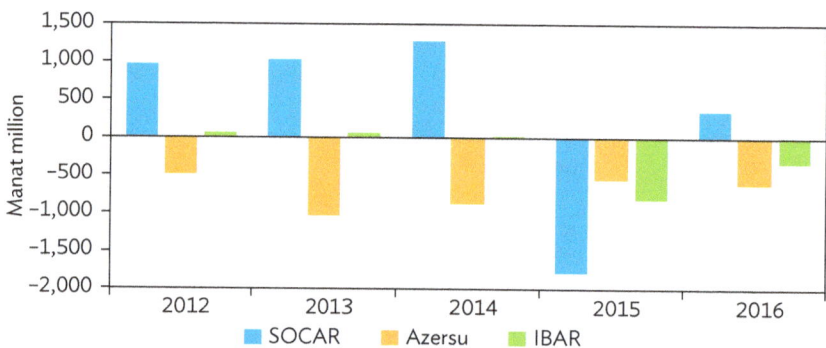

Figure 5.3: State Oil Company of Azerbaijan Republic, International Bank of Azerbaijan, and Azersu Revenue, 2012–2016

IBAR = International Bank of Azerbaijan, SOCAR = State Oil Company of Azerbaijan Republic, SOE = state-owned enterprise.
Source: Authors' calculations.

The economic downturn caused by the collapse in oil prices exposed the financial challenges faced by several of Azerbaijan's largest SOEs. Falling oil prices, coupled with poor debt management, caused the default of one major SOE and the near default of another—and declining SOE profits all round. In 2015, International Bank of Azerbaijan needed a public bailout of AZN5.6 billion ($3.3 billion) and Azerbaijan Railways one for AZN1.1 billion ($600 million) for restructuring. In 2016, the government's fiscal support to SOEs accounted for 12% of state budget expenditure, and 7% in 2017.

The macroeconomic significance (in terms of economic employment, GDP contribution, financial performance, and sector dominance) of the 14 SOEs covered in this chapter can be seen in their high level of debt. For the largest SOEs, this is estimated to have risen from 30% of GDP in 2013 and 2014 to just over 100% in 2016 (Figures 5.4 and 5.5).

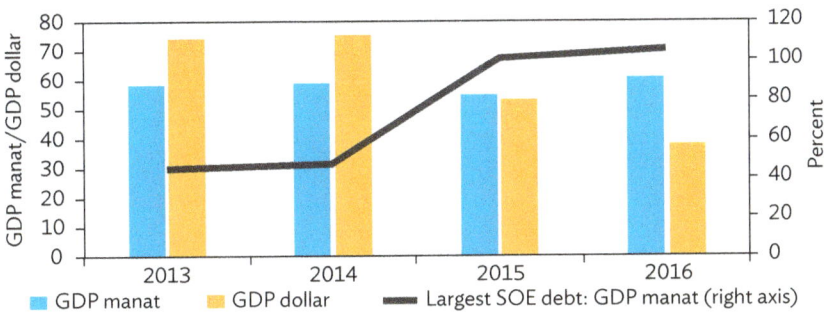

Figure 5.4: SOE Debt Levels, 2013–2016

GDP = gross domestic product, SOE = state-owned enterprise.
Source: Authors' calculations.

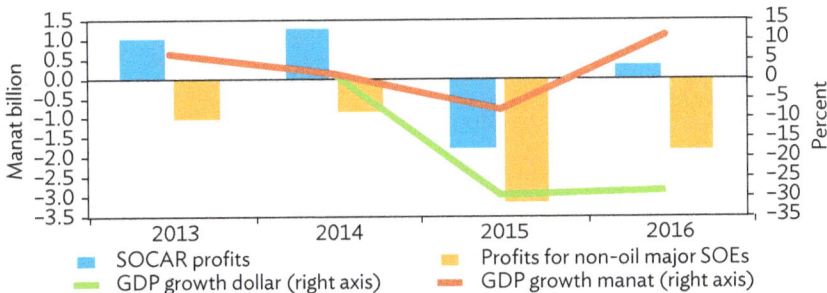

Figure 5.5: Profitability of Non-Oil SOEs and Economic Growth, 2013–2016

SOCAR = State Oil Company of Azerbaijan Republic, SOE = state-owned enterprise.
Source: Authors' calculations.

5.2   Government Reforms to Raise SOE Efficiency

The fall in oil prices also revealed the need to shift from state-led to private-led diversified economic growth. The government earnestly recognizes the need to diversify the economy through greater private sector participation to achieve sustainable development. To this end, under the Strategic Road Map on the National Economy Perspective, the government has developed a comprehensive cross-sector SOE reform agenda to raise the efficiency of SOEs, and ready for privatization and privatize selected nonstrategic SOEs, including attracting foreign direct investment.

Under this agenda, the government, in 2016 and 2017, initiated important reforms to improve the centralized financial control and financial transparency of SOEs. These reforms included implementing a comprehensive action plan to increase the transparency and efficiency of the financial activities of large SOEs, and to set up a committee to supervise the revenue and expenditure of large SOEs.[2] The government has successfully set up a database on SOEs, evaluated proposals to improve the sector's regulatory and legal framework, and classified assets in priority sectors for privatization.[3] Forty SOEs were identified as suitable for privatization; 11 out of 13 SOEs within the 2017 pipeline were privatized.[4] In 2018, the government introduced significant restrictions on loans and state guarantees to SOEs and government financial institutions, and strengthened institutional arrangements and business processes for appraising and approving these loans and guarantees.[5]

Under Presidential Decree No. 2300, dated 5 September 2016, the government initiated the development of the critical elements of the SOE oversight and governance frameworks. These included procedures for evaluating the efficiency of SOEs, rules and standards for the corporate governance of SOEs, and rules for the performance-based remuneration of SOE managers.[6] Formalizing the SOE performance evaluation framework will enable oversight agencies to proactively inform the government of potential risks and to come up with targeted responses if problems arise.

---

[2]   Presidential Decree No. 2300, dated 5 September 2016; Resolutions of the Cabinet of Ministers No. 636s, dated 1 December 2016, and No. 534, dated 30 December 2016. On the Asian Development Bank's (ADB) support to SOE reforms in Azerbaijan, see ADB. 2017. *Report and Recommendation of the President to the Board of Directors: Proposed Programmatic Approach and Policy-Based Loan for Subprogram 1 to the Republic of Azerbaijan for the Improving Governance and Public Sector Efficiency Program.* Manila.

[3]   The database of large SOEs is at http://e-emdk.gov.az/idm/. The database information on about 22 large SOEs includes personnel records and financial and accounting indicators, including real estate information.

[4]   In line with the Presidential Decree No. 1003, dated 19 July 2016.

[5]   Presidential Decrees No. 424, dated 24 August 2018, and No. 410 dated 18 December 2018.

[6]   The decree envisaged the approval of these items within 4 months of the issuance of the decree.

The Law on Accounting was amended in May 2018 to require (i) SOEs to prepare their financial statements in accordance with International Financial Reporting Standards, (ii) SOE chief financial officers to be certified professional accountants,[7] and (iii) all state-owned legal entities, excluding educational and medical ones, to submit their financial statements with an auditor's opinion to the Ministry of Finance and Ministry of Taxation each year by 31 March. With just a few exceptions, the largest SOEs have started to publicly disclose their annual and consolidated financial reports, together with the audit opinion. These measures emphasize the government's determination to instill a strong corporate governance culture in SOEs and boost their performance.

Slow progress is being made on the privatization of SOEs, despite its prominence in the Strategic Road Map on the National Economy Perspective. From 2015 to 2017, proceeds from SOE privatizations were only AZN124.1 million ($72.8 million)—AZN104.9 million ($61.5 million) below projections (Table 5.1).

Table 5.1: SOE Privatization Revenue, 2015–2017
(manat million)

Item	2015	2016	2017
Expected revenue from privatization	29.0	100.0	100.0
Actual revenue from privatization	24.1	31.2	68.8
Fulfillment rate	83%	31%	69%

SOE = state-owned enterprise.
Source: Central Bank of Azerbaijan.

5.3   Overview of SOE Inefficiency

This chapter covers 14 SOEs that were chosen on the basis of the following criteria: (i) economic significance (share of a major sector, employment, and contribution to GDP); (ii) level of inefficiency (significant underperformance and capacity for improvement); and (iii) their strategic importance (potential impact on national security, trade, and systemic risks) (Table 5.2).

---

[7]   A professional accountant is a person who has successfully passed the Azerbaijan State Examination Center's exam, obtained a professional accountant certificate, and is a member of professional accounting organization.

Table 5.2: The 14 Assessed SOEs

State-Owned Enterprise	Sector	Economic Significance, Strategic Importance, Level of Inefficiency
Infrastructure state-owned enterprises		
State Oil Company of Azerbaijan Republic (SOCAR)	Oil and gas	SOCAR is of high economic significance given its importance for the country's export revenue, tax revenue, employment, and providing oil and gas for domestic consumption.
Azerenerji	Power generation and transmission	Monopoly power generator and transmission company, with the potential to financially underperform.
Azerishiq	Power distribution	Monopoly power distribution company.
Azerbaijan Airlines	Passenger and freight airline, airports, air fuel provision, and air navigation services	The national flag carrier does not make its financial information public.
Azerbaijan Railways	Railway transport	A vertically integrated SOE that owns all rail infrastructure and related assets, and is the only rail operator of both passenger and freight services. The company holds significant debt and received a government bailout in 2016 to restructure debt.
Azersu	Water supply and sanitation (except for Nakhchivan Autonomous Republic)	One of Azerbaijan's most vulnerable SOEs.
Baku Metropolitan	Underground rapid transit system in Baku	Receives significant subsidies from the state budget, which have increased over time.
State Agency of Azerbaijan Automobile Roads	National and regional roads	Has large levels of debt and receives budget support.[a]
Port of Baku	Ports	Strategic asset for trade in the region. Financial statements are not made public. Responsible for the Port of Alyat and Alyat Free Economic Zone.
Services state-owned enterprises		
Azercosmos	Satellite services	Strategic asset.
Azerpost	Postal services	Financial reports only available for 2009, 2015, and 2016.
Azerbaijan Caspian Shipping Company	Marine merchant fleet, shipyards, and offshore support	Strategic asset for trade in the region. Plays connecting role in the Transport Corridor Europe Caucasus Asia. Provides marine transportation of goods and passengers in the Caspian Sea, and offshore support services for oil and gas operations.

Continued on next page

Table 5.2 continued

Agrolizing	Agriculture machinery, cattle sale, and leasing finance	Sole provider of government-subsidized inputs and financing for operating equipment for the agriculture sector and one of Azerbaijan's most vulnerable SOEs.[b]
Government financial institutions		
International Bank of Azerbaijan	Banking	The country's largest bank defaulted in 2015 and received a bailout to restructure.

SOE = state-owned enterprise.
[a] Hashimova, K. and Z. Kadyrov. 2017. *The Current Situation and Problems of State-Owned Enterprises in Azerbaijan.* Baku: Center for Economic and Social Development.
[b] Under Presidential Decree No. 413, dated 19 December 2018, the sale of machinery and cattle to farmers was opened to other suppliers, and agricultural leasing finance will be done through authorized banks. The decree also envisaged the gradual privatization of Agrolizing's agrotechnical extension services.
Source: Authors.

Financial and performance analysis

Overall, there is no consensus on how to evaluate SOE performance: some studies focus on productivity and efficiency dimensions, while the others look at financial and profitability indicators. Taghizadeh-Hesary et al. (2019) show that solvency per employee costs and productivity have more deterministic power over the success or failure of SOEs than profitability.

Taking into account the limited availability of data, several financial and operational performance metrics were used for the financial analysis of the sample SOEs and to shed useful light on the challenges these firms face (Table 5.3).

Underperforming SOEs

This section briefly discusses the problems of Azerbaijan's five most underperforming SOEs: Azersu, Azerbaijan Railways, Azerenerji, Azerishiq, and International Bank of Azerbaijan. All have incurred large financial losses or faced significant challenges.

Only SOCAR and Azerbaijan Caspian Shipping of the 14 SOEs for which financial data were available during 2014–2016 made a profit. Azersu imposes the heaviest fiscal and financial burden of the 14. This overleveraged and highly inefficient SOE has a negative 170% return on equity. For Azersu to get a positive return on equity, it would need to massively increase its net operating cash flow through tariff increases and cost reductions.

Table 5.3: Financial Performance of SOEs

	SOCAR	International Bank of Azerbaijan	Azersu	Azerishig	Azerenerji	Baku Metropolitan	Azerbaijan Railways	Azerbaijan Caspian Shipping	Azercosmos	Azerpost	Azerbaijan Airlines	Agrolizing
ROE (%)	3.4	(33)	(170)	(0.16)	(63)	(2.3)	(59)	11.5	(82.7)	0	(65)	(5.4)
ROA (%)	1.67	0.1	(52)	(0.15)	(13.5)	(0.02)	(22.52)	9.7	(13.1)	(0.1)	(5.76)	(2.7)
EBITDA margin (%)	4.02		(32.7)	5.02	45	24	(66.8)	43	(40)	19.6	(7)	(12.36)
ICR	4.05			0.1	5.3	1.64	0.39	12.2		0.4		
Quick ratio	1.12				0.76				0.32	1.42		
Enterprise value to EBITDA	21.85			27.5	11.06			6.46		9.6	17.9	
Debt to capital (%)	66	93	100	42	73.5	31.8	69.8	10.47	84.5	41.4	94	52
Debt to EBITDA	15.17			11.49	8.01	5.96		1.26		2.3	10.8	
NPL (%)		8.51										
CET1 (%)		12.86										

( ) = negative, CET1 = common equity tier, EBITDA = earnings before interest, tax, depreciation, and amortization, EV = enterprise value, ICR = interest coverage ratio, NPL = nonperforming loan, ROA = return on assets, ROE = return on equity, SOCAR = State Oil Company of Azerbaijan Republic, SOE = state-owned enterprise.
Notes: Values reflect most recently available 3-year average of metrics in 2014–2016 or 2015–2017. Blank cells imply data unavailability or that the metric is not used for the state-owned enterprise.
Source: Authors' calculations.

Azerbaijan Railways' financial performance has been impaired by the lack of a supporting sector policy and institutional mechanisms, and only rising indebtedness has allowed the company to continue operations.[8] Since 2015, however, Azerbaijan Railways has been the first nonfinancial SOE to undergo comprehensive reforms to (i) strengthen governance, management, and financial autonomy, (ii) conduct an effective financial restructuring of its debt liabilities, (iii) improve financial management, internal controls, and reporting, and (iv) raise operational efficiency and undergo effective corporate restructuring (ADB 2017).[9] Given Azerbaijan Railways' strong commitment to reform, it is well positioned to become self-sufficient and profitable in the medium term. In the meantime, further government financial support may still be needed to overcome difficulties in managing its operations and for asset maintenance.

The two SOEs in power delivery, Azerenerji (electricity generation and transmission) and Azerishiq (electricity distribution), are working to improve governance and operations.[10] The power sector's profitability declined after the 2008 global financial crisis as the government reduced tariffs of essential services. Least-cost optimization remains a problem in the power sector, as are its aging assets that will require substantial capital outlays for them to be maintained or replaced. Indeed, a sizable proportion of Azerenerji's losses during 2014–2017 were incurred by impairment losses and the cost of replacing assets.

International Bank of Azerbaijan, in May 2017, ceased repayments on its foreign debt and filed for bankruptcy following the devaluations of the manat. Because of the bank's dominant position in the finance sector, its default adversely affected the country's financial stability. The bank had to restructure $3.3 billion of foreign debt ($2.3 billion was explicitly assumed by the government), and revise its policy on debt, liquidity, and investment management.

The restructuring resulted in the bank's debt being transferred to a special purpose vehicle, Aqrarkredit.[11] Its net short foreign currency position—despite

---

8   Azerbaijan Railways manages the country's railway network. It changed from being a government railway department to a government-owned, self-accounting closed joint stock company in 2009. Most of Azerbaijan Railways' revenue comes from freight; its passenger services lose money but are socially important.

9   The status of the implementation of railway sector and corporate reforms supported under this program can be seen at https://ady.az/ru/content/index/75/73. The Azerbaijan Railways' reform program includes piloting of new financing schemes with the government.

10   Both are open joint stock companies.

11   Most of the domestic sovereign guarantees, estimated at 14.6% of GDP at the end of 2018, are related to the purchase of the bank's toxic assets by Aqrarkredit.

a substantial decline—was still large at $0.9 billion (1.9% of GDP) at the end of 2018. The corporate governance reforms and financial restructuring, which included lowering funding and operational costs, and replacing problem loans with yielding liquid assets, enabled the bank to post net income of AZN426 million ($250 million) and a return on average assets of 3.5% in 2018. The government plans to eventually privatize International Bank of Azerbaijan, in which it holds more than 95% of shares.

Efficiency losses caused by SOE underperformance

This section looks at Azerbaijan SOEs in terms of efficiency losses to the economy, implying potential productivity gains that could result from a better performance of these firms.

The following four steps were taken to assess SOE performance on a portfolio basis against private sector benchmarks, and to quantify the efficiency loss of SOEs:

(i)   The emerging market private sector operator benchmarks were identified.[12] These were sourced from those identified by Aswath Damodaran, professor of finance at the Stern School of Business at New York University (NYU Stern), who used a return-on-equity decomposition by sector for emerging markets during 2010–2017.[13] The benchmarks are an aggregate of the pretax returns of private firms for a particular year in the review period.

(ii) The target pretax profits for SOEs were quantified on the basis of sector benchmarks obtained from step (i). For example, if the benchmark rate of return on equity is 8% and the SOE's equity is AZN100 ($58.6), then the SOE target pretax profit would be AZN8 ($4.7).

(iii) The difference between the benchmark-based (target) and actual SOE pretax profits is the efficiency loss. For example, if the target profit was AZN8 ($4.7) but the actual pretax profit was AZN4 ($2.33), the efficiency loss would be AZN4 ($2.35).

---

[12] Azerbaijan is categorized as an emerging market in the International Monetary Fund's 2018 *World Economic Outlook* report.

[13] For more information on the benchmarks, see http://www.stern.nyu.edu/~adamodar/pc/datasets/roeemerg. xls. Private sector operators are used as comparators to accurately reflect target equity returns (given that SOEs implement projects associated with risk), and because the SOEs should ideally be held to commercial performance standards. The government's cost of debt could be another potential, though lower, benchmark. Here, if the government injects equity in SOEs, the return on this equity must at least equal the cost of government borrowing. In 2018 and 2019, the government's borrowing cost in manats averaged 9.4% for 3-year bonds and 8.3% for 2-year bonds. Almost all SOEs in the sample would fail to meet this benchmark.

(iv) The potential efficiency losses were adjusted for foregone reinvestment gains. For example, had an SOE's performance reached a target level in 2010 and created additional value, the gain would be reinvested by the SOE or the government and earn cumulative returns on the investment until 2017. The summation of foregone reinvestment returns in each year in this period represents the aggregate efficiency loss incurred by the SOE to the economy.[14]

It is worth noting that losses because of underperforming SOEs are not merely because tariffs are not set to fully recover costs. These losses are also caused by poor corporate governance, inadequate financial management systems, and scant accountability of SOEs to shareholders. Combined, these factors create high levels of inefficiency independent of tariff levels.[15]

Applying the approach just described shows the high level of inefficiency in Azerbaijan's SOEs (Figure 5.6). In 2015 and 2016, this was equivalent to 7.64% and 3.65% of GDP, respectively. The average inefficiency during 2013–2017 was 4.2% of GDP. A large proportion of the efficiency losses in the water, transport, energy, and financial sectors occurred from asset impairment and foreign debt restructuring, poor asset maintenance, and inadequate operational performance and financial management.

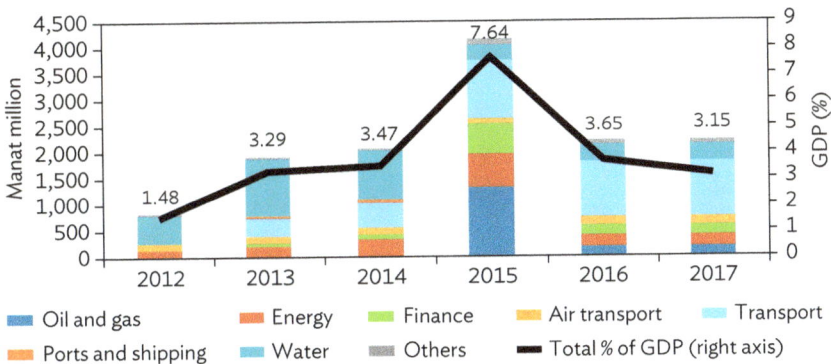

Figure 5.6: Inefficiency of SOEs by Sector

GDP = gross domestic product, SOE = state-owned enterprise.
Note: 2015 to 2017 are adjusted.
Source: Authors' calculations.

---

[14] The underperformance in 2015 and 2016 was adjusted downward by 100%—the approximate degree of devaluation of the manat from 2014 to 2016—to sterilize the devaluation's effect. It was also assumed that the SOE sector's performance in 2017 was consistent with that of 2016.

[15] If the inefficiency was only because of low tariffs, then making SOEs efficient by simply raising tariffs would result in an economic transfer; that is, the losses would be borne elsewhere without any net economic impact.

Many SOEs incur recurrent operational losses that are largely a result of ineffective policies and decisions at sector and national (cross-sector) levels. For various reasons, policy choices over the years have used SOEs as an instrument of specific economic and social policies.

The efficiency losses of underperforming SOEs are both allocative and dynamic in nature. Allocative efficiency losses are because SOE costs are too high (that is, the resources used by SOEs to produce services could be better used on more economically efficient production) or SOE revenue is too low (that is, revenue is less than the efficient cost of providing the service).[16] Another dimension of this economic loss has been the inefficient provision of implicit government subsidies to underperforming SOEs, because the costs of these subsidies were not known and the benefits were not quantified or appropriately targeted, resulting in below-cost prices for all users—in other words, a pure social policy instrument.[17]

5.4 Fiscal Implications of Underperforming SOEs

Impact on fiscal sustainability

Azerbaijan's poorly performing SOEs have a direct impact on fiscal sustainability and therefore negative consequences for the economy. Subsidies for SOEs have resulted in years of substantial fiscal losses and foregone spending. Table 5.4 shows the ways in which the performance of SOEs affects the government's fiscal position.

Table 5.4: Government's Fiscal Position and SOE Performance

Revenue	Expenditure
Dividend income from state-owned enterprises (SOEs)—requires profitability	Direct subsidies—underperforming SOEs require government support
Corporate tax revenue—SOEs account for 23% of total tax revenue	Explicit government debt guarantees on contingent liabilities—government must bear the cost if these liabilities materialize

Source: Authors.

---

[16] In both cases there is a loss of allocative efficiency: either underconsumption of services because the cost is too high or overconsumption because the price is too low. This leads to dead-weight losses. The dynamic allocative inefficiency is discussed in section 5.5.

[17] The government provides implicit subsidies through its foregone returns on equity and other support, including unpriced debt guarantees. Subsidies are only efficient if they are economically or socially justified; in other words, the economic benefits outweigh the economic detriment arising from a subsidy's distortion of pricing and consumption.

Profitable SOEs increase budget revenue through corporate taxes and dividend income paid to the government. On the expenditure side, the government bears the cost of providing budget support to loss-makers, and for subsidizing public services provided by SOEs. Provisions for explicit guarantees are also charged annually and the nonguaranteed debt of strategic SOEs can be a cost to the government if the collapse of a major state firm triggers an economic crisis.

If SOEs had been efficient in 2016 in terms of NYU Stern's emerging market private sector benchmarks, the corporate tax base would have been higher because of the increased taxable revenue from a profitable SOE sector.[18] Hypothetically, that could have enabled budget spending on education to have been 24% higher than it was, and 10% higher for health.

On the assumption that no tax credits are offset, it is possible to quantify the potential improvement in the budget position from higher taxes on SOEs. Table 5.5 shows the improved budget position arising only from increased corporate income tax revenue from the adjusted SOE profits (it means SOEs would have performed at benchmark).[19]

Table 5.5: Fiscal Impact of Improved SOE Performance
(manat million)

Budget Factor	2013	2014	2015	2016	2017
Revenue	19,496	18,400	17,498	17,505	16,516
Expenditure	19,143	18,709	17,784	17,751	17,538
Budget addition from corporate income taxation, assuming no offsetting tax credits	287	906	685	662	662
Gain as a percentage of GDP	0.49	1.54	1.26	1.10	0.94
Surplus/deficit	352	(308)	(286)	(245)	(1,021)
Adjusted budget surplus/deficit	640	599	399	416	(359)

( ) = negative, GDP = gross domestic product, SOE = state-owned enterprise.
Source: Authors' calculations.

The reliance of SOEs on government support reduces the benefits of oil revenue for future generations. This is because a sizable part of this revenue ends up being used, through the state budget, to cover the inefficiency losses of SOEs instead of being efficiently invested by SOFAZ.

---

[18] This would have been achieved by SOEs charging cost recovery tariffs and through better corporate governance to reduce inefficiencies.

[19] The corporate income tax rate is 20%. Other fiscal benefits that have not been quantified include dividend revenue, lower provisioning for contingent liabilities, and lower levels of subsidization of SOE activity.

The financing needs of Azerbaijan's SOEs are high. Loss-making state firms receive heavy government support to maintain and upgrade their assets. The periodic ex post outright fiscal outlays that become necessary to keep SOEs afloat are mostly provided in incentive- and performance-incompatible ways (that is, not in an ex ante defined or contractualized way, as is the case with public service obligations). This perpetuates corporate management decisions that are inefficient and cause fiscal risks.

Because several SOEs operate in strategic sectors, the government recognizes their special financial needs and provides budget support when adverse events occur. For example, when International Bank of Azerbaijan defaulted on its nonguaranteed bonds, the government had to intervene and move the bank's bad debts off its balance sheet. Although this debt was not guaranteed, the prospect of the country's largest bank defaulting was not an option for the government. The point here is to avoid creating an environment where SOEs can accumulate debt with little incentive to improve performance and assume that the government will come in with a bailout; in this case, by guaranteeing nonguaranteed debt.

Figure 5.7 shows how big a drain SOEs were on government resources in 2016 and 2017 in terms of budget support for these firms, which accounted for just over 12% of budget spending in 2016.

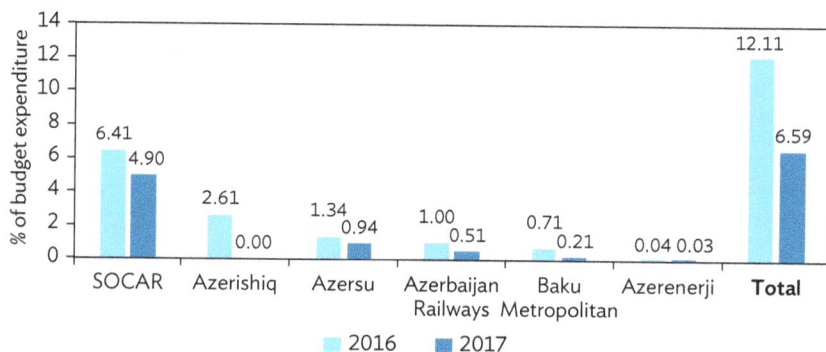

Figure 5.7: Support for SOEs as a Proportion of Budget Expenditure, 2016 and 2017

SOCAR = State Oil Company of Azerbaijan Republic, SOE = state-owned enterprise.
Source: Central Bank of Azerbaijan.

Fiscal risk from contingent liabilities and related-party risk

The reliance of the country's largest SOEs on budget support and the effects of their excessive debt is exacerbated by SOEs having numerous activities with related parties. This related-party risk implies, for example, that failures in the water sector can affect payments to energy distribution providers, creating large payables to generation providers. Table 5.6 shows the payables of several SOEs in 2016 and 2017.

Table 5.6: Related-Party Payables of SOEs, 2016–2017
(manat million)

State-Owned Enterprise	2016	2017
Azerenerji	3,426	2,417
Azerishiq	541	236
Baku Metropolitan	35	24
Azersu	889	903
Azerbaijan Railways	732	0

SOE = state-owned enterprise.
Source: Central Bank of Azerbaijan.

Fiscal risk assessment

The government's financial support for continually underperforming SOEs creates explicit and implicit risks to its fiscal position. Many of the SOEs assessed in this chapter are natural monopolies in their sectors and can be regarded as systemic because of the essential economic services they provide. Azersu is a case in point: it makes a loss and is kept afloat by the government.

Table 5.7 assesses the fiscal risk of the main SOE sectors. It looks at the risks from several angles, including (i) degree of guaranteed debt (the explicit level of debt the government is required to cover in the event of a default), and other obligations and liabilities,[20] (ii) foreign exchange exposure (the level of the sector's exposure to exchange rate fluctuations), (iii) financial performance (whether the sector is profitable), and (iv) debt serviceability (whether operating cash flows are sufficient to cover interest repayments). The fiscal risk profiles of transport sector SOEs and government financial institutions are in special need of attention because of their high level of contingent liabilities and risks related to financial performance and debt serviceability.

---

[20] According to the Ministry of Finance, the guaranteed debt obligations and commitments of SOEs in 2016 were 5.16% of GDP in oil and gas sector, 17.6% in government financial institutions, 1.16% in transport, 2.8% in air transportation, 0% in ports and shipping, 0.77% in communication, 3.11% in energy, 0.26% in water supply, and 0.04% in other sectors.

Table 5.7: Fiscal Risk Assessment of SOE Sectors, 2016

Sector	Guaranteed Debt; Obligations and Liabilities to GDP (2016 % GDP)	Foreign Exchange Exposure	Financial Performance	Debt Serviceability
Oil and gas	58.42	High exposure to foreign exchange in short-term positions	Low risk (positive operating returns)	Low risk due to high operating cash flows in relation to service debt
Government financial institutions	23.23	High exposure to foreign exchange, but trend is declining	Moderate risk (positive operating returns)	Moderate risk
Transport	10.52	High exposure to foreign exchange (Azerbaijan Railways)	High risk (financial losses)	High risk
Air transport	3.94	Low exposure (exposure of 5% or less)	High risk	High risk
Ports and shipping	0.16	Low exposure	Low risk	Low risk
Communications	1.31	Low exposure	Moderate risk (operating losses of Azercosmos, break-even of Azerpost)	Low risk
Power	6.38	Moderate exposure	Moderate risk (Azerenerji operational losses, Azerishiq break-even)	Moderate risk
Water	1.61	Low exposure	High risk (Azersu financial losses)	High risk
Others	0.65	Low exposure	Low risk	Low risk

GDP = gross domestic product, SOE = state-owned enterprise.
Source: Authors' calculations.

The underperformance of SOEs also creates a fiscal risk to the government through the balance sheet of state banks' loan defaults, which reduce the assets of these banks and, consequently, government's equity position in them. It is necessary to review the loans issued to state-owned institutions, including the loans received with state guarantee. In this respect, a Commission was established to ensure fiscal sustainability in financial and economic activities in large state-owned institutions, to further strengthen forecasting of revenues and expenditures, and monitoring its execution, as well as to improve governance in this area and to enhance transparency (through Order #534, dated 30 December 2016). The Commission keeps the activities under its control. It should be noted that 81% of loans in Azerbaijan are made by these banks. SOEs hold 16% of all loans in the financial system. The power, water, air transport, and rail sectors are particularly risky for state banks given their financial underperformance.

5.5   Impact of the Performance of SOEs on the Economy

This section examines how the performance of Azerbaijan's SOEs affects the economy. It finds substantial potential output losses because of the underperformance of the largest SOEs that are dominant in the provision of public infrastructure and infrastructure services.[21] The associated dynamic efficiency losses caused by this underperformance imply the economy has foregone GDP growth.

Figure 5.8 shows the potential GDP gain from public investment funded by SOE profits at benchmark levels using the International Monetary Fund's approach for quantifying growth from public investment.[22] The figure shows the differential in actual year-on-year GDP growth and potential GDP growth with efficient SOEs. It shows that economic growth would have likely risen had SOEs invested efficiently and obtained benchmark returns, and then reinvested this capital in public infrastructure.[23]

To calculate the potential GDP gain from public investment funded by SOE profits, this analysis assumes that all potential revenue from an efficiently functioning SOE sector—that is, taxes from SOEs—are fully spent on public infrastructure investments (by SOEs themselves or the government). The analysis also assumes that increases in investment spending equivalent to 1% of GDP in a particular year would increase growth by about 0.75% in that year. Take 2013, if SOE losses for that year of AZN1.9 billion ($1.1 billion)—3.3% of

---

[21]   Improving power, transport, communication, and water supply and sanitation infrastructure spurs economic output. The direct effect of improved infrastructure is raising the productivity of land, labor, and other physical capital.

[22]   The International Monetary Fund (IMF) offers an approach to quantify the dynamic efficiency impacts of public investment. Here, an increase in public infrastructure investment affects output both in the short term (by boosting aggregate demand through the fiscal multiplier and potentially crowding in private investment) and in the long term (by expanding the productive capacity of the economy with a higher infrastructure stock). IMF. 2014. Is It Time for an Infrastructure Push? The Macroeconomic Effects of Public Investment. Chapter 3 in World Economic Outlook: Legacies, Clouds, Uncertainties. Washington, DC.

[23]   It is assumed that had SOEs performed at benchmark levels and returned their costs of capital, these returns could have been reinvested in public infrastructure. This does not imply that all returns should necessarily be reinvested in infrastructure (by the government or SOEs). Some returns could, for example, be used by the government to invest in public health services.

Figure 5.8: Actual versus Potential Gross Domestic Product Gain from SOE Performance, 2012–2017

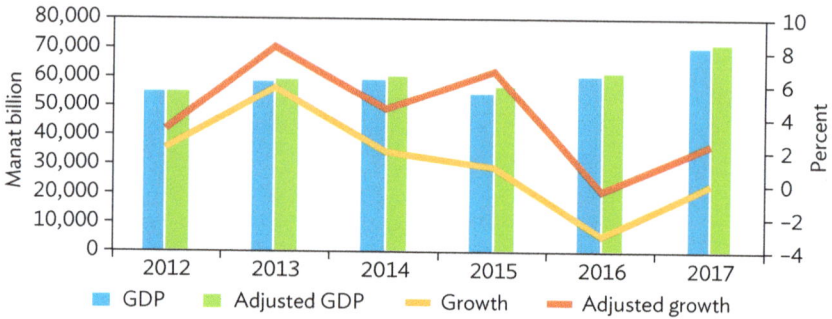

GDP = gross domestic product, SOE = state-owned enterprise.
Notes: The GDP gain was revised downward by 100% in 2014, 2015, and 2016 (approximate manat devaluation in this period) to sterilize the impact of devaluation. For 2017, because of data limitations, the performance of SOEs was assumed to be the same as in 2016.
Source: Authors.

GDP—had been fully reinvested, GDP would have been 2.5% higher than it was (that is, an adjusted growth of 8.3% compared with unadjusted growth of 5.8%).

This shows that a more profitable SOE sector could help create an economy that is more resilient to economic shocks, given the difference in the 2013 GDP position and an even larger difference in 2015. And had SOE profits been at benchmark levels within the sector, the burden on SOFAZ to transfer oil revenue to the national budget to fund government spending would have been reduced.

Benefits of improved SOE efficiency

Raising the efficiency of SOEs will be important for raising the low productivity of the non-oil private sector, to which SOEs provide inputs and services.[24] On the fiscal side, improving the efficiency of SOEs would (i) facilitate the privatization of financially viable SOEs (SOEs that perform at benchmark levels could be privatized, thereby increasing the sources of budget revenue); (ii) improve the government's budget position (increased corporate tax revenue and a broader tax base would reduce the budget deficit); and (iii) lessen the need to provide debt guarantees for SOEs (state firms will require less secured debt from the government). Ensuring that SOEs perform at benchmark levels and are self-sufficient will help the government to adhere

---

[24] For example, productivity in Azerbaijan's agriculture sector is reported to be about three times lower than in Turkey and about six times lower than in Poland.

to the fiscal rule, adopted in July 2018, mandating that transfers of oil revenue to the state budget are rules-based. It could also open additional fiscal space for social sectors and agriculture.

Corporate governance

Azerbaijan's SOEs largely do not meet the benchmarks of the 2015 Organisation for Economic Co-operation and Development's (OECD) Guidelines on Corporate Governance of State-Owned Enterprises (OECD 2015). The guidelines are widely used as an international benchmark to help governments align the management and regulation of their SOEs with standards used in the private sector. The guidelines take into consideration the special nature of SOEs as instruments of public and social policy. But they also emphasize that SOEs should operate in an environment that closely resembles the private sector. The OECD guidelines cover (i) legal and regulatory frameworks, (ii) the state acting as an owner, (iii) the equitable treatment of shareholders, (iv) relations with stakeholders, (v) transparency and disclosure of company information, and (vi) the responsibilities of SOE boards.[25]

Although the government formulated general corporate governance standards in 2011, its provisions are not legally binding and are voluntary. Currently, there are no corporate governance standards that nonfinancial SOEs would be required to comply with and to report on their adherence to these standards. Neither is there an explicit SOE policy that—supported by legal and regulatory frameworks—would enable SOEs to operate as businesses in a market environment.

Gaps in governance practices

Benchmarking Azerbaijan's SOEs against the OECD guidelines revealed that 73% are nonconforming, 25% are partially conforming, and only 2% are fully conforming (that is, they apply the corporate governance principles recommended by the OECD). Among the shortcomings are a lack of clear reporting and monitoring on SOE performance between state firms and supervisory public bodies. These lines tend to be fragmented and are often unclear, leading to some public sector agencies and institutions raising concerns over possible risks and weaknesses emanating from SOEs. Some SOEs do not publicly disclose their annual financial reports, despite a legal requirement to do so. And when financial information is disclosed, it is often limited.

---

[25] State banks are mandated to adhere to standards of corporate governance in banks which is based on international practice.

Many SOEs do not disclose annual external auditor reports—and in some instances the independence of external auditors may be questionable. This has allowed many SOEs to conceal substantial performance weaknesses that pose serious fiscal risks to the state budget. These reports, when they do exist, are often outdated in that they are released long after the audit period covered in the report.[26] Table 5.8 shows the lack of independent externally audited financial reports for 2016 for several SOEs.

Table 5.8: Availability of Externally Audited Reports, 2016

Nonfinance Sector	
State Oil Company of Azerbaijan Republic, closed joint stock company	✓
Azerenerji, open joint stock company	✓
Azerbaijan Airlines, closed joint stock company	X
Azerbaijan Railways, closed joint stock company	X
Azersu, open joint stock company	✓
Azerishiq, open joint stock company	X
Azerbaijan Caspian Shipping, closed joint stock company	✓
Baku Metropolitan, closed joint stock company	X
Port of Baku, closed joint stock company	X
Finance Sector	
International Bank of Azerbaijan, open joint stock company	✓
Azer Turk Bank, open joint stock company	✓
Aqrarkredit, closed joint stock company	X

Note: ✓ = latest independent auditor's full financial report is publicly available; X = latest independent auditor's full financial report is publicly available only in part or is not publicly available.
Sources: Company financial reports available online as of March 2018.

A lack of public ownership policies; fragmented management and oversight

Azerbaijan has no legislation that provides a rationale for setting up SOEs and their objectives. This ambiguity creates unclear and sometimes conflicting mandates for SOEs—to achieve loss-making public policy goals while operating commercially, for example.[27]

---

[26] In addition to 2016, audit reports of Azerpocht LLC for 2017 and 2018 were also published on their official website.

[27] There are SOEs in the form of a public legal entity. These are nonstate or nonmunicipal organizations set up on behalf of the state or municipality, or by a public legal entity, to engage in activities of national and public significance. Public legal entities have their own charter, property and equity capital formed by property contributed to them by their founders. Public legal entities may engage in commercial activities provided they comply with the goals established within their charters. Neither the state nor municipalities are responsible for the obligations of these entities, and shareholders are only liable for their contributed capital. Article 5.4 of the Law on Public Legal Entities No. 97-VQ, dated 29 December 2015, stipulates that these entities cannot be declared insolvent.

No public ownership policy distinguishes the state's function as owner, manager, policy maker, financier, and sector regulator. But the separation of these functions is necessary to ensure that SOEs can make independent decisions that are free from state interference. Having a state ownership policy would help the government determine why, when, and how the state should own assets, and provide the justification for whether an SOE should remain in government hands or be privatized. Under current conditions, public ownership functions are scattered across several government agencies that lack clear coordination channels. The responsibility for SOE oversight, and implementing and enforcing legislated SOE reforms, is also spread across several government agencies (Table 5.9).

Table 5.9: Institutions Responsible for SOE Oversight and Management

Agency	Responsibility
Line ministries	Appointments of CEOs, strategy setting
State Committee on Property Issues	Asset management, data collection, privatization
Ministry of Economy	Performance monitoring, monitoring the implementation of action plans
Ministry of Finance (Treasury)	Use of budget funds, financial statements
Ministry of Finance (Public Debt Management Agency)	Guarantees and guaranteed debt monitoring
Chamber of Accounts	Periodic checks of SOEs
Cabinet of Ministers	Budget approvals, appointments
President's Office	Appointments
Special Commission on Large SOEs	Income and expenditure monitoring of the 20 largest SOEs

CEO = chief executive officer, SOE = state-owned enterprise.
Source: Authors.

This fragmentation does not allow for the comprehensive oversight and monitoring of SOE functions, which are often duplicated, thereby reducing their accountability. No central authority is responsible for evaluating the performance standards of SOEs, oversight of financial risk, and ensuring that SOEs that break the standards are made accountable.[28]

Weak board governance and accountability

Another shortcoming that emerged from benchmarking Azerbaijan's SOEs against the OECD's guidelines is the lack of transparent rules for the composition of independent board members, their qualification requirements,

---

[28] For this and the following section, it is necessary to take exception to state banks, Azerpocht LLC and Agrarkredit CJSC.

nomination, appointment, and remuneration; and criteria for dismissal.[29] Although it is natural for governments to participate in the selection of SOE board members, they should not intervene in daily management. In Azerbaijan, it is common for SOEs to follow unclear procedures for appointing members and determining remuneration, which often means board autonomy may not be guaranteed.

While multiple entities monitor and collect different data on SOE performance, no one agency is responsible for centralizing this information; reporting on financial risks being faced, including sector ones; and ensuring noncompliant SOEs disclose all required information. Without this centralized function, there is a risk that the government is prevented from having a clear picture of the real contribution and fiscal risks emanating from SOEs.

International lessons from best practices

This section looks briefly at SOE reforms in five countries: Australia, Georgia, Indonesia, Lithuania, and Malaysia. All of them have taken steps to improve the performance of their SOEs and, in most cases, introduced regulatory practices in line with OECD guidelines.

Australia's experience shows how developing a comprehensive policy framework for SOEs can advance the professionalization of the state as a corporate owner. The Australian Commercial Policy Framework defines procedures for shareholder oversight, corporate governance, financial management, capital planning, debt management, internal controls, and risk management. Setting up a similar framework could help Azerbaijan establish a comprehensive system when applying private sector practices and incentives to SOEs.

Georgia's experience is useful for how it handled fiscal transparency reforms. In the 2015 state budget, the government disclosed and analyzed the country's fiscal risks by publishing fiscal risk statements that included risks emanating from SOEs. Both the budget and the fiscal risk statements disclosed transfers between the government and SOEs. The information included all direct transfers to SOEs, such as subsidies, equity injections, loans, and contingent exposures associated with nondebt guarantees.

---

[29] In many instances, the interpretation of the OECD's benchmarks on SOE corporate governance needs to be seen in the wider country context given the political, social, institutional, and even cultural dimensions, as well as the time needed for certain concepts to establish themselves. For example, an effective institutionalization of the SOE supervisory board concept requires time to facilitate changes in the corporate culture of SOEs and governance in general to ensure that important and often influential stakeholders (SOE management, for example) are convinced about the value addition of supervisory boards.

Lithuania's experience in reforming its state-owned railway company offers useful lessons for Azerbaijan Railways on structural and management changes to improve efficiency and performance. Lithuania's railway reforms emphasized good corporate governance and a commercial orientation. As a result of these reforms, Lithuanian Railways' revenue rose by 93% from 2001 to 2009.

Malaysia is an example of how to use key performance indicators for SOE operations and linking the performance of state firms to management remuneration. Malaysia instilled a performance-based management culture that is reflected in higher profits. From 2004 to 2014, the 20 largest Malaysian SOEs operating overseas tripled their market capitalization.

Indonesia's experience offers a particularly useful lesson for Azerbaijan. Indonesia's SOEs are compensated for unprofitable activities, and below-cost tariffs mandated by law to deliver public services. PT Perusahaan Listrik Negara, an SOE that has a monopoly on electricity generation, transmission, and distribution, is compensated in this ex ante contractualized way. The government informs the firm on the level of compensation it will receive to offset the impact of below-cost tariffs so that it can operate with a high degree of commercial and investment certainty.

5.6   Conclusions and Policy Recommendations

The government has taken important measures to increase the efficiency and accountability of its SOEs to help transform the sector from being a drag on public resources to an engine of economic growth and diversification. Initial progress is being made, but more needs to be done to close the SOE sector's many regulatory, institutional, and operational gaps.

Over the short term, it will be important to sustain the reforms initiated in 2017 to improve the financial oversight and transparency of SOEs through the adoption and effective rollout of the SOE corporate governance rules and standards, by conducting regular SOE performance monitoring and reporting, and implementing efficiency-enhancing sector-specific reforms.

Addressing SOE issues requires comprehensive, well-sequenced, and coordinated reforms at the macro, sector, and SOE levels. These reforms are inherently complex and are sensitive issues for the government, SOEs, and other stakeholders. The following is a four-step reform approach for the government to consider over the medium term that builds on the ongoing reforms. This approach was developed with the specific challenges that Azerbaijan's SOEs face in mind, as well as drawing on the applicable experiences of SOE reforms in other countries.[30] Each step is a building block for the next step.

First step: Define a clear state ownership policy

The government needs to define and formally document a clear ownership policy for SOEs that demarcates the commercial (asset management, operations, service delivery) and noncommercial functions (policy, regulatory, social) of all public corporations, including SOEs that are fully or partially owned or controlled by the government.

Noncommercial functions should either be vested in separate bodies to ensure the commercial performance of SOEs can be assessed or, if they remain the responsibility of SOEs, they should be appropriately compensated through transparent subsidies. Doing this will avoid distorting commercial performance. Formulating a clear ownership policy for SOEs will ensure that services or projects delivered via SOEs at below-cost recovery levels require either direct subsidies, credit enhancement, or capital injections.

Second step: Align SOEs' legal and regulatory frameworks with the state ownership policy

All existing and proposed legislation and governance arrangements for SOEs should be reviewed to ensure they are consistent with the state ownership policy. Any revisions of the legislation and governance arrangements for SOEs should provide a clear governance framework for the performance of SOEs. This will bring consistency and certainty to the application of good corporate governance standards, and the framework can be the mechanism to ensure the state ownership policy is implemented. The provisions should set up a structure for the division of roles and responsibilities of SOEs and their ownership and oversight agencies, and this should be applicable to all state firms.

This should be coupled with actions to professionalize SOE boards to strengthen the new governance framework. SOE boards lack decision-making autonomy and clearly established functions and responsibilities. In addition, their expertise may not be relevant to the sector in which the SOE they represent operates (as in the case of politically appointed boards).

---

[30] On the global experience in reforming SOEs, see ADB, Independent Evaluation Department. 2018. *State-Owned Enterprise Engagement and Reform*. Thematic evaluation. Manila. pp. 10–13.

Professionalizing SOE boards will also require independent regulators to take on the policy-making and regulatory functions that are currently undertaken by SOEs. The role of independent regulators will be to ensure a fair operating environment for SOEs in which they are appropriately compensated where prices are set by the government. For example, the Tariff Council sets electricity prices below the efficient costs of supplying electricity to users. Independent regulators can have a positive impact on the commercial performance of SOEs in the network industries, including water, electricity, gas, and transport.

Third step: Set up a commercial performance and monitoring framework

After the government has defined and separated the regulatory and policy functions that govern SOEs, it will be necessary to set up a commercial performance and monitoring framework that helps SOEs operate as efficient businesses. This framework should establish the principles for how SOEs plan and coordinate with the government to set short- and medium-term targets and performance indicators, such as target rates of return or credit ratings. The framework would also determine how SOE boards report the performance against these targets to shareholders.

Setting up a commercial performance and monitoring framework would help impose financial discipline on Azerbaijan's SOEs and create incentives through performance-based remuneration to promote commercial practices and outcomes comparable to the private sector. To improve the monitoring of the risks that SOEs face and to flag fiscal risks, an operational and institutional framework should also be set up that regulates how the government— through the Ministry of Finance, the Ministry of Economy, or other oversight body— would monitor and deal with underperforming SOEs, and disclose fiscal risks.

In developing the operational framework, the government should require SOEs to formulate comprehensive annual business plans and medium-term projections that are approved by the Ministry of Finance. It is important that SOEs are credit rated to better gauge their financial sustainability and help focus the attention of their managements on project sustainability. Capital investment plans can provide further detail and context on the performance indicators and targets. SOEs, in their investment plans, should provide details of their long-term capital investment plans and how they will be implemented.

The government should ensure there are performance incentives for senior SOE management and ensure management is accountable to shareholders. The global practice is to incentivize board members and senior management by linking performance to remuneration. For senior management, this should be based on well-defined financial and nonfinancial indicators that are agreed on in an SOE's business plan.

As SOEs start publicly disclosing their performance against agreed benchmarks and are accountable to shareholders if they fail to meet them, the Ministry of Finance should report on the impacts to the government's financial position. For large SOEs, it is recommended that the Cabinet of Ministers, after the Ministry of Finance has approved business and investment plans, monitors the performance of SOEs against their performance indicators and targets, and report on this to the presidential administration and the public.

The Ministry of Finance should oversee the reporting and monitoring functions related to the fiscal risk of SOEs. The ministry should issue periodic risk reports that evaluate the impact of underperforming SOEs on the fiscal position and provision funds for these risks. The reporting of public debt should include nonguaranteed SOE debt and SOE debt that is guaranteed but not provisioned in the state budget. Doing this will enable government decision-makers to be timely informed on the size of debt and its associated risks.

For SOEs operating in economic sectors with regulated tariffs (power, water, transport), an independent regulator should be given the authority to ensure that in addition to earning regulated profits, SOEs across economic sectors are monitored and held accountable for service quality.

Line ministries should use project pipelines and screening procedures consistent with commercial performance and the monitoring framework to ensure service and quality. That is, when line ministries allocate projects to SOEs, they need to evaluate whether these projects are consistent with the screening frameworks and commercial practices so that SOEs can internally finance projects and be repaid by project revenue. If projects are inconsistent with commercial practices, the government must compensate SOEs for providing public services at below cost.

Fourth step: Preparing state assets for greater private sector participation

When the circumstances are right, the government should consider selectively divesting SOEs and attracting private sector participation to deliver SOE investments or services through public–private partnerships (PPPs). The prerequisites for doing both will be setting up effective legal, institutional, and regulatory frameworks for promoting competition and regulating public utilities.

The privatization of SOEs should be guided by a well-designed strategy that (i) creates an overall privatization plan setting out the SOEs and types of assets that could be considered for divestment; (ii) categorizes SOE assets into nonstrategic and strategic assets (divesting the noncore functions of SOEs would be a less controversial start); and (iii) develops a comprehensive strategy for each strategic asset (nonstrategic assets could be divested quickly on the basis of the assets that would fetch the most from a sale; strategic assets would require a well-considered evaluation making the case for their possible privatization).

Another option is to attract private sector participation in SOE projects through PPPs. A private partner can help the government achieve better value for money and more efficient management of public infrastructure and services. Because Azerbaijan does not have a comprehensive legislative framework for PPPs, it should try to learn from the experience in these partnerships of other countries in the region and advanced economies with well-defined PPP frameworks.

The government needs to define an optimal institutional framework for PPPs and formulate a PPP strategy by identifying priority sectors, geographical areas, modalities, and government support mechanisms for PPPs, among other things. Having a sound PPP strategy has helped many other governments advance their national development programs at a lower cost to the public and with higher efficiency.

Although PPPs differ from full divestment through privatization, good corporate governance is essential for both modalities to attract private investors. By improving the governance of SOEs, and implementing better contingent liability management processes, the government will be able to better protect state assets and enhance their performance, and ensure higher valuations.

In the short term at least, private investors are unlikely to be attracted to many of the SOEs covered in this chapter. The government needs to acquire the capability and capacity to privatize SOEs. Factors that appear to be contributing to the "unattractiveness" of Azerbaijan's SOEs from an investment perspective include years of underinvestment, dependence on government subsidies (or on below-market rates for goods and services from other SOEs), the limited control that SOEs have had on their own financial health, weak corporate governance, a lack of commercial orientation, and ad hoc tariff-setting.

Because of these impediments, the privatization of SOEs should only proceed once the four recommended steps have been taken. SOEs operating within well-defined commercial frameworks and regulatory structures will reduce the risk of anticompetitive behavior with private ownership.

References

ADB (Asian Development Bank). 2017. *Report and Recommendation of the President to the Board of Directors: Proposed Programmatic Approach and Policy-Based Loan for Subprogram 1 to the Republic of Azerbaijan for the Improving Governance and Public Sector Efficiency Program*. Manila.

_____. Independent Evaluation Department. 2018. *State-Owned Enterprise Engagement and Reform*. Thematic evaluation. Manila.

Hashimova, K. and Z. Kadyrov. 2017. *The Current Situation and Problems of State-Owned Enterprises in Azerbaijan*. Baku: Center for Economic and Social Development. http://cesd.az/new/wp-content/uploads/2017/12/State-Owned-Enterprises-Azerbaijan.pdf.

IMF (International Monetary Fund). 2014. Is It Time for an Infrastructure Push? The Macroeconomic Effects of Public Investment. Chapter 3 in *World Economic Outlook: Legacies, Clouds, Uncertainties*. Washington, DC.

Khazar University, Eurasia Extractive Industries. 2018. *State-Owned Oil Company Case Studies: SOCAR*. Baku. http://eurasiahub.khazar.org/pdf/EN_SOCAR.pdf.

OECD (Organisation for Economic Co-operation and Development). 2015. *OECD Guidelines for Corporate Governance of State-Owned Enterprises*. Paris.

Taghizadeh-Hesary, F., N. Yoshino, C. J. Kim, and A. Mortha. 2019. A Comprehensive Evaluation Framework on the Economic Performance of State-Owned Enterprises. *ADBI Working Paper*. No. 949. Tokyo: Asian Development Bank Institute.

World Bank. 2017. *Republic of Azerbaijan: Corporate Governance and Ownership of State-Owned Enterprises*. Technical Note. November 2017. Washington, DC. http://documents.worldbank.org/curated/en/741211532553730650/pdf/AUS0000257-Ajarb-PUBLIC-2018-JUNE-AZE-Final-Technical-Note-AZ-SOEs-FINAL.pdf.

CHAPTER 6

Concluding Remarks

The fall in international oil prices in 2014 from which Azerbaijan is staging a modest recovery put the country's vulnerability to external shocks and its lack of economic diversification into a harsh light. The government's Strategic Road Maps on the National Economy Perspective and Main Sectors of the Economy (Strategic Road Maps), launched in 2016 to tackle these and other economic and development challenges, is in the process of being implemented. Importantly, the Strategic Road Maps recognize the private sector as the "engine for economic development."

This Country Diagnostic Study aims to contribute to achieving the objectives of the Strategic Road Maps by examining the most binding constraints to achieving sustained and diversified economic growth, and the areas that should be prioritized to advance the government's reform efforts. The study does this by using growth diagnostics and a detailed analysis of the identified constraints in the broad economy (Chapter 2) human capital (Chapter 3) and infrastructure (Chapter 4) sectors, and for state-owned enterprises (SOEs) (Chapter 5).

The findings on the growth diagnostics in Chapter 2 point to macroeconomic risks and high finance costs as the main short-term binding constraints. Both resulted from the dependence on oil exports and the heavy use of oil revenues that have made the country highly vulnerable to external shocks. High finance costs—a binding constraint caused by low domestic savings and lack of availability to local and foreign finance—are a massive barrier to affordable credit. The infrastructure stock and market failures are the main medium-term binding constraints. Although Azerbaijan has generally good infrastructure compared with some other countries in the region, there are many gaps, which, unless narrowed, will impede efforts to diversify the economy. Azerbaijan's range of exports shows a low level of sophistication, and poor market coordination is hindering industrial development. A low level of human capital that has led to skills mismatches in the labor market is the main long-term binding constraint.

The findings on education and skills development in Chapter 3 are important because youth will remain a large segment of the population in the coming years. Even though Azerbaijan has a high literacy rate, its preschool and vocational education and training enrollment rates—and public spending on the latter—are low compared with some other similar countries in the region. Low job creation and labor productivity in non-oil sectors are causing young professional Azerbaijanis to seek work outside of the country. Most of the working-age population is either in informal employment or lack the skills to properly do the type of work they are engaged in. The country's education institutions have tried but failed to respond to the skills mismatch, and the links between education policies, education and training institutions, and the private sector are weak.

Chapter 4 showed that Azerbaijan has made significant investments in infrastructure development since independence. The country is developing north–south and east–west transport corridors, and oil and gas pipelines, to take advantage of its potential as a regional hub and to provide a critical mass of basic public infrastructure. It is important that the infrastructure plan is set within the medium-term fiscal framework and state investment program needs to support economic diversification. Stronger public investment management systems are needed to help the government invest more efficiently and smartly in infrastructure. Tariff and institutional reforms are needed for public utilities to improve services and maintain infrastructure assets. Involving the private sector in infrastructure sectors, such as railways and electricity, would help improve the efficiency of infrastructure services and the performance of SOEs.

The findings on Azerbaijan's SOEs in Chapter 5 draw attention to the sector's inefficiencies—a worry given the size of its contribution to gross domestic product (45% during 2014–2016). During 2013–2017, the level of SOE inefficiency (revenue loss) was equivalent to wasting 4.2% GDP. Azerbaijan Railways, Azersu, International Bank of Azerbaijan and Azerenerji contributed heavily to the sector's poor performance. The 12% in government spending that was used to support underperforming SOEs in 2016 could have been redirected to social services and education. Moral hazard among Azerbaijan's SOEs will continue to be pervasive for as long as they are permitted to accumulate debt and assume an implicit guarantee on nonguaranteed debt by the government. The reporting standards of the country's SOEs do not come close to international standards, and this is concealing the true state of the financial health of many SOEs and posing serious risks to the state budget.

The findings on the education, infrastructure, and SOE sectors all point toward the central recommendation of this Country Diagnostic Study—the government must press on with its reform strategy and ensure that it is aligned with the Strategic Road Maps. The findings support a reform strategy that pursues economic diversification beyond oil to augment Azerbaijan's growth potential. Maintaining the policy space to fine-tune reforms as needed to help the economy diversify is essential. For example, policy space is needed to identify a sustainable level of the Strategic Road Maps' planned restrictions on transfers from the State Oil Fund of Azerbaijan Republic and the state budget to better protect public spending and economic growth from oil price fluctuations—the maps' Golden Rule. At the time of writing, the policy space to do this had not been created. Since fund transfers comprise a significant share of the state budget, a sustainable level needs to be determined to operationalize the Strategic Road Maps. Policy space is also needed to refine and improve approaches to the target of human capital development in the Strategic Roads Maps. For example, while skills development and labor productivity targets are key objectives in the Strategic Road Map on Vocational Education and Training, and also embedded in the other sector road maps, the overarching strategy to link education to jobs remains weak.

A transparent approach to the reform process will be crucial to its success. For example, the government's large-scale restructuring of financial markets as a response to the economic downturn resulted in several specialized institutions being set up that need to achieve a wide spread of interconnected targets. Achieving these targets will require extensive coordination and information exchanges across all concerned institutions, and consideration of the mandates of others.

Economic diversification into non-oil sources of growth should be *part* of Azerbaijan's reform agenda but not its *core*. Policy makers need to prioritize interventions that tackle macroeconomic risks and the high cost of finance. Small- and large-scale reforms are needed to augment infrastructure and human capital—the fundamental building blocks of economic development. Poorly performing SOEs need to be made more efficient, and a better climate for doing business is needed to promote entrepreneurship.

Beyond these critical areas, frameworks need to be created that provide strategic directions for reforms. Policies on infrastructure development, state ownership, and market development still need to be formulated. Planning and coordination among a large number of institutions is important to advance the reform agenda. The objective, regular, and transparent measurement of successes—and failures—in the reform process is vital for policy maneuvering. Ensuring that Azerbaijan undergoes a sustainable economic transformation should be at the forefront of the government's reform agenda.

Identifying Azerbaijan's binding constraints in the short, medium, and long term is an essential step for a more impactful reform process. Chapter 2, which identified binding constraints, and the theme chapters (3, 4, and 5), close with substantial sections on conclusions and policy recommendations. These aim to help the government and its development partners remove constraints to growth, diversify the economy, and promote sustainable economic development.

Using the growth diagnostics framework proposed by Hausmann, Rodrik, and Velasco (2005), the main policy recommendations for tackling the constraints to growth are to (i) reduce macroeconomic risks—and this chapter already highlighted the importance of implementing the Golden Rule; (ii) tackle the high cost of finance—among the numerous interventions needed for this are better protection for property rights, ending monopolies, and strengthening reporting on nonperforming loans; (iii) plan infrastructure as a network of complementary assets; (iv) tackle market failures with measures to create a more enabling business environment and identify areas of the economy where skills are lacking the most; (v) invest in human capital; and (vi) and regularly assess Azerbaijan's performance against the indicators and targets in the Strategic Road Maps.

Azerbaijan is making good progress on education reforms. But an important area that needs addressing is striking a balance between supporting vocational education and training and higher education. To get this balance, the approach to human capital development needs to be holistic, systematic, and institutionalized. Adopting this approach should help increase the interoperability of certification and expertise between vocational education and training and higher education. Aligning worker skills to labor market requirements will mean giving providers of vocational education and training more authority to decide on operational matters. It also means allowing selected vocational education and training services to be provided by the private sector and recognizing the legitimacy of this training. Further study on Azerbaijan's labor market using better-quality data is needed, including for monitoring and evaluating labor market indicators and for studies that forecast market demand for skills. Because the government's human development and skills development agenda is ambitious, it needs closer coordination among stakeholders and prioritizing education reform in fiscal expenditure frameworks.

The quality of Azerbaijan's core infrastructure has improved significantly because of sustained high investment. But, as noted earlier, many gaps remain, especially in transport, energy, and water and sanitation infrastructure. Interlinked approaches are needed for strategically managing public infrastructure. Setting up an interministerial infrastructure agency would help the government to plan physical infrastructure and infrastructure services as a network of complementary assets, as recommended in a policy recommendation for removing binding constraints, which included gaps in infrastructure and public goods. A cohesive policy framework for infrastructure needs to replace the current fragmented approach that involves various polices on infrastructure development. To attract greater private participation in infrastructure, as envisioned in the Strategic Road Maps, durable policies and effective regulatory oversight will be needed to attract these typically long-term investments.

The government wants to instill a strong corporate governance culture to help turn around its underperforming and inefficient SOEs. The sector road maps in the Strategic Road Maps set out actions to do this, but more is needed to strengthen the many regulatory, institutional, and operational weaknesses of the country's SOEs. The Country Diagnostic Study offers a four-step approach—formulated with the specific challenges that Azerbaijan's SOEs face and the valuable experience of SOE reform in other countries—to build on ongoing SOE reforms. The first two steps involve defining an explicit state ownership policy that sets out the commercial and noncommercial functions of the country's SOEs, and aligns legal and regulatory arrangements for these enterprises with that policy. A commercial performance and monitoring framework is formulated in the third step to help SOEs operate as efficient businesses. Each step is a building block for the next step, with the fourth step suggesting ways for the government to increase private participation in the provision of public infrastructure and services.

Azerbaijan has made remarkable progress through often difficult times. From a collapsed economy after independence, the country has achieved a high level of human development and strong economic growth. Despite the bruising oil price shock, the economy is recovering, with the government undertaking bold macroeconomic and fiscal reforms, and a program of economic diversification under the Strategic Road Maps. Azerbaijan's gradualist approach to its reform strategy under the sector road maps has similarities with Australia's policy reforms in the mid-1980s, and Azerbaijan can draw useful lessons from that experience, especially how it helped Australia accelerate growth, increase productivity, and weather two financial crises in a decade. Appendix 2 looks at how Australia diversified its resource-rich economy.

The team that worked on this Country Diagnostic Study hope the policy recommendations will be useful for helping the government achieve the objectives of the Strategic Road Maps that will help lead to a strong, sustainable, and inclusive economic future.

References

Hausmann, R., D. Rodrik, and A. Velasco. 2005. Growth Diagnostics. *Faculty Working Paper*. Cambridge, MA: John F. Kennedy School of Government, Harvard University.

The Basic Economics of Dutch Disease

According to the workhorse theory of comparative advantage, the trade in primary products is expected to take place between lightly populated economies that are well-endowed with agriculture land or mineral and energy resources and those that are densely populated with few natural resources per worker (Krueger 1977; Deardorff 1984).

Leamer (1987) develops this model further and relates it to paths of economic development. If the stock of natural resources is unchanged, the rapid accumulation of produced capital (physical plus human skills and technological knowledge) per unit of available labor tends to strengthen comparative advantage in nonprimary products. Conversely, a new discovery of minerals or energy raw materials would, all things being equal, strengthen a country's comparative advantage in mining and weaken its comparative advantage in agriculture and other tradable products.

This would also boost national income and, hence, the demand for nontradables, causing mobile resources to move into the production of nontradable goods and services. This would further reduce farm and industrial production (Corden 1984). Conversely, resource depletion or a fall in the international price of oil would strengthen the comparative advantage of other sectors producing tradables and weaken the demand for nontradables in a petroleum-exporting country.

At early stages of economic development, countries with high trade costs are, typically, agrarian, with most gross domestic product (GDP) and employment in the agriculture sector (when home-produced food is included in the estimates). If these countries have a large stock of agriculture land and other natural resources per worker, the primary sector's share of GDP falls slower than in countries that are growing equally rapidly but are less abundant in natural resources. If this group of countries chooses to invest more in capital specific to oil and gas production rather than in farming or manufacturing, the development of a comparative advantage in non-oil tradables would be impeded. The agriculture sector's share of GDP, for example, would decline faster if its productivity growth lagged behind that of other sectors by more than the average global rate.

A boom in an oil-rich country's oil sector has the effect of strengthening the real exchange rate. This, in turn, draws resources to that sector and also to sectors producing nontradables, such as services, and thus away from other sectors producing tradables. A boom raises national income and so boosts the domestic demand for both locally produced and imported products. Together these forces reduce the volume of exports from nonbooming sectors and the domestic-currency price of those exports, and hence their aggregate value (Corden 1984).

Such a boom in an export sector could be supply driven (for example, the discovery of additional oil or gas deposits) or demand driven (a rise in the international price of oil, for example). For the latter, it will show up as an improvement in a country's international terms of trade and encourage new investment in that sector. The more the capital funding for new investment comes in from abroad, the earlier and larger will be the initial appreciation in the real exchange rate. Later, the exchange appreciation will reverse as the boom moves from its investment phase to its export phase and starts to return dividends and, possibly, capital to foreign investors (Freebairn 2015). The depreciation will be even greater if and when the export price declines, as has happened globally since 2014.

References

Corden, W. M. 1984. Booming Sector and Dutch Disease Economics: Survey and Consolidation. Oxford Economic Papers. 36 (3). pp 359–80.

Deardorff, A. V. 1984. An Exposition and Exploration of Krueger's Trade Model. Canadian Journal of Economics. 5 (4). pp. 731–46.

Krueger, A. O. 1977. Growth, Distortions and Patterns of Trade Among Many Countries. Princeton, NJ: International Finance Section.

Leamer, E. E. 1987. Paths of Development in the Three-Factor, N-Good General Equilibrium Model. Journal of Political Economy. 95 (5). pp. 961–99.

Freebairn, J. 2015. Mining Booms and the Exchange Rate. Australian Journal of Agricultural and Resource Economics. 59 (4). pp. 533–48.

Diversification and Growth of Resource-Rich Economies: Australia's Experience

Many resource-rich economies have performed poorly, often because of poor policy choices and sometimes because those policies were aimed at diversifying the economy. This suggests those that dramatically reform growth-sapping policies should perform very well once these reforms are carried out; and then they should keep growing at a faster rate relative to other economies than before the reforms were taken. But do the exports of such reforming economies become less diversified and make the economy more vulnerable to terms of trade volatility? In the experience of Australia, evidence suggests reforms of its growth-sapping policies led to greater diversification of Australia's economy and thus less vulnerability to external shocks. But the Australian reform approach took time to evolve, the community needed to be brought along, and institutions had to be strengthened before the optimal policy mix was able to achieve its goals.

This Appendix summarizes that Australian experience, and draws out the following implications for Azerbaijan:

- Trade-restricting policies do not necessarily diversify a resource-rich economy, and in Australia's past they made its exports more concentrated which meant the economy was more rather than less vulnerable to fluctuating terms of trade;

- Building evidence using pertinent data and sound economy-wide empirical analysis of alternative policy options, and distributing draft reports and hosting community consultations before reforms are decided, helps to build societal support for worthy reforms.

- A market-driven flexible exchange rate system helps greatly in allowing the economy to adjust promptly to fluctuating terms of trade and to reforms to trade-related policies;

- Evidence-based policy analysis can also help anticipate which minorities are most vulnerable to losing from policy reforms, allowing generic safety nets/trampolines to be amended or strengthened to minimize any such harm and thereby reduce resistance to reforms that might otherwise be politically unsustainable.

The key policy thrust of Australia's efforts to diversify its economy was through import-tariff protection to boost industrialization and reduce the country's reliance on primary products. It was a strategy that proved disastrous for economic growth. Instead, it was the country's subsequent market liberalization policy, supported by a range of microeconomic reforms and the move to a flexible exchange rate from the 1980s, that led to more diversified exports and less vulnerability to terms of trade volatility. This paper focuses on Australia's experience in diversifying its economy, because it offers lessons for Azerbaijan's efforts to diversify its sources of growth.[1]

When the Australian Federation formed in 1901, a protectionist trade policy was adopted. It was argued that this would diversify the economy away from agriculture and mining, and would increase employment and raise wages and so attract more immigrants. At that time primary products were 95% of merchandise exports, with gold and wool accounting for more than two-thirds (Anderson 2017). For several decades, import tariffs rose to protect manufacturing and some of the more labor-intensive, import-competing farm industries. Protection was further increased in the 1940s and 1950s with the adoption of quantitative import restrictions, which were converted to similarly protective tariffs in the 1960s. Exports of iron ore were banned from the late 1930s to the early 1960s, again with the aim of diversifying the economy by aiding the import-competing steel industry. By 1970, Australia was rivalled only by New Zealand in having the highest manufacturing tariffs among advanced industrial countries (Anderson 1987; Anderson et al. 2007).

Seven decades of import-substituting industrialization (along with other protectionist interventions, such as those in the labor market) cost Australia dearly in terms of its comparative standard of living. In 1900, Australia was arguably the highest-income country in the world on a per capita basis (McLean 2013). By 1950 its rank had slipped to third, by 1970 to seventh, and by 1990 Australia was not even in the top 30 (Table A2.1). While protectionism may have contributed to Australia's overall gross domestic product (GDP) by attracting more immigrants and industrial capital, many have argued it depressed growth in productivity and hence in GDP per capita—and led to a less rather than more diversified mix of exports (Anderson 2019).

---

[1] A complementary analysis of Australia's experience is provided by Wilkie and McDonald (2008).

Table A2.1: Ranking of Economies by Gross National Income per Capita, Purchasing Power Parity, Current International Dollars, 1950–2017

1950	1970	1990	2017
United States	United States	United Arab Emirates[a]	Qatar
Canada	Sweden	Qatar[a]	Macau, China
Australia	Canada	Kuwait[a]	Singapore
	Switzerland	Brunei Darussalam	Brunei Darussalam
	Denmark	Luxembourg	Kuwait
	Germany	Saudi Arabia	Luxembourg
	Australia	Switzerland	United Arab Emirates
		Bermuda	Bermuda
		Macau, China	Switzerland
		Aruba	Norway
		United States	Hong Kong, China
		Oman	Ireland
		Singapore	United States
		Iceland	Saudi Arabia
		Sweden	Denmark
		Japan	Netherlands
		Germany	Iceland
		Austria	Austria
		Canada	Germany
		Bahrain	Sweden
		Bahamas	Belgium
		Belgium	**Australia**
		Netherlands	
		Italy	
		Norway	
		Finland	
		Denmark	
		France	
		Hong Kong, China	
		United Kingdom	
		Australia	

[a] This is the ranking of these three oil states in 2000, when their data first became available. They may not have been top in 1990, but were certainly well above Australia's rank.

Sources: For 1950 and 1970, K. Anderson and R. Garnaut. 1987. *Australian Protectionism: Extent, Causes and Effects.* Boston, London and Sydney: Allen & Unwin. For 1990 and 2017, World Bank, World Development Indicators (accessed 29 May 2019).

Australia's comparatively poor economic growth performance for most of the 20th century contrasts with that of the final decade, when Australia outperformed all other advanced economies other than Ireland and Norway in terms of GDP per capita growth.[2] This was a period of especially rapid productivity growth (Parham et al. 1999; Dowrick 2001). Australia also grew faster than the average of countries in the Organisation for Economic Co-operation and Development (OECD) during the first two decades of the 21st

---

[2]   World Bank, World Development Indicators.

century, avoiding a recession even during the global financial crisis that began in 2007.[3] As a result, Australia had risen in income per capita rankings to 22nd by 2017 (Table A2.1).

The difference between the Australian economy's recent and earlier relative performances is due very substantially to the country's economic policy reforms that began in earnest when the Hawke Labor Government was elected in 1983. In the 1990s alone, both the mean and the standard deviation of Australia's import tariffs on goods halved. A continuation of the reform process brought the country's average most-favored-nation applied tariff down to 1.2% for agricultural goods and 2.7% for nonfarm products by 2016. That was lower than almost any other country, in contrast to 1970 when Australia's manufacturing tariffs were the highest among advanced industrial countries (Table A2.2).

The belated opening of the Australian economy to the rest of the world, and the floating of its currency in December 1983, coupled with many domestic microeconomic reforms to financial, labor and other markets and the strengthening of supportive institutions from that time, did more than reverse the decline in the country's income per capita ranking. In particular, it helped Australia weather the 1987 stock market collapse, the 1997–1998 Asian financial crisis, and the 2007–2008 global financial crisis. By making the economy and its exchange rate far more flexible and market-responsive, it also made it easier for Australians to adjust to the commodity price slump in 1985–1986, the commodity price boom in the decade to 2014, and the easing of commodity prices during 2015–2019.

Table A2.2: Average Most-Favored-Nation Tariffs on Agricultural and Non-Agriculture Products, 2016

(%)

Product Groups	Australia	New Zealand	United States	European Union	Japan	PRC
Agriculture	1.2	1.4	5.2	11.1	13.1	15.5
Non-agriculture	2.7	2.2	3.2	4.2	2.5	9.0
All products	2.5	2.0	3.5	5.2	4.0	9.9

PRC = People's Republic of China.
Source: WTO, International Trade Centre, and UNCTAD. 2017. *World Tariff Profiles 2017*. Geneva.

These events had a remarkable influence on the pattern of Australia's production and trade. The natural resource rich, lightly populated Australian economy (as revealed in the per capita factor endowments in Table A2.3) has had continually high export shares, and thus a strong comparative advantage,

---

3   In the 23 years leading up to the new reformist Labor Government (1961–1983), Australia's simple average of annual growth in GDP per capita was less than two-thirds that for the OECD as a whole (1.9 % versus 3.0% per year). By contrast, in the most-recent 23 years (1995–2017), Australia's growth rate was well above the OECD average (1.8% versus 1.4%). World Bank, World Development Indicators.

in primary products (Table A2.4). Australia's main trading partners are natural resource poor, heavily populated countries. The United Kingdom was the key one initially, assisted by Commonwealth trade preferences (Table A2.5). But that rapidly switched to East Asia once the United Kingdom joined the protective European Economic Community (now European Union) in 1973, and the economies of Japan and its newly industrializing neighbors grew dramatically.

Table A2.3: Per Capita Value of Resources, Wealth and Income, Australia, Azerbaijan, and Other Countries, 2014

Country	Agric. Land	Mineral Resources	Produced Capital[a]	Total Wealth[b]	Total Income[c]
Azerbaijan	**135**	**495**	**21**	**51**	**73[d]**
Australia	202	1,584	500	621	571
Canada	137	384	626	603	466
United States	117	119	640	583	503
Europe and Central Asia	97	138	228	218	241
Japan	25	1	355	339	350
Other East Asia	138	55	50	54	59
South Asia	60	12	9	11	14
Sub-Saharan Africa	78	39	11	15	17
Latin America and Carib.	139	122	73	82	91
Middle East and N. Africa	83	2,287	19	94	108
World	**100**	**100**	**100**	**100**	**100**

[a] Produced capital refers to all forms of nonnatural (including human) capital.
[b] Total wealth is calculated by summing the estimates of each component of wealth: agriculture land, mineral resources, forests, protected areas, nonnatural produced (including human) capital, and net foreign assets.
[c] Gross domestic product (GDP) based on 2014 dollars at market exchange rates.
[d] Azerbaijan's GDP fell to 39% of the global average by 2017.
Source: Appendix B of G-M Lange, Q. Wodon, and K. Carey, eds. 2018. *The Changing Wealth of Nations 2018: Building Sustainable Future.* Washington, DC: World Bank.

Table A2.4: Sector Shares of Exports and Revealed Comparative Advantage Index, Australia, 1950–2016

Item	Agriculture	Mining	Manufacturing	Services
Export Shares (%)				
1950	86	6	3	5
1970	44	28	12	16
1990	26	41	12	19
2016	15	48	19	23
RCA[a]				
1970	2.2	2.4	0.2	0.9
1990	2.3	4.3	0.3	1.0
2016	2.0	4.8	0.2	1.0

RCA = revealed comparative advantage.
[a] The index of revealed comparative advantage is defined as the sector share of Australia's exports divided by that sector's share of the rest of the world's exports, from B. Balassa. 1965. Trade Liberalisation and "Revealed" Comparative Advantage. *Manchester School of Economic and Social Studies.* 33 (2). pp. 99–123.
Source: Compiled by the author from Department of Foreign Affairs and Trade data. www.dfat.gov.au (accessed 31 July 2017).

Table A2.5: Trade Propensity, and Direction and Index of Intensity of Australia's Merchandise Trade, 1951–2016
(%)

a. Trade Propensity (%)

Item	1968–1972	1990–1992	2014–2016[c]
Exports + imports of goods and services as % of GDP	26	34	42

b. Direction of trade (%)

Trade Partner	Trade Direction[a]	1951–1955	1968–1972	1990–1992	2014–2016[c]
United Kingdom	X	36	11	4	1.9
	M	45	21	6	2.6
Other Europe	X	27	11	12	3.5
	M	15	19	20	15
North America	X	10	16	12	7
	M	15	27	26	14
East Asia + NZ	X	18	43	61	82
	M	10	22	42	59
Other countries	X	9	19	11	3
	M	15	11	6	9
Total	X	100	100	100	100
	M	100	100	100	100

c. Index of intensity of trade[b]

Trade partner	Trade Direction[a]	1951–1955	1968–1972	1990–1992	2014–2016[c]
United Kingdom	X	3.3	1.7	0.7	0.5
	M	5.0	4.1	1.2	1.0
Other Europe	X	0.8	0.2	0.3	0.1
	M	0.5	0.4	0.5	0.4
North America	X	0.5	0.9	0.6	0.4
	M	0.6	1.6	1.5	1.0
East Asia + NZ	X	1.5	3.0	2.7	2.3
	M	1.1	1.8	1.7	1.9
Other countries	X	0.4	1.3	1.0	0.4
	M	0.6	0.6	0.6	0.6
Total	X	1.0	1.0	1.0	1.0
	M	1.0	1.0	1.0	1.0

NZ = New Zealand.
[a] X refers to exports and M refers to imports.
[b] Index of export (import) trade intensity is the share of a region in Australia's exports (imports) divided by that region's share in world minus Australia's imports (exports).
[c] In the 2014–2016 column, the Other Europe rows are the 28 members states of the European Union, and the North America rows include Latin America.
Source: Updated from K. Anderson. 1995. Australia's Changing Trade Pattern and Growth Performance. In *Australia's Trade Policies*, edited by R. Pomfret. London and Melbourne: Oxford University Press; Department of Foreign Affairs and Trade data. www.dfat.gov.au (accessed 31 July 2017).

This evolving pattern of trade specialization depends not only on comparative advantage but also on policy choices and their changes over time, and on international terms of trade shocks. In Australia's case, its long history of industrial protectionism, together with its ban on iron ore exports until the early 1960s, ensured a smaller share of Australia's GDP was traded than would be normal for an economy of its size. It also ensured a bigger manufacturing sector than would have emerged under free trade, which was possible in Australia's full-employment setting only at the expense of other sectors. The manufacturing sector's share of GDP by 1960 was the same as the average (29%) in OECD countries, even though Australia has always been lightly populated and so has had a weak comparative advantage in manufactures. This was corrected by lifting the ban on iron ore exports in the early 1960s; the lowering of costs of shipping coal, iron ore, and other minerals; and the trade, exchange rate and other microeconomic policy reforms of the 1970s, 1980s and 1990s. Since 1960, manufacturing's share of GDP fell much more rapidly for Australia than for the average of OECD countries: to 15% compared with the OECD average of 22% in 1990, and to 6% compared with 14% for OECD countries in 2017 (Figure A2.1).

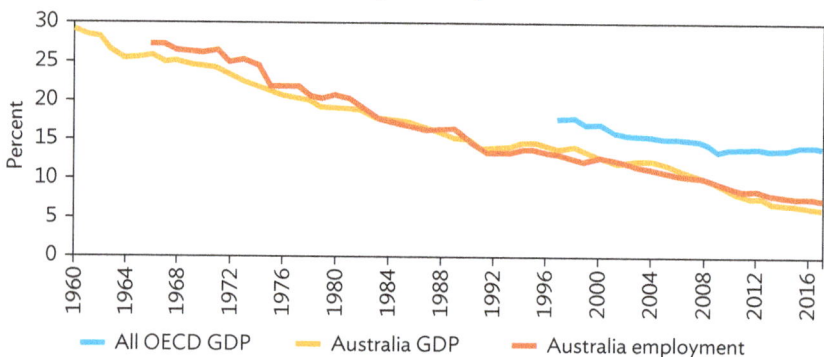

Figure A2.1: Share of Manufacturing in Gross Domestic Product and Employment, Australia and Other OECD Countries, 1960–2017

GDP = gross domestic product, OECD = Organisation for Economic Co-operation and Development.
Sources: GDP compiled by the author from M. Butlin, R. Dixon, and P. J. Lloyd. 2014. A Statistical Narrative: Australia, 1800–2010. In *Cambridge Economic History of Australia,* edited by S. Ville and G. Withers. Cambridge and New York: Cambridge University Press, and updated from World Bank, World Development Indicators Database. OECD GDP shares from World Bank, World Development Indicators database. Data on Australia's employment by activity from OECD data at https://data.oecd.org/emp/employment-by-activity.htm#indicator-chart.

The excessive size of Australia's manufacturing sector as of 1960 was particularly at the expense of the natural resource-based sectors in which the country had its strongest comparative advantage. It has been known since Lerner (1936) that in a two-sector setting, import taxes can have the same effect as export taxes, but how import taxes affect the sector producing nontradables depends as heavily on the elasticities of substitution in production and consumption as between tradables and nontradables. Sjaastad and Clements (1982) suggest that in Australia, nontradables were relatively close substitutes for importables, so their production would have been encouraged by the protection of import-competing industries, further drawing mobile factors of production away from export industries.

It was not only the natural resource-based exportables that Australia's protectionism discouraged, however. Export industries within the manufacturing sector were discouraged, as were services exports. Together those two sectors contributed only one-twelfth of Australia's exports of goods and services in the early 1950s. Even by 1980 their combined contribution was barely above one-quarter. But by 2000 it had risen to 44%, or 22% each, with each sector therefore surpassing agriculture's share (21%) for the first time, and mining accounting for the other 39% of exports (Table A2.2); Anderson [2001]).[4] That is, by making the Australian economy more market-friendly, its exports became far more diversified than they had been under the previous protectionist regime—even though an ostensible aim of that earlier policy was to diversify the economy.

Australia's trade with East Asia boomed following the opening of the Australian economy, especially since the decline of the most protective tariffs to no more than 5% and the elimination of the last quotas on imports.[5] Not only was this a huge boost to Australia's primary product exports but also to imports of manufactures from emerging Asian economies. The latter accounted for barely 10% of Australia's imports in the 1950s and less than 20% in the late 1960s, but by the early 1990s their share reached 40%—and are now close to 60% (Table A2.5).

Accompanying this remarkable transformation in Australia's production and trade patterns was the already-mentioned boost the reforms gave to economic growth. A likely source of that growth was the stimulation the opening up gave to private-sector investment in research and development. As a share of GDP, business research and development rose fivefold: from just 0.2% in the decade before the reforms got underway in 1984 to an average of 1% in the decade to 2018 (Figure A2.2).

---

[4] The mining investment boom from 2000 to 2012 reduced the shares of all other sectors in Australia's exports, such that by 2013 shares for manufacturing, agriculture, and services were 12%, 13%, and 17%, respectively, before they began to recover when the Australian dollar's real exchange rate depreciated from 2014. World Bank, World Development Indicators.

[5] The ERAs to textiles, clothing, and footwear, and to motor vehicles and parts, both peaked at more than 140% in the mid-1980s before quotas on their imports were removed (Productivity Commission 2003).

**Figure A2.2: Research and Development Expenditure
by Business Sector, Australia, 1967–2018**
(% of GDP)

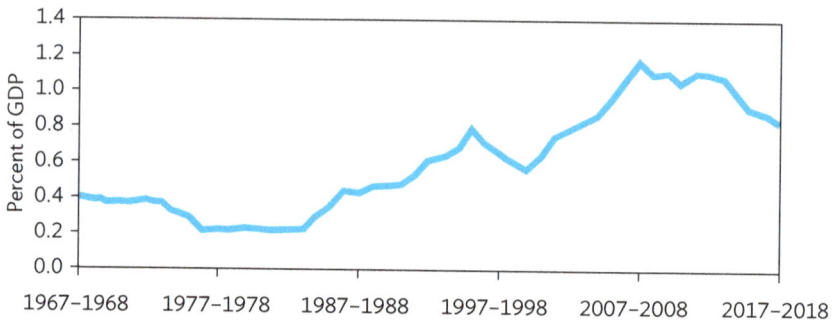

Source: Australian Bureau of Statistics. 2018. *Australian System of National Accounts, 2017–18*. Cat No. 5204.0 Canberra.

Extent of protectionism

An important contribution to the reform process was setting up a new government agency in 1973 whose mandate is to bring more transparency to trade and industry policy debates. Initially named the Industries Assistance Commission, it was renamed the Industry Commission and then the Productivity Commission as its mandate broadened to include a focus on growth. One early and crucial aspect of the agency's published empirical work involved yearly estimates of the nominal and effective rates of government assistance (NRAs and ERAs) to industries not only in manufacturing but also in agriculture and eventually mining.[6]

Productivity Commission (2018) summarizes almost 50 years of official estimates of ERAs for key sectors. For the first half of that period, the average ERA for manufacturers fell steadily, from 35% in 1970 to 20% by 1988, and by 1999 it had fallen to 5%. Agriculture's ERA fell even more rapidly, from 28% in 1970 to an average of barely 10% during 1975–1990 before falling to 5% by 1999—although it fluctuates because of year-to-year movements in international food and fiber prices that are less than fully passed through to the domestic market within a year. Since 2000 the ERAs for both manufacturing and agriculture have averaged 5% (Figure A2.3). Australia's mining sector has

---

[6] These built on the partial equilibrium concepts of nominal and effective rates of import protection promoted by Corden (1971). The NRA can be thought of as the percentage increase in the price of an industry's product due to, for example, an import tariff on a like product. The ERA also takes account of distortions to prices of an industry's inputs, and so can be thought of as the percentage increase to value added in that industry as a result of government interventions in its product and input markets.

been mostly taxed rather than supported by the government. The lifting of the export ban on iron ore in the early 1960s allowed the inevitable minerals and energy raw materials trade with Japan to belatedly get underway. It was some time before efficient tax instruments, such as resource rent taxes, were applied. There have been further mining policy reforms since then, and Productivity Commission (2018) estimates of mining's ERA were close to zero during 2000–2018.

Figure A2.3: Effective Rates of Government Assistance to Agriculture and Manufacturing, Australia, 1970–2017 (%)

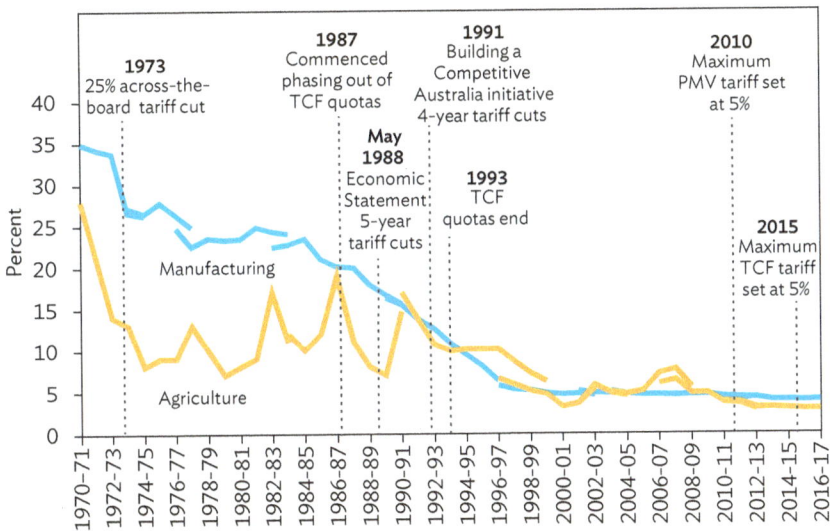

PVM = passenger motor vehicles, TCF = textiles, clothing, footwear.
Source: Productivity Commission. 2018. *Trade and Assistance Review 2016–17*. Canberra.

Australia's mining sector has been mostly taxed rather than supported by the government. The lifting of the export ban on iron ore in the early 1960s allowed the inevitable minerals and energy raw materials trade with Japan to belatedly get underway. It was some time before efficient tax instruments, such as resource rent taxes, were applied. There have been further mining policy reforms since then, and Productivity Commission (2018) estimates of mining's ERA were close to zero during 2000–2018.

Service sector interventions were dismantled, initially by the Labor Government following its election in 1983 but supported by the conservative Opposition, which continued the process after it displaced the Labor Party at the 1996 election. Markets for banking, post and telecommunications, ports, higher education, health, rail and air, and to some extent sea transport were opened up, and there has been the progressive outsourcing of many government services. Substantial reforms to competition policy and practice, including the privatization, corporatization, and de-monopolization of numerous government enterprises, were well advanced by the start of the 2000s (Forsyth 1992 and 2000; numerous Productivity Commission reports).[7]

To get a fuller sense of the extent of the bias against primary production in Australia before 1970 when the Industry Assistance Commission estimates begin, Anderson, Lloyd, and MacLaren (2007) provide NRA estimates back to 1946. Anderson et al. (2008), following a World Bank methodology used in intercountry comparisons, also used production-weighted average NRAs for non-agricultural tradables. The latter are compared with the NRA for agricultural tradables via the calculation of a percentage relative rate of assistance (RRA), defined as:

$$RRA = 100*[(100+NRAag^t)/(100+NRAnonag^t)-1],$$

where $NRAag^t$ and $NRAnonag^t$ are the percentage NRAs for the tradables parts of the agricultural and non-agricultural sectors, respectively. Since the NRA cannot be less than -100% if producers are to earn anything, neither can the RRA. And if both of those sectors are equally assisted, the RRA is zero. That same analysis has since been extended back to 1904 by Lloyd and MacLaren (2015), and Figure A2.4 updates those RRA calculations to 2017 and expands the agriculture sector to including mining. The RRAs in that figure thus provide an estimate of the extent to which relative prices of tradables in Australia have been distorted by government policies against primary production to favor manufacturing. They suggest that in the 1930s, for example, it was as if Australia's primary production was taxed about 30% relative to what would have prevailed under free trade. Those estimates also make clear that so far in the 21st century the average NRA for each of the main tradable sectors is very close to zero: the past intersectoral policy bias has nearly disappeared.

---

[7] For these reports, see www.pc.gov.au.

Figure A2.4: Nominal Rates of Government Assistance to Manufacturing, Primary Production, and Relative Rate of Assistance to Primary Sectors, Australia, 1904–2017

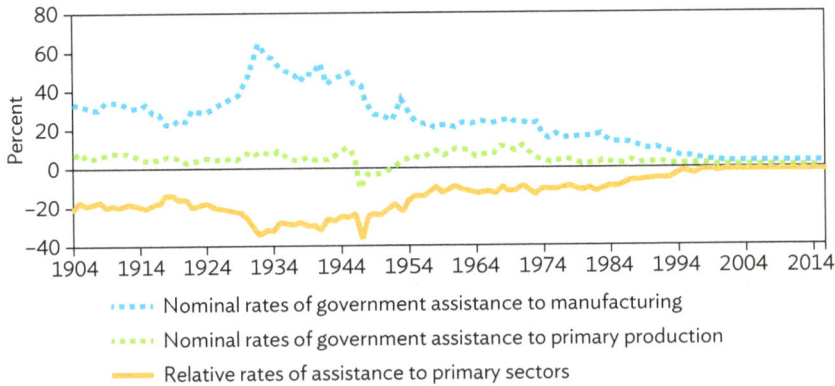

Nominal rates of government assistance to manufacturing

Nominal rates of government assistance to primary production

Relative rates of assistance to primary sectors

Sources: Compiled by the author based on data in K. Anderson, P. J. Lloyd, and D. MacLaren. 2007. Distortions to Agricultural Incentives in Australia since World War II. *Economic Record*. 83 (263). pp. 461–82; P. J. Lloyd, and D. MacLaren. 2015. Relative Assistance to Australian Agriculture and Manufacturing since Federation. *Australian Journal of Agricultural and Resource Economics*. 59 (2). pp. 159–70, updated from Productivity Commission. 2018. *Trade and Assistance Review 2016–17*. Canberra.

Modelling the economic effects of protectionism and reform

The availability of estimates of the extent of price distortions resulting from Australia's protection policies opened the way to model their effects on production, consumption, trade, and economic welfare, especially as economy-wide, computable general equilibrium (CGE) models developed. Powell and Snape (1993) review the first two decades of economy-wide CGE policy modelling in Australia. The development and applications of the ORANI family of models (Dixon et al. 1982), which was largely funded by the two predecessor institutions of the Productivity Commission, included extensive training of economists on how to use the models and how to communicate their results to policy makers and the public. It was unlike any previous Australian venture in policy analysis in that it welded academics and public servants into an interagency research team that cut across the usual civil service silos and controls. More than that, the modelers developed a capacity to routinely enhance the core ORANI model with greater details for any particular industry being analyzed. This involved two-way communication between the modelling team and business practitioners, which convinced commissioners at two of the Productivity Commissions' predecessor institutions that such formal modelling has real-world relevance.

By exposing not only which groups might be hurt by a policy reform or changes in export prices but also which ones could gain and by how much, a more comprehensive economy-wide perspective was obtained. That made it easier to "sell" policy reform proposals and to argue against demands from vested interest groups for populist policies that would harm national welfare. For example, leaders in the farm sector realized that ORANI could be used to estimate the extent of the damage done to farmers by protecting manufacturing. In a study commissioned by Australia's National Farmers' Federation, manufacturing protection in the early 1980s was estimated by Parmenter (1986) to reduce real farm incomes by one-sixth. The federation used this estimate very effectively to press for a continuing commitment to tariff reductions.

Dixon (2008) updates by 15 years the Powell and Snape (1993) review on the use of CGE modelling in Australian trade policy making. Dixon (2008) argues that such policy modelling flourished because Australia had an appropriate important initial issue to focus on (that is, import protectionism), the right institutions for ensuring a sophisticated policy dialogue, and the right type of model of the economy to provide credible empirical estimates. Australian modelers expanded the dimensions of model results to include estimates of outcomes not just by industry and product but also by region, occupation, household, and electorate. And they analyzed changes not only in policy but also in producer technologies, factor endowments (including mining booms), international terms of trade, and consumer preferences, among other things.

Disaggregating results by region and occupation within Australia has been important in two respects: First, it makes it easier to identify which household groups might lose from a structural or policy change, thereby allowing fine-tuning of social safety nets in advance. Second, by identifying more precisely which groups are likely to gain from a policy improvement, the government can point to and seek support from the beneficiaries. By then making the models dynamic, CGE modelers were able to suggest how adjustments to shocks trace out over time.[8] And by entering the forecasting arena, they can provide insights into prospects for different industries, occupations, and regions, thereby aiding investment decision-making.

Banks and Nankivell (2010) summarize some of the many benefits Australia has reaped from opening up its economy. They acknowledge that trade liberalization has been only one element of the policy transformation, but stress that trade reform played a pivotal role. In addition to offering consumers

---

[8]   The dynamic MONASH model is a 113-industry dynamic successor to ORANI (Dixon and Rimmer 2002).

lower-priced goods and a wider variety of products, reductions in tariffs have lowered costs of myriad services bought by households and firms. The depreciation of the real exchange rate that accompanied the opening up has made virtually all industries that received less-than-average assistance more profitable. In addition to these reallocation effects, all industries became more dynamic, not least because lobbying for special assistance was made far less worthwhile than before the reforms, so entrepreneurial effort was redirected to raising productivity to boost competitiveness internationally, including through much greater private investment in research and development (Figure A2.2). Further, by announcing policy reforms in advance and phasing them in simultaneously over several years for many industries during the 1980s and 1990s, businesses had time to adjust—and less scope to argue for exemption. Adjustments by firms and workers in the most-protected industries were eased by adjustment assistance programs in extreme cases, further reducing the prospect of successful lobbying for exemptions.

A striking outcome of the reforms was the increased diversity of production and exports in Australia. It shows up in the rise in the share of both manufacturing and services in the country's total exports (Table A2.4). It also shows up in the declining shares of traditional exports of wool, grains, meat, and sugar, with other rural exports increasing their aggregate share from 22% in 1984 to 49% in 1999 as the opening up stimulated productivity growth in numerous farm industries that had not been competitive in exporting previously (Figure A2.5).

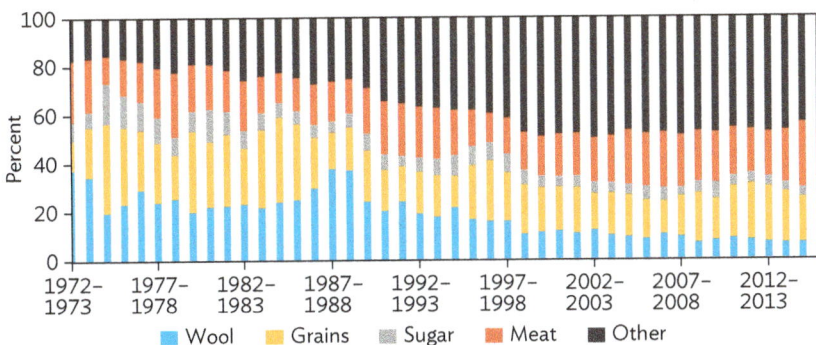

Figure A2.5: Shares of Agricultural Products in Total Rural Exports, Australia, 1972–2016
(%)

Source: Australian Bureau of Agricultural and Resource Economics and Sciences. 2018. Agricultural Commodity Statistics. Canberra.

Why the eventual liberalization?

Why Australia was so protectionist for so long, and why it eventually decided to reform unilaterally, has been the focus of much speculation and empirical analysis. Garnaut (1994) stresses the increasing disenchantment with interventionist trade policies. The efforts of Corden and other academics, and of the Productivity Commission and its predecessor institutions, were crucial inputs in the process of gradually changing the climate of opinion of economics and business media toward one of advocating trade liberalization. But the economic reform process—which involved far more than just trade liberalization—is mostly due to the initiatives of the Hawke-Keating Labor Government, which came to power in March 1983, and the willingness of the Opposition to support the process and continue it following its coming to power in 1996. Australia early in 1983 had just seen its largest fall in employment and rise in unemployment since the Great Depression. The Hawke-Keating reform program was vindicated by a subsequent rise in employment that was stronger than in any other 7-year period in the 20th century, and was helped by a compact with the labor union movement. The trade-liberalizing part of the reforms was facilitated by the political and intellectual leadership agreeing to the need for a more open economy, the rise in organized countervailing lobbying from farmer and mining export interests, and the desire to build what would inevitably become closer and more cooperative trade relations with East Asia (Table A2.5). The gradualist reforms were greatly assisted by former prime minister Bob Hawke's extensive public discussions and consultations with key industry and labor groups, complemented by many substantive government publications on the benefits of reform and the growth in Australia's trade with emerging East Asian economies. Also helpful to reform have been generous generic social safety nets/trampolines ensured adjustment assistance to those households initially harmed by the reforms, and a fiscal equalization mechanism that redistributes uneven gains from growth across States within the Australian Federation.

Corden (1996) stresses also the importance of floating the Australian dollar early in the Hawke Government, so the exchange rate could devalue as the tariffs were gradually reduced. In this work, Corden notes that the Productivity Commission has not been subject to "regulatory capture" by protectionists. Indeed, the Commission continues to be influential in its public inquiries and published reports on an ever-wider range of microeconomic policy issues. Corden also points out that the nature and timing of Australia's reform were influenced by the global move to flexible exchange rates, and by the spectacular economic success of earlier liberalizations by East Asia's newly industrializing, outward-oriented economies—in contrast to the evident failure of an import-substitution strategy in Latin America and, albeit to a much lesser extent, Australia.

Lessons for Azerbaijan

Azerbaijan and Australia are equally blessed with a relative abundance of natural resources per capita (Table A2.3). Azerbaijan is seeking to diversify its economy to reduce its vulnerability to volatility in the prices of its primary export items. Australian governments had a similar goal during the first seven decades of the 20th century. In Australia's case the heavy hand of government intervention in markets was seen as the panacea, particularly in providing protection from import competition for the least-competitive manufacturing and farming industries. In hindsight, that policy failed not only in diversifying exports but also in inhibiting investment and economic growth. When that protectionist regime was eventually replaced with one that was more market-friendly, many more firms and industries became export-focused, production and exports became more diversified, the share of private investment in GDP rose fivefold, and Australia's rate of growth in GDP per capita shifted from being 35% below to being 28% above the OECD average (footnote 3). More than that, the increased flexibility of markets and the floating of the currency ensured the economy was far more resilient to external shocks: despite the 1997–1998 Asian financial crisis, the 2007–2008 global financial crisis, and the commodity price downturn during 2015–2018, Australia has not had a recession since 1992 and the unemployment rate has been stable at around 5%.

The key lessons for Azerbaijan and other resource-rich economies are that these economies are likely to be more diversified the less governments seek to protect and assist their least-competitive sectors, and that a flexible exchange rate allows producers and consumers to adjust more rapidly to external shocks. Moreover, with the information and communication technology and robotics revolutions making services far more tradable (Baldwin 2016, 2019), all economies—including resource-rich ones—are going to see services become more important in their export mix, and more so the more open and market-friendly are their economies. Evidence-based policy analysis can contribute greatly to community consultations before reforms are decided, helping to build societal support for worthy reforms. Such analyses also help anticipate which minorities are most vulnerable to losing from policy reforms, allowing generic safety nets/trampolines to be amended or strengthened to minimize any such harm and thereby reduce resistance to reforms that might otherwise make be politically unsustainable.

References

Anderson, K. 1987. Tariffs and the Manufacturing Sector. In *The Australian Economy in the Long Run*, edited by R. Maddock and I. McLean. Cambridge and New York: Cambridge University Press.

_____. 1995. Australia's Changing Trade Pattern and Growth Performance. In *Australia's Trade Policies*, edited by R. Pomfret. London and Melbourne: Oxford University Press.

_____. 2001. Australia in the International Economy. In *Restoring Australia's Economy*, edited by J. Nieuwenhuysen, P. J. Lloyd, and M. Mead. Sydney: Cambridge University Press.

_____. 2017. Sectoral Trends and Shocks in Australia's Economic Growth. *Australian Economic History Review*. 57 (1). pp. 2–21.

_____. 2019. Introduction and Summary. Ch. 1 in *Agricultural and Manufacturing Protection in Australia*, Vol. 2 of *World Scientific Reference on Asia-Pacific Trade Policies*, edited by K. Anderson, Singapore: World Scientific.

Anderson, K., and R. Garnaut. 1987. *Australian Protectionism: Extent, Causes and Effects*, Boston, London, and Sydney: Allen & Unwin. Re-published in *Agricultural and Manufacturing Protection in Australia, Vol. 2 of World Scientific Reference on Asia-Pacific Trade Policies*, edited by K. Anderson, Singapore: World Scientific, 2019.

Anderson, K., M. Kurzweil, W. Martin, D. Sandri, and E. Valenzuela. 2008. Measuring Distortions to Agricultural Incentives, Revisited. *World Trade Review*. 7 (4). pp. 675–704.

Anderson, K., P. J. Lloyd, and D. MacLaren. 2007. Distortions to Agricultural Incentives in Australia since World War II. *Economic Record*. 83 (263). pp. 461–82.

Australian Bureau of Agricultural and Resource Economics and Sciences. 2018. *Agricultural Commodity Statistics*. Canberra.

Balassa, B. 1965. Trade Liberalisation and "Revealed" Comparative Advantage. *Manchester School of Economic and Social Studies*. 33 (2). pp. 99–123.

Baldwin, R. 2016. *The Great Convergence: Information Technology and the New Globalization*. Cambridge MA and London: Harvard University Press.

_____. 2019. *The Globotics Upheaval: Globalization, Robotics and the Future of Work*. London and New York: Oxford University Press.

Banks, G., and T. Nankivell. 2010. Gaining from Trade Liberalization: Reflections on Australia's Experience. In *An Economy-Wide View: Speeches on Structural Reform*. Canberra: Productivity Commission.

Butlin, M., R. Dixon, and P. J. Lloyd. 2014. A Statistical Narrative: Australia, 1800–2010. In *The Cambridge Economic History of Australia,* edited by S. Ville and G. Withers. Cambridge and New York: Cambridge University Press.

Corden, W. M. 1971. *The Theory of Protection.* Oxford: Clarendon Press.

_____. 1996. Protection and Liberalization in Australia and Abroad. *Australian Economic Review.* 29 (2). pp. 141–54.

Dixon, P. B. 2008. Trade Policy in Australia and the Development of Computable General Equilibrium Modeling. *Journal of Economic Integration.* 23 (3). pp. 605–30.

Dixon, P. B., B. Parmenter, J. Sutton, and D. Vincent. 1982. *ORANI: A MultiSector Model of the Australian Economy.* Amsterdam: North-Holland.

Dixon, P. B., and M. T. Rimmer. 2002. *Dynamic General Equilibrium Modelling for Forecasting and Policy: A Practical Guide and Documentation of MONASH.* Amsterdam: North-Holland.

Dowrick, S. 2001. The Australian Productivity Miracle. In *Restoring Australia's Economy,* edited by J. Nieuwenhuysen, P. J. Lloyd, and M. Mead. Cambridge and Sydney: Cambridge University Press.

Forsyth, P., ed. 1992. *Microeconomic Reform in Australia.* Sydney: Allen & Unwin.

_____. 2000. Microeconomic Policies and Structural Change. In *The Australian Economy in the 1990s,* edited by D. Gruen and S. Shrestha. Sydney: Reserve Bank of Australia.

Garnaut, R. 1994. Trade Liberalization and the Washington Consensus in Australia. In *The Political Economy of Policy Reform,* edited by J. Williamson. Washington, DC: Institute of International Economics.

Lange, G-M., Q. Wodon, and K. Carey, eds. 2018. *The Changing Wealth of Nations 2018: Building a Sustainable Future.* Washington, DC: World Bank.

Lerner, A. 1936. The Symmetry Between Import and Export Taxes. *Economica.* 3 (11). pp. 306–13.

Lloyd, P. J., and D. MacLaren. 2015. Relative Assistance to Australian Agriculture and Manufacturing since Federation. *Australian Journal of Agricultural and Resource Economics.* 59 (2). pp. 159–70.

McLean, I. W. 2013. *Why Australia Prospered: The Shifting Sources of Economic Growth.* Princeton NJ: Princeton University Press.

Parham, D., T. Cobbold, R. Dolamore, and P. Roberts. 1999. *Microeconomic Reforms and Australian Productivity: Exploring the Links.* Canberra: Productivity Commission.

Parmenter, B. R. 1986. What Does Manufacturing Protection Cost Farmers? *Australian Journal of Agricultural Economics*. 30 (2–3): 118–27.

Powell, A. A., and R. H. Snape. 1993. The Contribution of Applied General Equilibrium Analysis to Policy Reform in Australia. *Journal of Policy Modeling*. 15 (4). pp. 393–414.

Productivity Commission. 2003. *From Industry Assistance to Productivity: 30 Years of "The Commission."* Canberra: Productivity Commission, December.

———. 2018. *Trade and Assistance Review 2016–17*. Canberra: Productivity Commission.

Sjaastad, L. A., and K. W. Clements. 1982. The Incidence of Protection: Theory and Measurement. In *The Free Trade Movement in Latin America*, edited by L. A. Sjaastad and H. Hesse. London: Macmillan.

Wilkie, J. and T. McDonald, (2008). Economic Geography and Economic Performance. In *Economic Roundup*, Canberra: The Treasury. http://unpan1.un.org/intradoc/groups/public/documents/apcity/unpan035849.pdf

WTO, International Trade Centre, and UNCTAD. 2017. *World Tariff Profiles 2017*. Geneva: WTO.

www.ingramcontent.com/pod-product-compliance
Lightning Source LLC
Chambersburg PA
CBHW041145230326
41599CB00039BA/7174